MW00424937

Sexism & Sensibility

Sexism & Sensibility

Raising Empowered,
Resilient Girls in
the Modern World

Jo-Ann Finkelstein, PhD

NEW YORK
HARMONY

This is a work of nonfiction. To protect the privacy of others, certain names have been changed, characters conflated, and incidents sometimes condensed.

Published in the United States by Harmony Books, an imprint of Random House, a division of Penguin Random House LLC, New York.

Harmony Books is a registered trademark, and the Circle colophon is a trademark of Penguin Random House LLC.

Library of Congress Cataloging-in-Publication Data
Names: Finkelstein, Jo-Ann, author.
Title: Sexism & sensibility / Jo-Ann Finkelstein, PhD.
Description: New York: Harmony, [2024] | Includes bibliographical references and index.
Identifiers: LCCN 2024008288 (print) | LCCN 2024008289 (ebook) |
ISBN 9780593581162 (hardcover) | ISBN 9780593581179 (ebook)
Subjects: LCSH: Girls—Social conditions. | Girls—Psychology. |
Girls—Public opinion. | Child rearing. | Parenting.
Classification: LCC HQ777 .F56 2024 (print) | LCC HQ777 (ebook) |
DDC 649/.133—dc23/eng/20240321
LC record available at https://lccn.loc.gov/2024008288
LC ebook record available at https://lccn.loc.gov/2024008289

Printed in the United States of America

harmonybooks.com

10 9 8 7 6 5 4 3 2 1

First Edition

Book design by Diane Hobbing

For Jonah and Gabi
and every child deserving a more equitable world

CONTENTS

The moment seemed innocuous enough at the time. I was eight or nine, baking brownies alongside my mother. The envelope was lying next to the double boiler, addressed to her in perfect, flowing cursive handwriting. I picked it up, smearing it with chocolate, and asked the obvious question: Why did it say "Mrs. [My Father's First and Last Name]"? I knew enough to know Mrs. meant it was for my mother. But why was she referred to by my dad's name and not her own? I wasn't a precocious feminist pointing fingers, but my sense of justice had been violated. My mother told me matter-of-factly, even proudly, this was simply how it was done once a woman gets married. It seemed clear and uncomplicated to her. But I couldn't let it go: Why was my amazing mother, gourmet chef extraordinaire, and a woman raising four small children while completing college, content to be tucked away behind her husband's name? As the only girl in a family of four kids, I needed to know. When I pressed, though, her words, tone, and body language made it clear this was something I wasn't supposed to ask.

· This wasn't the only time I encountered something that seemed unfair, yet the grown-ups around me avoided discussing it, leaving me bewildered. In my synagogue, the seats for boys and men flowed down the center, while those for girls and women were situated on the sides, making clear our place in a man's world was on the periphery. The rabbi and other important people onstage were all men. In the texts, "he" and "man" stood for both sexes, and stories of women were largely absent. If

I raised the issue, I was told things were done this way because of tradition, which I now understand to be code for "stop questioning."

The same ethos pervaded my education: My brilliant high school English teacher, a Black woman, put thick red slashes through the "her" portion of "his/her" that I'd used in an essay. She explained, "To avoid confusion, use 'his' instead of 'his/her,'" and then added, notably, "It's not sexism, it's accepted practice."

Tradition. Accepted practice. To avoid confusion. But nothing was more confusing to me than having authority figures, especially those authority figures, tell me in ways large and small it was okay to erase girls from the conversation. It would take a long time to understand that "sexism" and "accepted practice" are categories that can and do routinely overlap and that a person's discomfort with that overlap is often dismissed as oversensitivity.

Sex and gender would be part of my studies at Harvard and Northwestern as I trained for a PhD in clinical psychology and launched a career rooted in an understanding of how gender bias, social justice, and mental health intersect. But my own therapy is where I came to understand how those early experiences of having my innate sense of justice invalidated had affected me. Growing up, I'd often felt that if I peeked my head out, someone would whack it down. At some point I'd picked up the mallet and begun doing it to myself. I kept the most genuine parts of myself underground because a lifetime of training told me it wasn't only unsafe to emerge but unfair. Unfair because I'd be claiming space not meant for me and because the women before me hadn't had that opportunity.

I would come to feel a mix of betrayal and wistfulness about those early experiences. I met peers with similar experiences, and together we wondered: Why hadn't the grown-up women in our lives shared our curiosity and anger? Or at least acknowledged *we* had a right to feel those things? It took until graduate school for someone to name my experience, and I felt the storm clouds part. In a paper for my developmental psychology class, I mentioned how I was often accused in my family of being too sensitive and dramatic, rather than being acknowledged, as I see it now, as highly attuned to my environment. The professor scribbled in the margin, "That's what people say to talk girls out of their feelings!" When your feelings are denied or disbelieved, especially as a child, it's an existential threat. My anger sharpened but eventually dissipated as I realized many women of that era had even fewer resources than I did to help them identify sexism. And don't all parents comfort children by telling them not to worry about things that scare them? For some situations, it's a reasonable strategy: that shot will only pinch; Grandma died, but I'm not going anywhere. But for others—and maybe especially big systemic problems like sexism and racism—it can be patronizing, and even destructive. Today, as a seasoned psychologist and a parent of both a son and a daughter, I have a lot more empathy for those grown-ups who swept gender issues under the rug.

As parents we're stuck between a rock and a hard place when it comes to nurturing and shaping our children's innate sense of justice while still preparing them to live in the world as it truly exists. We're faced with a hundred little choices about what to share, what to explain, what to ignore in the name of expediency every day. Even if my mother had felt indignant about the erasure of her name on that envelope, she still had to make a choice about whether and how to share that with a little girl. Would affirming things were unfair upset me? Would it make me less prepared to function well in a world that expected girls and women to accept such things without question and punished them for stepping out of line? Which battles are worth fighting, and when do we instead quietly encourage our children to be flexible, respect tradition and accepted practice, and avoid confusion?

All parents make these calls, but mothers of daughters have an extra task as we untangle our own early experiences from the situations our girls now face. We must sort out our perceptions and memories so as not to pass on the disbelief, denial, or accusations of hysteria we encountered. We tread a difficult line between preparing our daughters for the world and instilling fear. We don't want to unfairly color the way they see the world, but not knowing what to expect could be worse. It's vital they trust their instincts, whether that curdled feeling in their stomach comes from a teacher's snide comment in class or from being approached by a carful of teenage boys. They need to know what to do when they feel their hearts racing but their feet are glued to the pavement. It's our job to teach them to navigate bodily autonomy in a world where their bodies often don't feel like their own and aren't safe, to stand their ground when they need to, and to move on with grace and without guilt when they can't. My greatest wish for my daughter is that she knows what it feels like to trust herself, and to make sure she doesn't feel "less than" even if she's sometimes treated that way. I want that for all of our daughters.

As a psychologist, I advocate for the kind of personal responsibility that comes from understanding feelings and how those feelings affect behavior. But I also see patients who feel responsible for things outside their control: girls whose anxiety, depression, or daily struggles are caused or exacerbated not by what they do but by the way they're treated *because they're girls*. I hope this book will help you help your daughter distinguish between what is and what isn't within a girl's control, what is and what isn't her responsibility, and what is and what isn't her fault—and what she can do when she faces sexist experiences that leave her feeling diminished.

Even the youngest children have a fundamental sense of fairness: research studying babies as young as twelve months old has found infants notice when resources are distributed unequally. By the time girls are forming a sense of self in the world, they can tell the playing field isn't level, but that's rarely made explicit for them. Worse, the world around them actively encourages them to dull their own "fairness detectors," as so many adults do for the same reason one might unplug a carbon monoxide alarm that keeps chirping after the authorities have issued assurances the air is safe to breathe. Time and again girls in my psychology practice tell me their attempts to report gender-based harassment are met by well-meaning adults who minimize the incident, admonish them, or invoke platitudes such as "He probably has a crush on you." This persistent dismissal by adults of situations that appear unjust to girls seems like a tacit endorsement of bad behavior, leaving them feeling abandoned, mistaken, or crazy. Girls need to hear what they're feeling is real and that they don't have to silently suffer through it.

Fairness is an integral part of a child's developing understanding of how the social world operates. However, when we model different expectations for different groups of people—whether grouped by race, sex, religion, or other categories—we distort the concept of fairness and dampen a child's natural ability to detect it. For example, if Stella protests having to help her mom cook while her twin brother, Zach, is allowed to go out to play, she might be told this is because Mom wants "girl time" with her or even because girls are better at preparing food (even though there's no evidence to suggest girls are better cooks than boys). Similarly, if little Zach protests always having to trudge through the snow to take out the garbage, his parents might explain it's his job because boys are so strong (even though at his age boys and girls don't differ in muscle mass). The explanations we give for differential treatment are often untrue and feed into children's conceptions of who they are and why they're treated as they are. When we treat girls and boys differently, or allow such treatment to pass without remark, we're teaching our children to recalibrate their fairness detector in a way that excuses sexism.

Didn't We Solve This Sexism Thing Years Ago?

The short answer is no.

The long answer is no, no, no, no, no.

It's true there have been worse times and places to be a woman. Women in the United States today can decide if and when they get married, and they can work, wear pants, play sports, go to college; they can even open a bank account, buy a house, and take out a business loan without the say-so of a husband or father, which wasn't true in my mother's generation. Same-sex marriage is legal, and the last decade has seen a raft of new federal and state laws protecting transgender and non-binary teens and people assigned female at birth.

And yet.

Evidence of progress is too often used to shut down questions about the work still to be done. In fact, a recent five-decade study finds progress toward gender equality has slowed down, stalled, or even reversed in key areas since the 1990s. Legal protections in some areas have been turned back decades—as when federal guidelines in 2020 abruptly narrowed the definition of campus sexual misconduct and when the Supreme Court overturned federal abortion protection in 2022. Even as we tell girls they can be whatever they want to be when they grow up, equal pay protections are being hollowed out; even as we tell them they can balance ambitions for both careers and families, the legislatures in many states are working to outlaw contraception; and even as a rainbow of positive role models for LGBTQ+ kids is more visible than ever, more than a dozen states (and counting) have proposed "don't say gay" bills that ban teachers and administrators from supporting their needs in school.

Though the double binds and double standards are head spinning, girls face them day in and day out. They hear talking heads on the news ask if #MeToo has gone "too far" even as they go to school expecting harassment and heed warnings to take their drinks with them to the bathroom at bars and parties. One in six women—the majority between twelve and thirty-four years old—experience an attempted or completed rape, and 98 percent of rapists aren't held accountable. Teens are often considered too young to have sex but old enough to parent should they become pregnant.

Equal pay has been the law for decades, but research shows women are still being paid less than men "due to no attributable reason other than gender . . . and the pay gap is even wider for women of color." Women work long hours outside the home yet still do two and a half times the amount of domestic and childcare work of their male counterparts. Women have outnumbered men in colleges for decades, but the halls of power are still overflowing with men. Women make up just 10 percent of CEOs at Fortune 500 companies and only 28 percent of members of the U.S. Congress. Only 13 percent of directors in Hollywood are women, and a mere 11 percent of top-grossing movies in 2022 featured more women than men, making 2023's *Barbie* a major anomaly.

More statistics abound, but I'll stop here for now and remind you that despite all the evidence, people still insist sexism no longer exists. In a large-scale survey, 87 percent of eighteen-to-twenty-five-year-old women reported having been sexually harassed and half of men reported that they'd harassed a woman, yet nearly half of all those respondents agreed "society has reached a point that there is no more double standard against women." The dissonance is staggering.

As parents, we want our daughters to both fit in with the culture and be protected from it. The mixed messages that result can be confusing. We tell our daughters one day it's what's inside them that counts, not their looks, and the next day tell them they're asking for trouble because their shorts are too short. (If we comment on their shorts, we end up doing the very thing we're trying to protect them from—sexualizing them—but if we hold our tongues, we worry we're leaving them unprepared for how the world will see and treat them.) We grasp for control in a world that finds so many ways to diminish and hurt our daughters that we end up making them feel responsible for how they're treated. Even if we tell them explicitly it's unfair that close-minded people will acknowledge only their body and not their whole humanity, we're sending the message this state of affairs is up to them to manage. The last thing we want is to add to the chorus that tells girls it's their job to figure out how to survive sexism. Rather, we want to raise boys who treat them with dignity and are intolerant of sexism. For that reason, you'll find much in here about raising boys too, alongside the tools and support girls need to reconsider the stories they've adopted about themselves.

This book isn't about casting girls and women as victims or boys and men as villains. It's about preventing girls from internalizing the limiting and distorting messages of our culture and from privileging others' feelings, perceptions, and comfort over their own. My aim is also to help us figure out what part we play as adults in both clarifying and muddying the waters for our daughters as to what's fair and how they should expect to be treated.

Why Talk About This Difficult Stuff?

"I just don't want her to see herself as a victim," one mother told me. I understood exactly what she meant. As parents, we find it easier to focus on telling our daughters how strong, equal, and powerful they are. Talking about how the world can be particularly difficult or scary for them can feel like robbing them of their innocence, or teaching them to look for darkness around every corner. But when we don't address the challenging or creepy experiences most girls endure, we rob them of context and the permission to name what they're experiencing, and so contribute to their confusion. A sunshiny "girls can do anything!" mindset is far from enough to protect them.

We have names for the type of treatment we hope to protect them from: misogyny, sexism, prejudice, discrimination. Helping our daughters become familiar with these terms will help them understand the small slights—or massive injustices—aren't their personal failures but a failure of the system. And we've got our work cut out for us. They'll be chronically underestimated, dismissed, and talked over. They'll watch television that offers mostly superficial, trivial reflections of themselves, read books in school featuring mostly male protagonists, and receive history lessons that will essentially be a record of men's lives. They'll read news pieces written mainly by men about personally relevant issues that were decided almost exclusively by male politicians. The systems they rely on—modern democracy, medicine, and the justice system— were all created by and for men. Heck, even their playing cards will tell them kings are more powerful than queens. But we can give them the tools to assess the power structures that lurk behind every human inter- action before second-class treatment erodes their self-esteem.

Some of you may be thinking, "Wait, my daughter already knows more about this stuff than I do." Thanks to social media or progressive educations, girls today are often savvier than their mothers were at that age about the cultural ambivalence toward women. Some can even artic- ulate a feminist argument about their bodily autonomy—one they've probably used against you when you insisted no rips in their pants when going to church. But maybe all this awareness is also making them anx- ious because it amplifies the mixed messages aimed at girls, making the world seem harder to navigate, sex seem traumatic, and the task of equal- ity feel heavy on their shoulders.

Awareness alone isn't sufficient to handle actual sexism; young people don't yet have the cognitive, emotional, and social skills to really manage it. Their budding feminism is more of an identity politics. They believe all choices are valid and empowering—my body, my choice! Their will- ingness to stand up for their and others' choices is impressive and gives me hope for a truly inclusive future. Their confidence in their ability to say "hands off!" is comforting. The problem is their mantra can lack analysis and real-world experience. Consent, for example, is far more difficult during a confusing, pressured moment. And it's true, most choices *are* valid, but without an understanding of the unseen forces at play, they're often not real choices. It's one thing to discover sexism as a teen and feel alone and hopeless; it's another to experience it knowing you've got a parent in your corner.

As adults raising girls, we want to interrupt these harmful dynamics while they're still young. The confusion wrought by the mixed messaging that tells girls they're equal while routinely objectifying and degrading them doesn't disappear with adulthood. These psychological paper cuts accumulate, becoming festering wounds of self-doubt. In my psychology practice, I see many seemingly high-functioning adult women struggling with the same problems as their teenage daughters. They pour their creative energy into their appearance rather than into a sense of purpose; they avoid leadership roles due to shaky confidence; they view themselves from the outside, nitpicking their bodies, skin, faces, and appetites in ways I rarely hear from boys and men. The competition and envy between women, born of a culture toxic for women, destabilize their relationships. Trauma doesn't have to be an event; it can be the invisible residue of growing up in a world that believes you're weak, inferior, irrational, overly emotional, and incapable of leadership and of making important decisions. More than seventy years after Simone de Beauvoir coined the term, our daughters are still the "second sex."

What Can Parents Do?

Even those of us who ensure our daughters have books with strong female characters, bring them to Women's Marches, and buy them RBG paraphernalia often feel at a loss when it's time to get down in the weeds of gender bias and sexism with them. "Girl power" is wonderful for building a can-do attitude and self-respect for the female gender, but it neither prepares girls for unfair and unsavory behavior nor addresses the hurt and resulting confusion girls confront when they do encounter poor treatment just for being a girl. That's where this book comes in.

We've all heard a single discussion about tough topics—like "the talk" about the birds and the bees—is ineffective, not only because kids tune out in horror, but because different pieces of the topic need to be covered at different ages. Like sex, sexism should be an ongoing conversation. Primarily, we want to help girls identify the biases inherent in coming-of-age in a male-centric world and to find strategies to help them avoid internalizing them. My aim is to give you the language girls need to express how sexism affects them and to highlight the confusion wrought when their experiences are patronized and discredited. And I offer guidance on how to have conversations about (and model behavior around) tough situations where girls encounter sexism in their lives at various stages of development.

An essential part of interrupting sexism is exploring our own internalized sexism (even those of us who equally distribute chores have it!) and how it shows up in our parenting, because those are also the places we can create the most change. Just as a toddler looks to a parent to see if they should be scared upon hearing a loud noise, girls look to us to signal whether their instincts can be trusted. By recognizing the ways we've unconsciously been reinforcing toxic messages, we create new opportunities to combat them. Throughout, I'll share actionable steps we can take to undo the "traditions" that no longer serve us, individually and together as allies seeking a more just world.

By exploring the subtle, chronic, cumulative indignities girls experience and believe are normal, you'll come to see this barrage of derogatory messages as the gateway to the more brazen sexual harassment and violence that we as a society increasingly condemn—the kinds we hear about daily in the news. I also offer commentary on the roots of sexism so that we might nudge ourselves out of current gender-stereotypical thought patterns and effectively intervene on our daughters' behalf. I hope this book will help you better understand her and support your efforts to help her fine-tune her "sexism detector" so that she can make a meaningful and vivid life; so that she knows she can be the main character, not just the eye candy, the one who makes the jokes, not just laughs at them.

PART 1 OF this book will explore how we set the stage for gender bias and sexism to flourish in girls' lives by colluding with the culture via our own implicit biases and the narrow scripts we hold for ourselves and for them. Part 2 will delve into two major cultural forces that create and intensify sexism: beauty culture and the media, focusing on the most common concerns I hear from parents. Part 3 will examine common experiences in girls' lives that teach them they're less deserving, intelligent, and powerful than boys, impeding their right to reach their full potential. In part 4, we'll focus on sex and sexuality, discussing how to set girls up for true body autonomy and sexual agency. Throughout, I use stories from my own life and the lives of my therapy patients to make the concepts and the research come alive. The stories I draw on from my work have been altered to disguise any identifying details and in a few instances are composites to protect the privacy of those who've confided in me. But in each instance, I worked hard to preserve the integrity of what transpired. I chose from the most common challenges girls and their parents face, so if you see yourself reflected in these accounts, it's both happenstance and deliberate.

My hope is by the end of these pages you'll have a clearer path forward for helping your daughter manage the dissonance between who the world says she is and who you know her to be: powerful, astute, and full of potential.

Part I

The Path We Put Her On

CHAPTER 1

Egalitarian Relationships, Equal Parenting

Interrupting the Generational Transmission of Sexism

Exposure to sexism begins at home, so that's where we'll begin to unravel it. Many mothers have swallowed whole the definition of the stereotypical good woman, and they expect the same of their daughters, namely to be pleasant, skinny, and self-sacrificing above all else. Conforming to sexist systems has many benefits, including the sense you've mastered something other women find challenging—gaining the approval of the dominant culture. Many fathers are in "the awkward position of loving a gender they have been taught to devalue"—a chilling line that's stuck with me from *Reviving Ophelia,* the 1994 groundbreaking book about saving the selves of teenage girls. When a father disparages an assertive woman, makes a misogynistic crack about his son throwing like a girl, or communicates in a demeaning way with his wife, he diminishes his daughter.

Implicit bias may be thriving in the unconscious of well-meaning parents and caregivers, but it's hard to spot. After all, we grew up in a culture even more sexist than the one in which we're raising our daughters. We're often blind to the roles our everyday behavior, ways of relating, traditions, religious doctrine, and language play in diminishing girls' positive sense of their selves. Eager for them to belong, we might inadvertently encourage them to conform to traditional feminine norms. Or maybe we push these norms onto them because of our own unconscious envy. We compliment our daughters on their looks far more than our sons, tease them about boys before they even know what a crush is, silence their strong opinions, and encourage them to lose weight, all of which teach them their appearance and sexuality are what's important. Yet when they hit puberty, we worry they're too preoccupied with these things and in danger of being shallow or "slutty."

As (seemingly asymptomatic) carriers of the sexism virus, we emphasize emotional appearance in boys as much as we emphasize physical appearance in girls. The pressure to appear strong and in control grows as boys grow. We teach them to stifle their emotions, empathy, and tenderness so they might avoid suffering that greatest of all insults—being called girlie—thereby creating a culture of toxic masculinity. We ask boys not to notice what they feel, to separate their minds from their hearts. And we ask girls not to know what they know, to separate themselves from their minds. We're asking both boys and girls to sacrifice core parts of themselves.

How do boys and girls grow up and develop emotional and sexual connections under these circumstances?

One gender expert calls straight relationships the "misogyny paradox," referring to the difficulty boys and men face in liking and respecting women in a culture where they're seen as more masculine for objectifying and demeaning them. The subordination of women, then, isn't an unintentional by-product of masculinity but indispensable for its very existence.

In their 2018 book, *Why Does Patriarchy Persist?*, Carol Gilligan and Naomi Snider explain that patriarchy, defined as a culture based on a gender binary and hierarchy, is harmful to both sexes because it forces men to act as if they don't need others or care about what, in fact, they care deeply about, and women to choose between having a voice or having a relationship. We internalize these patriarchal codes of conduct and artificial scripts and, in the process, lose something essential to our very beings. We take our selves out of relationship in order to have relationships that are culturally sanctioned and are left with a "crisis of connection." This psychologically harmful pattern is compelling, not only because people in positions of economic and institutional power can retain their privilege, but, as the authors explain, "by requiring a sacrifice of love for the sake of hierarchy . . . patriarchy steels us against the vulnerability of loving and by doing so, becomes a defense against loss." In other words, patriarchy both creates loss and hardens us against experiencing the full emotional effects of it.

These dynamics show up in therapy again and again. They were especially true for Camila and Drew, a couple in their late thirties who'd been married for ten years. When they arrived in my office for couples counseling, they were on the verge of losing their marriage, and their relationships with their young children were deteriorating. Before we really dig into kid stuff, it's worth exploring some adult interactions because they provide an opportunity to see how unconscious gender norms can eat away at a relationship and how we transmit subtle gender bias and sexism to the next generation. After all, when our children are present, everything we do is parenting.

From the waiting room, Drew took Camila's hand, pulled her up from her chair, and led her into my office as you might a child. But I had the sense she was less like a child and more like a rag doll. Each session began similarly with Camila settling in quietly, crossing her legs, and remaining poised and alert. Drew, on the other hand, would stretch and noisily plop onto the couch. He wasn't a particularly large man, but he filled the room with big gestures and unselfconscious body language, adjusting his testicles, responding to texts, picking his nose, clipping his fingernails, flossing his teeth, and once, during a video session, using the camera to pop a zit. I noted how differently—and stereotypically—they moved in the world.

Drew opened that first session saying, "I'm not sure what Camila told you already, but basically everything's fine. I don't want you to think we're unhappy, and I want Camila to know I'd never leave her. The major problem is intimacy. She's just not into it." I noticed Camila adjust her face and smile, as if taking her cue from Drew about how to feel. She agreed with Drew, their sex life was in shambles. On the phone, she'd mentioned other problems like communication, parenting, and feeling disrespected by Drew, but I sensed it wasn't safe yet to mention those things.

Their first session centered on an argument they were having over a party, which, it turned out, revealed a lot about their troubling dynamic. They'd agreed to throw a fundraiser in their home for their kids' school. Attendees were parents from the school who'd donated $50. Camila felt pressured to make it worth the money, and Drew had gotten frustrated with her attention to detail, explaining she spent too much time worrying about something that didn't matter "in the grand scheme of things." Camila crossed her arms at that last comment and looked at the ceiling. I asked her what was happening. "Drew thinks these events just magically happen. Just like our wedding." It turns out, their sexual issues began during their engagement, because, Drew claimed, Camila's planning was a turnoff. As therapy progressed, I noticed that despite his critiques of Camila's style of hosting parties, he was frequently effusive afterward.

In this day and age of two working parents and less defined domestic roles, Camila wasn't happy about doing all the work, and Drew could feel her resentment. Rather than step up, he just told her to do less work. And indeed, if she wanted parties and he didn't, the therapy would've turned to more of a negotiation about how to handle this difference. But as is often the case, a little more exploration into this stated difference between them revealed overlapping feelings that had gotten polarized. Both Drew and Camila were experiencing conflicting desires within themselves: They *both* wanted and didn't want to throw nice parties. But Camila was left "holding" the wanting and Drew the not-wanting.

While an argument about how to throw parties can seem frivolous, in this case parties were a metaphor for desire. Parties symbolized many things in their life that required planning and effort; it takes planning and effort when you *want* something, whether it's a nice evening out (gas in the car, reservations, babysitter) or a relatively smooth day trip to the beach with kids (sunscreen, sand toys, towels, hats, lunch). Camila and Drew would become polarized in these situations: she was the one who wanted something, and he was the one who didn't care much. Drew insisted Camila overthought things, and Camila insisted Drew refused to learn from experience—that things almost always went better when they'd planned, especially when it involved the kids. It infuriated her that Drew didn't think finding the kids' hats to shield their tender skin from the sun was a big deal, and he was frustrated Camila "was obsessed" with that. Camila called Drew a "typical guy": thoughtless, unempathetic, and self-centered. Despite this, she couched her criticism in the fear she probably was just asking too much. Drew knew "in the grand scheme of things" he benefited from Camila's planning and that he should "accept women fixate on things that seem trivial" to him. With that comment Drew not only devalued Camila and women in general but minimized his own feelings and preferences by saying they weren't important.

Camila and Drew defaulted to viewing their relationship through the prism of gender. Deciding men are from Mars and women are from Venus may offer easy shorthand for explaining gender differences, but in fact these ingrained conceptions of gender contributed significantly to their marital troubles. Socialization and persistent gender role division are what allow sexism to persist and be transmitted from generation to generation. As the only son in his family of origin, Drew's sole chore had been to mow the lawn a few times in the summer. Camila, on the other hand, was responsible for many household details including helping with her younger sister. This led to differences in their expectations and attitudes toward household responsibilities. The unequal division of childhood labor is still true today. Girls between the ages of fifteen and seventeen spend nearly twice the amount of daily time cleaning, cooking, and running errands as boys that age. This is no small thing when you consider research showing women fall behind in their careers and are paid less because they're overburdened at home.

Gender socialization alone didn't explain everything, though. Camila told us, "When I met Drew, he was living with two roommates and his place was immaculate. I mean, well, not immaculate, but really clean for guys, and Drew would get annoyed if his roommates ever left dishes around the house. Now Drew thinks nothing of leaving dishes in the basement for days. It's like now that I'm here to clean up after him, he doesn't have to do anything." She paused, then added, wrinkling her nose, "As if I'm his mother." Camila was hitting on something important often found in heterosexual relationships. Women are most often the ones in families to carry the "mental load"—the never-ending to-do lists and the relentless awareness of everyone's unique needs required for households and families to run smoothly. Even if they work outside the home—even if they earn as much as their male partners—they shoulder 60 percent of the caregiving and household responsibilities. With a "mom" present, the fantasy of perpetual boyhood can be played out. It wasn't Drew's maleness per se that rendered him incapable of picking up after himself, helping plan the parties, or finding the hats. It was that he could rely on Camila to do it. And she did, rarely mentioning her dismay to him, at least not verbally. But it's not sexy to think of your husband as a child. When Camila did complain, Drew cast her in the role of the castrating mother. No wonder couples who share chores and childcare equally have more sex.

Men often wish their partners would just worry less. It's true, women often feel pressured to "perform gender"; that is, they've internalized society's values of what makes a "good" mother or "good" homemaker. In part, Drew was impatient with Camila's commitment to detail because he sensed it was driven by her need to perform gender well. But letting that go is difficult because it's almost always the woman who's judged when her house is messy, parties or events aren't up to snuff, or, say, her three-year-old shows up at school without underwear on under her skirt (true story; her dad had been on kid duty, but I was the one who got the call). People in queer relationships also experience this problem of an imbalanced mental load, suggesting binary gender roles infiltrate everyone everywhere. Why, then, does it so often divide along gender lines in hetero relationships? Maybe, as Camila suggested, Drew had gotten used to women picking up after him, that he was just taking advantage of gender expectations by employing "weaponized incompetence." No doubt that was part of it, but because he'd taken good care of his home before marriage, I wondered if there was more to it. Drew told us, "I do want a neat house, but sometimes I just don't register the mess. And I just don't care as much as Camila." There it was again: "I don't care."

This disavowal of desire is something I run into often when cisgender straight men begin therapy. Sometimes they come in at the demand of their partner and sometimes because they want something but they're not sure what it is or how to get it. On several occasions I heard Drew reiterate, "I make a ton of money; I have a big house and a hot wife. What more could a guy want?" I always got the sense he was looking at himself from someone else's point of view or from a cultural perspective rather than from a felt sense of himself. One time I wondered aloud, "Yes, what? And also, would it be okay to want whatever more is?" Drew wanted support from Camila for his hard work and the lifestyle it afforded them but didn't expect it for his emotional struggles. He didn't even seem to know he could hope for that. He told himself he wanted sex, but he didn't realize he also wanted the connection that can come with the intimacy of sex. He'd learned from his father he had to put on a brave face whenever he got upset. "God," Drew said, "he razzed me so much. I think he was trying to protect me, prepare me for people like him." With his needs and emotions frequently rejected, Drew withdrew, figured out how to soothe himself, and told himself the story he didn't really need anyone. It was as if he understood manhood to be about possessing things—money, objects, people turned into objects—things that compensated for the unmasculine wish for tenderness and care that men are expected to renounce.

As the therapy turned toward a deepening exploration of their respective intimacy issues, it became clear that it was Drew who'd withdrawn from sex, humiliated by unpredictable performance issues. The narrative, though, had transformed to align with traditional gender norms. Camila said, "I sort of forgot about his part of the intimacy stuff." She'd felt a core issue in their marriage was too touchy to talk about because she sensed a fragility in Drew that, when poked, he'd conceal with anger, "like he has to explode so he won't break." To avoid Drew's anger, she said, "I'd go limp, quiet, so we could just move on"—the rag doll effect I'd seen that first day in the waiting room. She'd learned from her parents it was best to remain pleasant and inconspicuous, so she avoided conflict and hurt by splitting off what she knew about Drew and what she wanted from him. And Drew stopped caring about things he actually cared about in order to feel safe and accepted.

Gilligan and Snider explain that the patriarchal push for masculine detachment (not caring) and feminine self-silencing (not knowing) forces us "out of relationship," which is a necessary dynamic for establishing hierarchy. Put another way, "hierarchy requires a loss of empathy by those on top and a loss of self-assertion by those below." That's why Drew (like even feminist men can) got angry and ashamed when his vulnerability threatened to be exposed by any loss of status or autonomy and why Camila (like so many women) felt guilty prioritizing her own needs. Internalized gender roles and expectations were killing not just their sex life but also their ability to communicate, co-parent, and appreciate each other. These ways of being (or not being) relational simultaneously created aching loss and offered them the psychological defenses needed to protect themselves from some of their deepest fears and shameful desires.

It's far too simplistic to say that Camila wanted closeness and Drew didn't, that Camila was controlling and Drew rejecting. In reality, both Drew and Camila were desperate for closeness, but neither was aware of the barriers to intimacy they'd erected. A turning point came via a realization Drew had in therapy: his engagement to Camila had terrified him, since he imagined himself unworthy of "the Latin goddess." Idealizing someone usually leads to disappointment in that person, or fear you won't live up to their standards, and it seemed as if Drew had pushed Camila away in preparation for the inevitable loss. Hearing this, Camila felt enormous relief. Her relief, though, turned to anger at Drew for making her feel inadequate and crazy during the engagement. In a culture that codes the communication of feelings and fears as feminine, Drew hadn't been able to open up emotionally and instead blamed her for his issues. But because Drew was learning to tolerate her anger and felt genuinely sorry for what he'd put her through, she could get mad directly, rather than be passive-aggressive, without worrying he was going to leave or explode. He was much more willing and able to be vulnerable, so Camila no longer had to pretend she didn't know what she knew for fear of breaking him, which had secretly made him seem less of a man to her, not more. She could be reassuring about his fears of inadequacy and loss. As Drew integrated his vulnerability and need for care and Camila found her voice and sense of agency, their capacity for closeness and sex grew.

From this glimpse of Drew and Camila's life, we can see the pressure put on boys to be strong and to repudiate both their need for care and

their own gentleness or kindheartedness, and the pressure on girls to be good, to keep their anger and their agency under wraps. We can see the cues Camila and Drew took from their parents and the havoc it wreaked when they replicated this in their connection to each other. Harmful gendered socialization is handed down through the generations; Lucas and Sofia, Camila and Drew's children, were in danger of inheriting it as well.

Passing the Gendered Torch

Lucas and Sofia often took center stage in their parents' therapy. Lucas was withdrawn, and Sofia was increasingly irritable. Drew complained Camila was too coddling of Lucas and too critical of Sofia, and Camila felt Drew was the opposite—overindulging Sofia and too hard on Lucas. They described arguments in front of the kids where Drew seemed to be modeling his disavowal of desire and Camila the swallowing of her voice. By doing so, they were unwittingly socializing their kids to do the same.

Camila began a session, glancing nervously at Drew, by saying, "We should talk about what happened with Lucas yesterday." I sat quietly as they shifted in their seats and said nothing. Drew spat, "Why don't you just say it, since you seem to think it's such a big deal," and Camila responded by trying to smooth things over, "Hon, I'm not saying it's a big deal, but he was pretty upset." "Whatever," said Drew dismissively, the usual charm he used to avoid uncomfortable topics gone. After some time had passed, I spoke: "You seem pretty upset yourself, Drew. Can you say what's wrong?" "Jesus," he snapped. "None of this matters in the grand scheme of things." I didn't react and allowed him to sit with what he said. After a while he shook his head and muttered, "Goddamn it." I pushed him gently: "That expression is usually our cue you're trying to make something that matters to you not matter." "Yeah, yeah. I heard it." He put his head in his hands and cried silently. "Goddamn it," he repeated over and over.

Eventually, he told me the story, with some additions from Camila. They'd been visiting friends at a lake house, and seven-year-old Lucas and another boy a year older were walking on the edge of a stone wall about five feet off the ground. Lucas hadn't wanted to follow his friend onto the wall, because he was scared, but Drew repeatedly encouraged him to give it a try. In Camila's words, Drew had pushed him into it. Camila had tried to intervene by telling Lucas he didn't have to if he didn't want to, and Drew had snapped at her, demanding she stop treating him "like a princess." That's when Lucas either gathered his courage or stopped listening to his feelings and began putting one foot in front of the other to balance as he walked. He made it about halfway across when he fell and landed hard at the bottom of the bushes flanking either side of the wall. The left side of his face and his arm were scraped and bleeding, but he was otherwise physically okay.

It's what Drew said next that seemed to wound Lucas the most.

According to Camila, he said to Lucas, "Jesus, kid, what happened?" as if disgusted. Then he turned to the other boy, as if to make a point, and said, "Great job, Matt!" Drew protested this interpretation and claimed he was just trying to take care of both the boys in the moment. As we unraveled Drew's feelings about the incident, he admitted he'd been thinking "what a pussy" when Lucas had initially refused to walk the wall. When Lucas fell, Drew immediately felt scared and guilty but also mad at Lucas for making him feel that way by being "unable to perform" (sound familiar?), especially compared with the other boy. So, Camila was partly right; Drew was disgusted by Lucas, but he also felt awful and concerned. Pushing Lucas was his way, like his own father's, of trying to help him avoid feeling unmasculine.

Camila was angry with Drew but also with herself for not insisting Lucas take a pass. She'd felt sure it wasn't a good idea because Lucas was more than a year younger than the other boy and had "coordination issues." But with Drew taking responsibility for his part, she was able to acknowledge that sometimes she's too quick to intervene, which had caused her to doubt herself and remain silent in the face of Drew's princess comment. Being reflective and considering alternate options is important for ourselves and when raising kids, but too often Camila didn't trust herself and held back, only to feel regret, anger, or self-loathing later.

Nine-year-old Sofia was with them when all this happened. Drew often called her Princess, but unlike with Lucas it was meant as a term of endearment. Drew showed a deep pride in and affection for Sofia. He'd use "Princess" in place of her name—"How was school, Princess?"—and to compliment her appearance: "You look like a princess today." This kind of special treatment of girls can stir envy in boys and complicates sibling relationships. Most likely, hearing her father derogatorily use "princess" for Lucas would've been confusing: be a princess, yet princesses are wimpy. Camila admired Drew's attachment to Sofia and had liked the term when Sofia was younger. But in more recent years she'd also hear him complain about her acting like a princess when she got upset about things he found trivial, like the time they didn't have fries at a restaurant and Sofia threw a fit. Exasperated, Drew had told her to stop behaving like a spoiled princess.

Like Sofia, lots of little girls are referred to as princesses just as they're building a set of ideas of what it means to be a boy or girl. They use stereotypes as a guide for how they should behave, what they should look like, and what things they should like. Research shows when kids think of princesses, they think of beautiful, nurturing creatures who often require rescuing. Princesses are valued for those qualities rather than for being brave, smart, and strong. Referring to your daughter as Princess can convey the idea what you love about her is what's traditionally feminine about her. Worse, for some, "feminine" is synonymous with "incompetent." Not only does calling her Princess reinforce certain qualities over others, but then, as Drew exhibited, the term is just as often used disparagingly.

In the next session, I learned that a few days after the incident with Lucas, Sofia asked her father to stop calling her Princess. Camila had shown up alone to our session because Drew had to take a last-minute call. Camila told me Sofia had had a dance recital, and when it was over, Drew told her she'd danced like a princess. Sofia responded in front of a group of other parents, "You don't even like princesses, which is probably why you were on your phone and don't even come sometimes to my dancing." Camila's eyes flashed. "It was like someone burned me with fire. I was instantly infuriated and told Sofia to 'zip her lips.' She knows why Daddy can't always be there." I was struck by her using "Daddy" with me instead of "Drew" and recalled her telling me of her own father's unavailability.

Drew had been hurt by Sofia's words and stayed quiet. In the car, however, he'd tried to explain why he'd needed to be on his phone. When Sofia wouldn't look at or speak to him, he confirmed her fear that princesses were not actually admirable by saying, "Here comes Princess Bratty." The message seemed to be only girls without negative feelings are good princesses. When we miss the opportunity to understand and empathize with our kids' feelings, they're more likely to feel hurt, angry, and misunderstood. I wasn't surprised to hear Sofia proceeded to have an epic meltdown.

"That girl's getting out of control!" Camila huffed, shaking her head, though she'd admitted she'd been irritated with Drew herself. She explained Sofia needed to learn to be respectful, "especially to her father," and to show poise and self-control.

"Like *you* do, even when you're mad at Drew; like you did with your father, and really do most of the time," I stated.

I'll never forget the wry, pained look on Camila's face at that moment. After a long time she said slowly, "I'm so *good*, aren't I? And now I'm teaching my daughter to be good." It's not as if we hadn't discussed previously her tendency to please, to swallow her voice and her desires. But because she was seemingly more aware of the generational transmission of gender norms, it hit her on a new level. "Say more about being good," I said. "Well," she said, "I'm a fake, really. It's not like I always feel good inside. I have some pretty shitty thoughts actually, but I've always wanted to be that quintessential gracious, warm woman. I used to think if my mother could just relax and be affectionate with my father, he would've stayed." Then she added, regurgitating the sexist stereotypes she'd internalized, "I was going to be the girl who lets things roll off her back . . . not the crabby, naggy wife who lets herself go."

Camila could relate to Sofia feeling neglected and hurt, but she'd aligned herself with Drew's feelings and jumped to his defense. Camila found the immediacy of Sofia's feelings so disturbing it burned. Her daughter hadn't yet been socialized to take them underground, or just grin and bear it, and that made Sofia seem unrefined and reflected poorly on Camila's mothering. Beneath that interpretation, though, we discovered Camila envied her daughter's ability to speak her mind.

Camila had been alluding to not feeling fully seen or respected by

Drew, and this event opened the door for her to explore her own feelings of being called queen, sometimes sarcastically, and treated like "some shiny thing," valued for her beauty and sexuality but not her mind and feelings. In the early years when things were easy between them, Camila loved the flowers he'd bring after an argument, even if he didn't attend to her feelings or attempt to resolve the conflict beyond that. It was romantic. She explained, "It made me feel like a queen. It's what I always thought guys were supposed to do even though my father never did." In more recent years, Camila found herself feeling annoyed by the predictable flowers, aware on some level she was being bought, but felt selfish and ungrateful and so kept it to herself. I noted she thought she had to choose between being a queen—a good woman, a wonderful wife—and being fully human. Putting someone on a pedestal robs them of being a real person with real feelings. And as we saw with Drew's versions of queen and princess, it's far too easy to tumble off that pedestal.

What's a Parent to Do?

Chauvinism is a value, and like any value it's often passed on to our children. But chauvinism isn't always conscious, and when we unintentionally model these behaviors and beliefs, our children absorb them. If we tell our daughters to be quiet and polite but don't tell our sons the same, we're perpetuating sexism. If we force our daughters to cover up and never teach our sons to respect girls, we're perpetuating sexism. If shopping and mani-pedis become a mom's primary activity with her daughter or if parents play ball or have political discussions only with their sons, we're reinforcing stereotypes. Dads who make sexist comments about hotties and jokes about women drivers and naggy wives crush their daughters' spirits and teach their sons to see women through this lens too. In well-intended attempts to stop girls from internalizing stereotypes, we may comment on a woman we think wears too much makeup or isn't sporty enough. But when we discourage them from being "girlie" or encourage them to be "tough like their brother," it's just another side of the sexist coin: the message is boys are better.

It's not only how we interact with and treat our kids that transmits sexism. Children soak up the dynamics between their parents—how they treat each other, whether they respect and like each other, and how they divide the household management and childcare. When one person, like Camila, is tasked as the air traffic controller, alerting everyone when and where to fly the planes while also flying some of the planes herself, it's not equality, and it rarely makes for a healthy relationship. Unknowingly placing gender and the accompanying sexist expectations at the center of their identities left Camila and Drew feeling lost and unhappy and at risk of compromising their children's development and well-being. In addition to working on your own unconscious stereotypes, you can beef up your children's sexism detectors by following these five suggestions.

> Children soak up the dynamics between their parents—how they treat each other, whether they respect and like each other, and how they divide the household management and childcare.

❥ Model Equality in Your Partnership

"Do you want to marry a mommy or a daddy when you grow up?" my friend overheard her six-year-old daughter asking her older sister. The older girl pondered and answered, "A mommy, they do more." Let that be a lesson!

One of the best ways to ensure you raise children who expect equality and notice its absence is to keep the power dynamics of your partnership equal, particularly in heterosexual relationships. When fathers share housework equally, studies show their daughters are less prone to limit their aspirations to traditionally female careers. But it's not a mathematical equation; it's caring. Said another way, it's important to ensure one parent doesn't feel overloaded and underappreciated, and neither partner feels as if they have to rigidly adhere to conventional gender roles. Make a point to switch up who serves the food, fills out the school forms, fixes broken electronics, or drives the car when the family is together. That last one is quite the metaphor if you think about the message it sends when Dad is always in the driver's seat.

Of course, as parents, we sometimes send mixed messages. My husband is our family driver because otherwise he gets motion sickness, and I'm perfectly happy ceding the driving to just about anyone else. When your children turn their impressive new critique skills on you and wonder about some of the traditional roles you've settled into, try not to get defensive. Validate their excellent observation, and explain that people tend to take on what they're good at, which, in part, is based on the uneven gendering of our childhoods and the uneven opportunities and income available to them.

One of the best ways to ensure you raise children who expect equality and notice its absence is to keep the power dynamics of your partnership equal. . . . But it's not a mathematical equation; it's caring.

Even for couples who largely divide along traditional gender lines, if you're modeling genuine respect for each other's contributions, you can model equality. It's essential to value each parent's work, regardless of what that work is and what it pays (or doesn't pay). Maybe equality looks like aiming for equal rest; maybe it's sharing all the tasks outside the hours of 9:00 to 5:00. Allow Dad to manage household tasks and decisions too so Mom is not always the go-to parent—power that can be hard to relinquish. Given women's lower social status generally, Dad can make a point of noticing Mom's contributions and insist the kids respect her wishes. Our kids absorb who and what are considered important, and if Mom consistently defers to Dad's decisions, schedule, and life path—which studies find is the case even among couples who say they've achieved equal partnership—it sends a clear message to girls that their voices, contributions, and interests don't matter.

➲ *Moms, Model Self-Respect, Not Perfection*

When women downplay their strengths and accomplishments, repeat-edly sacrifice themselves for the good of others, and make little time for themselves, they're teaching girls what's in store for them. Some girls embody that, giving up pieces of themselves without question. Others are confused and eventually become frustrated and angry. One sixteen-year-old patient of mine named Rebecca repeatedly complained about her mother being too nice. She wanted her mom to stand up for herself when her father asserted his preferences over hers, or even when Rebecca was being "bitchy" to her. Another patient, fourteen-year-old Mei, loathed that her mother always seemed exhausted yet never stopped to take a break. She'd saved up to buy her mother a professional massage for her birthday, and her mom still hadn't cashed it in by her next birth-day. Mei said, "No wonder she expects me to be so perfect." Rebecca and Mei worried this was what they could expect for their futures. They began recognizing those self-sacrificing qualities of their mothers in themselves. Rebecca, whom you'll meet again in chapter 6, started ther-apy because she was very anxious. It turned out she was chronically evaluating the effects of all of her small, everyday actions on her friends. Clearly her mother was not the only people pleaser in the family. Rebecca was so focused on making others happy she'd lost touch with her own wishes and needs. If we want our daughters to grow into self-respecting, strong women in healthy relationships, we need to model those qualities and connections.

Bias, the antecedent of sexism, infiltrates even our children's safest spaces, including their homes. Home is the easiest place to keep bias away, which isn't to say it's easy at all. Our cultural inability to see par-enting and domestic labor as *work* pressures women to make it seem effortless and contributes to its invisibility. Without close attention and an explicit investment in equality, sexism seeps into all hetero relation-ships. The younger me, who insisted she'd only marry a feminist man and raise kids free from gendered expectations, marvels at finding her older self constantly falling short of those egalitarian ideals. The climb to egalitarianism is a little like being in a game of *Donkey Kong,* but the barrels being thrown at you are lower pay for women, unsubsidized childcare, unpaid maternity leave, no sick leave, male entitlement, and women judged against impossible standards of motherhood and beauty, among other hard-to-navigate obstacles.

In my new-mom mind, mothers kept spotless homes and had fresh-baked goods on hand, spent quality time with their children, and volunteered at their kids' school while also working. How many working fathers feel the need to meet all the pressures of the stay-at-home mom? Something had to give, and for me that started with letting go of my resistance to a messy home and to leftovers or frozen pizza for dinner. We find comfort in doing things the way our mothers did and in the traditions we grew up with, so we're reluctant to let these ideals go. It can also seem unfair to ignore those domestic obligations and impossible standards when our own mothers weren't shown that grace. But if we want to stop passing on bias and sexism to the next generation, better to change our focus from perfectionism to evading fireballs and trying to save *Donkey Kong*'s hostage—our truer selves, our daughters' futures, Princess Equity.

➲ *Praise Your Prince for Being More Than Strong and Your Princess for Being More Than Pretty*

As we saw in the clinical vignette, Drew sent conflicting messages to his kids with his use of the word "princess," but the word itself isn't the problem; his limited definition of what one is was the issue. We need princesses to know they can be clever, interesting, tenacious, funny—anything other than just pretty and in need of protection. And princes need to hear they're valued for being kind, thoughtful, artistic, and sensitive. And that they deserve to be rescued too. In other words, strong and pretty are just single characteristics among many that make up complex human beings. By age ten, though, research shows kids have already internalized the myths and stereotypes about their gender.

A global study in fifteen countries found girls believe their most important asset is their appearance, and ten-to-fourteen-year-olds of all genders believe the myth that boys and men are the dominant sex, strong and independent, while girls and women are vulnerable. Whether you're a girl in Baltimore, Beijing, or New Delhi, you learn your body is a target that needs protecting from the boys, who've come to understand they're the aggressors. Researchers discovered that the constraints we put on girls in the name of protecting them are actually making them more vulnerable, not less, because they engender fear and subservience and restrict knowledge and power leading to profound disadvantages and health implications for girls. In chapter 3 we'll delve into how adults amplify small gender differences, morphing them to fit stereotypes— and how to avoid this.

➲ *Address Sexism Directly*

Pervasive sexism can be so subtle that girls don't realize why they feel less important, credible, and capable than their brothers and male classmates. Instead, they use their loss of voice, space, and dignity that comes with being discriminated against as proof of their inadequacy. Trauma can be prevented or healed only when it's acknowledged and understood. There's no shortage of everyday examples to draw from to help our children detect when sexism is at play. For example, a mother might point out, "The waiter was so deferential with Uncle Sid but ignored me and Aunt Tory until he realized I was paying and became extra nice." Or you can ask questions to stimulate thoughts on fairness: "What do you think about that character giving up her job once she got married? That was common in the 1950s when this show takes place, but did you know a woman's career is still sometimes considered less important than a man's?" And when they're old enough, you can talk directly with them about domestic violence, rape, female genital mutilation, historical injustices, and other undeniable misogyny.

We can encourage girls to speak up when they witness sexism or at least remind them they don't have to laugh or stay silent just to be polite. If they feel comfortable, they can question it ("Do you really believe *all* girls are [insert sexist comment here]?"), disagree ("That's not true"), or offer support ("I'd actually like to hear her thoughts on this"). The caveat here is to not overdo it so that talk about sexism starts to sound like a lecture to young ears. Like a smoke detector that beeps only when there's smoke, a sexism detector in good working order sounds when something is wrong and quiets when all is well. Such radar is essential so girls learn to trust their instincts and can decipher when danger is present.

Most girls are conditioned not to trust themselves and to deny sexist or abusive incidents. They repeatedly hear: you're overreacting, it has nothing to do with being a girl, you took it the wrong way, get a sense of humor, he meant it as a compliment, it's boys being boys. Or, worse still, they hear: What were you wearing? What were you doing? Maybe you led him on. This is widespread, socially sanctioned gaslighting. Despite the mounds of evidence of systemic oppression, girls blame themselves. They decide their comment really was stupid, they didn't deserve recognition, they must have made a mistake, they probably shouldn't have gone home with him, they should have been more forceful, they gave him the wrong idea. If they grow up in a household that actively discusses sexism, their sexism detectors will allow them to reject the gaslighting and to trust what they know to be true, realizing there's something wrong with the culture, not with them personally.

> If they grow up in a household that actively discusses sexism, their sexism detectors will allow them to reject the gaslighting and to trust what they know to be true, realizing there's something wrong with the culture, not with them personally.

⮕ Raise a Son Who Is Sensitized to Inequality

We hear much more about the effect of bias and stereotypes on girls than on boys because girls are the ones who've been marginalized, who have less safety, autonomy, and opportunity. But make no mistake, as we saw with Drew, boys suffer too because of masculine stereotypes. I've come to understand we need to raise boys differently not just to protect our daughters but to protect our sons.

My male patients struggle with so many of the same issues as my female ones—anxiety, self-esteem, friendships, romance, identity, depression, feeling misunderstood—but unlike the girls and women, who often disclose problems to close friends or family, a teenage boy or grown man is often confiding in me before anyone else. Camila had her mother and two best friends to talk to, but Drew had no one. He had friends, but meaningful conversation was rare. There's a loneliness in boys and men who must pretend they don't want connection as a masculine ploy to find connection. Boys can express affection or be complimentary toward other boys, but it's usually quickly followed by something like a punch in the arm or the slang phrase "no-homo," used to reassure others they're not gay. Boy code inhibits them from being emotionally vulnerable and forming the deep connections they may not even know they long for. Fathers can help fill these gaps in social-emotional skill building and intercept this destructive pattern by sharing emotion and affection with their sons. Drew worried affection would make Lucas soft, and Lucas probably noticed he was more tender with Sofia. Over time Drew recognized feeling envious of Lucas for getting fatherly affection that he hadn't gotten and for getting the tenderness from Camila that Drew wanted but couldn't ask for. When we split off our desires, they always manage to come out sideways and disrupt relationships.

Repressing feelings and needs is bad for mental and physical health and gets in the way of men seeking medical and psychological care. In 2018, the American Psychological Association (APA) published its first ever report on boys and men, drawing from an abundance of research. Historically, male psychology was the universal norm—men's behavior and emotions the baseline for humanity—and studying women was a separate consideration. But now psychology was recognizing that the rugged, stoic, self-sufficient ideal of masculinity could be damaging. The report showed those who conform to or experience pressure to embody this stereotype are more at risk of suicide, violence, drinking and driving, bullying and being bullied, and have a life expectancy five years less than women, to name only a few of the many consequences. It's difficult for cisgender straight men to see that a system that benefits them in so many ways isn't only undermining the health and safety of girls and women but also victimizing men.

"Toxic masculinity" is a term that gets thrown around a lot. It resonates with large swaths of girls and women who've been on the receiving end of it, but it tends to alienate boys and men because it sounds like a dump on masculinity in general. There are many great masculine qualities, ones we encourage our daughters to embrace, such as courage, leadership, ambition, and participating in public life. And there's nothing wrong with liking sports, cars, beer, and boys' nights. The last thing we want is boys being guilted for their gender and seeking a sense of belonging online among those who assure them their maleness (and their whiteness) make them extra special. Masculinity itself isn't toxic, but conforming to certain strands of masculinity can be. Toxic masculinity tells boys they're one misstep away from being a pussy or a pansy, so they must deny sadness, never admit doubt or a need for help, be straight and always want sex, see women primarily as sex objects, use violence to dominate, and be intolerant of anyone who doesn't conform to those same norms of masculinity. It encourages a "bros over hos" culture, policing men at risk of becoming "whipped" by a woman. As we saw with Drew, masculinity that divorces men from their vulnerability makes navigating their inner lives and interpersonal relationships difficult.

When we raise boys to fear femininity, as Drew was raised and was on his way to teaching his son, we heighten their "girlie detectors," increasing the odds they'll develop a masculinity lacking in empathy and respect. Indeed, men who grow up believing they have to adhere to a rigid masculine stereotype are more likely to sexually harass women and gender-nonconforming people and to commit physical and sexual dating violence and intimate partner violence. Masculinity is as much a performance as femininity. A study out of Duke found aggression was related to having a fragile sense of masculinity, especially among young men whose identities are still forming. This was what Camila experienced with Drew.

> When we raise boys to fear femininity . . . we heighten their "girlie detectors," increasing the odds they'll develop a masculinity lacking in empathy and respect.

Some say innate male aggression explains machismo, violence, and a drive for dominance. It's true, boys are more aggressive than girls. Actually, it's partially true because while two-thirds are more aggressive, that leaves a full third of boys who are less. Whatever the biological and hormonal differences, cultural and parenting influences are undeniable. By almost every measure, little boys are physiologically and emotionally more vulnerable than girls, yet research shows we tend to ignore their sadness, picking them up less quickly when they cry while also rewarding their anger more. Fathers give boys' anger more attention, and mothers give into it more than with girls. And one study observing toddler conflict found while mothers mostly instructed their children of both sexes to give up a toy to the other child in order to keep the peace, mothers of boys were significantly likelier to support their children in keeping the toy. Unintentionally, we may be teaching our sons they're entitled to whatever it is they want.

The media is an especially strong force in desensitizing our boys to violence and promoting aggression. The male characters in movies and television are much more likely to be violent and to be depicted as criminals than the female characters. I remember the day my son came home from a friend's house in fourth grade and asked me to explain what "prostituters" were. He'd been playing *Grand Theft Auto,* a video game rated for ages seventeen and older but that plenty of younger kids play, and they'd been killing prostitutes. Even the less gory games are full of heavy combat and devoid of emotional complexity; players are brutally defeated and the winner is the crowned champion. And although I appreciate that my son chooses a "more agile" female avatar, every one of them looks like a (fierce) supermodel.

For as long as I can remember, I was told girls can be anything boys can be. I've never heard, however, the phrase "boys can be anything girls can be." Entire books aren't devoted to fostering positive female qualities in boys. We must help boys see that sexism imposes limits on how they think and feel and on what they can be when they grow up. For these things to register as loss, however, we have to actually believe relational qualities like caring, connection, and cooperation are worth having, that they're aspirational for boys, not emasculating. But that requires doing something we don't as a culture do: value the behaviors and norms of girls and women. We can help by reading books to boys that feature girls or emotionally complex boys and be careful to avoid attaching gender to interests and abilities when we speak. As with our daughters, we must allow for and be responsive to the whole spectrum of human emotions in our sons so they can remain connected to their feelings; so they can be sweet, silly, roughhousing, nurturing, ball-throwing, princess/superhero-loving, fart-joking, deeply connected boys.

Often, the only acceptable feeling for boys is anger, which somehow escapes the label "too emotional" reserved for girls. We all have and deserve to feel all the feelings. Lots of my patients, but boys and men in particular who are supposed to be stoic, feel ashamed of their feelings. I often find myself giving them permission to have feelings by saying, "We don't get to pick our feelings. Our feelings are our feelings are our feelings, but once we understand them, we can better decide what we do with those feelings and how we want to behave."

It can be tricky to teach boys about structural privilege without shaming them. Male privilege is usually invisible to boys and men, but when they're made aware of it and its harmful effects, sexist attitudes are shown to diminish. They may be unaware that girls grow up learning to be vigilant, and if they're assaulted, they're blamed for being in the wrong place in the wrong clothes, while boys generally have the privilege of body autonomy. If they say something sexist, remember they're learning. Curiosity, compassion, and education go much further than shaming. Your relationship with them is more important than your, albeit crucial, argument. The overarching goal is to practice egalitarian parenting and build a sufficient sexism detector in boys too, such that denigrating all things feminine will no longer be an acceptable sport.

Of course, raising a son who is sensitized to inequality could also make life harder for him. If he dresses up like Wonder Woman for Halloween, or says he wants to be a nurse when he grows up, he'll probably be mocked. But at least he'll know you have his back and be able to explain the pitiful reasons he's being laughed at. If he tells his posse of other teenage boys to lay off the slut shaming, he may get shamed himself. With my own son, I'm in it for the long game. I suggest he speak up when he hears sexism, but I let him navigate his school life how he needs to, believing even if he doesn't stand up for it now, he at least doesn't participate in it and will one day have the confidence to speak up. Raising allies—kinder, gentler boys—could ultimately save their lives because boys too are beaten and raped by other boys and men. Thanks to the #MeToo movement, awareness about sexism is higher than ever among boys. One group of boys in Rhode Island created what they called a "Pedo Database" to document their teacher's harassment of the girls. When the teacher was later accused of stalking a preteen girl and being inappropriate with other girls, the boys spoke up and their evidence is being used in the investigation. Those are the boys we're trying to raise.

The overarching goal is to practice egalitarian parenting and build a sufficient sexism detector in boys too, such that denigrating all things feminine will no longer be an acceptable sport.

CHAPTER 2

Reconsidering Her Life Script

Challenging Tradition

Many of the women I see in therapy are there to reclaim pieces of themselves they've given up in the name of being feminine and marriageable and to avoid condemnation. They yearn for those bold, unedited, whimsical selves before a narrow definition of girlhood was thrust upon them, maybe at age three or six, but always by ten or twelve when their bodies changed. It's with these losses that they entered motherhood, and it's often in the name of their daughters that they enter therapy. They have a sense that if they can rediscover themselves, their daughters will be permitted fuller selves and bigger lives.

Before they even have sexual identities, we put our pink bundles of sugar and spice on the one-size-fits-all relationship escalator. No matter how successful they are in other regards, to get to the top without the (Tiffany) diamond, the (Vera Wang) dress, the Mrs. moniker, and a husband's last name is to be pitied. Meanwhile, our blue bundles of joy get to decide if and when they get on this escalator, whether they take the stairs instead or choose not to go up at all.

In the age of *smash the patriarchy*, how do traditions so deeply entrenched in sexism persist? By making romance disproportionately important to girls' well-being and sense of identity, we make it hard for them to resist the cultural defaults and seek instead more individually chosen happiness. Dating rituals, marriage proposals (and their teen analogue, promposals), wedding white, and relinquishing last names— sexism dressed up as tradition—can lead girls to subsume their needs and identities to follow a life script that research shows benefits them far less than boys and men. It may seem as though heteronormative scripts are losing their power, but my work with Gen Z girls has shown me those scripts are still alive, albeit more outside their awareness. Sure, they're saying "F—k the binary!" but the dominant culture holds sway. Almost all of the straight young women I see still unconsciously hold the fantasy of being swept off their feet, saved by a man who suddenly makes all their awkward pieces fit into a beautiful whole.

Given traditional pathways are often unfair and sexist for women, what's the alternative to the heteronormative escalator? The answer seems to lie in examining the following intricate ways misogyny has shaped our understanding of relationships and desire, rather than unconsciously imposing our choices onto our children. Attachment to this romantic fairy tale is tough to dismantle, but maybe our children, with assistance from us, will create other versions of relating and being.

The Heightened Importance of Romantic Relationships (for Girls)

Early in her therapy, Janine described why she felt compelled to marry someone two years prior who wasn't right for her. "As a kid I used to play 'Bride' using my pillowcase as a veil, and in middle school I doodled everywhere my first name with my latest crush's last name with a heart around it. But at some point I stopped wanting to be seen like some dependent girlie-girl and started playing the part of the independent woman who didn't need or even really want a man. I kind of even believed it. But I had a parallel belief there was something wrong with me if I didn't have a boyfriend, and it was always in the back of my mind if I didn't get married one day, it would be the ultimate proof of that." Janine was naming the double bind girls find themselves in: desperate for wanting a relationship, defective for not having one.

Janine's marriage was not entirely unhappy. Using an analogy fitting her chosen profession—a dentist—she described it as "more of a dull toothache than a cracked tooth, but it's slowly sucking the life out of me." Financially independent, she'd married at thirty to avoid becoming a sexist trope—a spinster, an old maid, a cat lady. We call an unmarried man a bachelor, maybe even an eligible bachelor, but there's no kind word or even neutral one for an unmarried woman. "Single woman" is a pitiable description if you're over thirty-five. Women who consciously forgo marriage are frequently met with disbelief: "Maybe you just haven't found the right guy yet." Not that long ago a woman's "choice" was either marriage, or poverty and stigma. While that isn't nearly as true today, the collective unconscious has a hard time catching up, and a patriarchal culture doesn't want it to.

I couldn't help thinking of what Janine had said when listening to a younger patient later that month. Lulu, a talented fifteen-year-old gymnast, shared similar frustrations about her struggle to make herself desirable to boys without letting go of her strength and intelligence. "It's like you're supposed to bat your fake eyelashes and go all giggly and pretend like I can't do a roundoff back handspring layout or whatever." She groaned, pitching her lithe torso forward in her chair and burying her head in her arms. "I really like Jake, but why do I have to be some dumb girl who he's going to be attracted to but probably not really respect?"

FROM AN EARLY age, romantic relationships are made important to a girl's sense of self in a way they aren't for a boy's, launching the imbalance and inequality found in future relationships. Marriage is the prize for girls—proof they're valuable—while boys learn it's something to endure, or maybe enjoy second to their career ambitions. Too often girls date and marry boys who haven't spent years preoccupied with marriage, while girls spend years dreaming of their wedding, rather than their life. No wonder women so often end up sacrificing too much and more of themselves than men. But like Janine and Lulu, many girls also have a vague and confusing awareness they're meant to be desirable to boys, but that being seen to care too much about boys or romance makes them seem ditzy or desperate.

Being in love is amazing. Relationships and intimacy are integral to our sense of fulfillment. The problem isn't romance. It's the expectation that all girls should care about is being desirable to boys. And the larger culture doggedly reinforces that notion. At this writing, *The Bachelor,* where women are portrayed as desperate to get married and having "cat-fights" over a rich, hot guy, was just renewed for its twenty-eighth season. Advice on how to get and keep a man is splashed on every second women's magazine cover (down from every cover), and boy troubles are depicted in nearly every TV show girls watch. The slow indoctrination into the virtues of marriage leads girls to believe they need marriage to be happy. Our daughters should hear marriage doesn't make people happy; happy marriages make people happy.

Our daughters should hear marriage doesn't make people happy; happy marriages make people happy.

The Rules of Dating and Relating

With Gen Z being the most progressive generation yet, you'd think the rules of dating would be extinct. But time and again I witness unnecessary hurt and confusion that come out of the stubborn belief that guys actively call the shots and girls passively wait for shots to be called.

"It's all okay!" Lulu said, dropping onto my office couch, picking up right where we'd left off the week before. "He didn't actually ghost me. He knew I was seeing other people and took it wrong. Didn't realize I was just waiting for him to make it official."

"Sounds like he was waiting for you to make it official," I said. Lulu wrinkled her nose. "That seems pushy." Was that her batting her fake eyelashes?

"Hmm, so when he says he's interested in being exclusive, it's not pushy, but when you do, it is?" I asked. Lulu laughed and said, "I know it sounds retro, but yeah, kind of. Or not pushy, but, like, pathetic."

I agreed with her it was a vulnerable position for anyone to be in but wondered if the wish to be chosen can get in the way of knowing what she wants and doesn't want. "Well, I know I like him enough to be with only him and want him to want that too. . . . What else is there to know?"

I suggested we take that as a real question. As Lulu thought about it, she realized she didn't actually know what she was hoping for beyond being called his girlfriend. "I like that he'll be off-limits to other girls, but that also worries me. I don't want to be too serious with someone because gymnastics takes a lot of my time and I still want to see my friends, but it's cool that someone's looking for you after school and, like, they'll pay for your dinner or whatever . . . not that I know if he's even like that." Of course, we all have to practice getting to know ourselves in relationships, but when the focus is more on being picked rather than how you feel and what qualities you want in someone, girls can get into bad relationships.

If we're going to talk about relationships, we need to talk about "benevolent sexism." Many of us, male and female, strongly believe hostile sexism is wholly inappropriate. But we're also raised to believe benevolent sexism is okay because it appears to compliment rather than insult women. Examples includes chivalrous behavior like men picking up the tab at a restaurant and giving up their seat for women. On the surface, it seems perfectly courteous, but it perpetuates a sexual narrative where a man's in control and a woman adopts a passive role. Chivalry is based on the ideal knight, ready to help the weak. Having dinner paid for may sound especially appealing to some girls, but if money is power (and it is), then paying is a way to exert that power. I'm not suggesting we instruct our daughters to never let a guy pay. I'm saying it shouldn't be about gender. Maybe the person who pays is the person who extended the invitation, or they take turns, or the person who makes more money pays. Cultural ideals of who men and women "should be" strongly influence preferences in heterosexual romantic partners, promoting the gender status quo and upholding traditional gender roles. In a phenomenon researchers have dubbed the glass slipper effect, the more a woman associates male romantic partners with chivalry, the less interest she shows in education, career goals, and earning money.

Another form of benevolent sexism is putting women on moral pedestals. It's based on stereotypes of women as more compassionate (read: don't be assertive), intuitive (you lack logic and rational thinking), nurturing (you take care of the kids), tidy (you're better at chores, and your house and body should be neat), and beautiful (no wonder we objectify your bodies). Of course, these qualities in and of themselves aren't bad, but they're used as a stranglehold on women and disguised as benevolence. Behave in these particular ways or you're aberrant.

If you've got an older teen or college student, then you might be thinking, "Who's dating?!" It's true, Gen Z is increasingly embracing "situationships"—relationships that remain undefined or aren't "going anywhere." In a sense, this is what Lulu was describing. It was hard to tell, though, if Lulu's proclamation about not wanting anything serious was a defensive stance against seeming needy. The week prior, she'd been heartbroken about being ghosted and had wondered, pulling out her phone, if she'd texted him back too soon, not soon enough, liked the right amount of his posts, and so on. "Oh gawwd," she'd drawled, "I double texted him. Ugh. But it was only because I wasn't sure if my first text made sense."

It's very possible she didn't want a serious relationship. I've certainly noticed, and the research shows, that relationship fever among these digital natives has been tempered compared with other generations. Having grown up alongside technology, they have constant companions and endless opportunities for finding someone new, a passive activity that can be done anytime, anywhere, creating the illusion they don't need intimacy, even as they wonder why they're so lonely. Perhaps in these tenuous times with worsening climate issues, financial instability, and a pandemic, kids are retreating from intimacy, too focused on their growing anxiety to make space for that which comes with dating. Maybe they're being pragmatic, focusing on fostering individual stability before diving into relationships. Or maybe situationships are lending kids the space they need to explore their gender and sexual identities.

Regardless, girls are still struggling with many of the same things we struggled with: differentiating lust from love; settling for a small amount of attention, hoping it'll become something more; fending off unwanted attention; trying to figure out how far is too far. In other words, many are still focused on what's appropriate or what scraps they can get, rather than on what they really want. The rules of sex for girls (as we'll discuss in the chapter on deconstructing girls' sexuality) still pit girls against guys, with guys trying to get what they can and girls playing defense. And they're heading toward a world of internet dating sites full of antiquated attitudes about women and relationships.

As I write this, SugarDaddy.com and MillionaireMatch.com still exist, both reinforcing a traditional male breadwinner–female homemaker model. WhatsYourPrice.com doesn't even attempt to hide the commodification of women: Men are the bidders, and women are auctioned off as dates. You might be surprised how many college students dabble on these sites. Even on the more commonly used dating sites like Bumble, you find disturbingly misogynist entitlement, despite the proliferation of men using "Feminist" in their profiles since #MeToo. Often used for one-night (or one-hour) stands, they've become a free-market economy for sex. Although sex is less taboo these days for all genders, and hookup culture insists girls can be conquerors too, guys who sleep with four different women in a week are players, and young women who hook up once with a guy they just met are whores.

A college freshman in my practice slept with one such "feminist" man after they matched earlier that night and had shared a fun evening over drinks. When he texted her to meet again, she wrote, "I had such a good time but I'm not interested in a relationship right now. I'm in exams and kinda nursing a broken heart so it's a bad idea anyway." His response: "Shoulda figured u were whoring when you were willing to get it in so quickly." Ouch. "Feelings?" I asked. "I want to say it rolled off my back because clearly he's got issues. But it stung. I mean, I thought he was a good guy and I would've seen him again if, well, you know . . . ," she said, referring to a painful breakup. "And things get around so, yeah, great. Now I'm a slut."

The profile pictures of young women on these sites are alarmingly homogeneous. Scrolling through my straight male friend's Tinder account, I saw almost exclusively skinny women with straight hair, fake eyelashes, and revealing clothing. Of course, they're not all like that in real life, but when I asked a friend's twenty-year-old daughter about it, she explained "Bombshell" is the name of the game if you want guys to swipe right. "And our self-esteem relies on those swipes," she said, only half mocking her generation. Our daughters are growing up in a dating age almost wholly dependent, at least initially, on their appearance. And when they do match, girls tell me they're inundated with unsolicited dick pics and requests for nudes.

The Romantic Proposal

As informal and different as teenage courting seems these days, not to mention demands for equality and same-sex marriage, you'd think the male-led proposal would wither. Yet it seems as vibrant as ever in the form of perfectly staged viral marriage proposals and now promposals and even homecoming dance proposals. The trope of the man who's afraid of commitment and needs to prove he's devoted to the woman who's desperate for a partner is being formalized as early as ninth grade. Girls learn men set the pace of relationships, knowing their time to hint at what they want, or should want, is coming. As Janine said, waving her wedding ring, "I waited for him to decide if I was worthy of his dowry."

Weddings, Maiden Names, and Motherhood, Oh My!

Weddings, last names, and motherhood might seem far off as we consider our daughters' lives now, but how they learn to navigate those are steeped in the traditions that conflate female adulthood with selflessness, that teach her that being female means her identity and value are defined by her relationship to men. It's well worth helping her think critically about each of these traditions and offer alternative solutions.

Traditional marriage rituals seem incompatible with nourishing equality. Janine's father "gave her away" in the white dress and veil symbolizing her purity (though she wore hot-pink shoes in mini-rebellion). The male officiant "permitted" her husband to kiss his bride and pronounced them "*man* and wife." Then the best man introduced the newly merged couple as "Mr. and Mrs. [His Name]." Just like that the name Janine had her entire life—the name associated with all her achievements and social media accounts, the name that would no longer turn up in a Google search by an old classmate or boss looking for her with important news or a fabulous job lead—was erased and followed by champagne and exuberant applause. Then all the single ladies lined up—heels off, dresses hitched—clambering to catch the bouquet and snag themselves a life.

FOR MANY WOMEN, relinquishing their name is symbolic of family unity, making it easier to know what to write on future children's birth certificates. It can also be a romantic gesture of commitment, or a woman may be influenced by her theology. Indeed, the Bible sees a woman giving up her own name and using her husband's as a symbol of a man and woman's legal and spiritual unity. But why, then, doesn't the husband take the last name of his wife? The answer is because for a man to become like a woman in any way is to sacrifice status. So, yes, we give up our names for many reasons, but it's also a choice to prioritize a man's name over our own.

Though there are many ways to put a positive spin on a woman's giving up her name, we can't ignore what it signals, not just to others, but to our daughters. When girls see their names as temporary, as less important than the name they'll finally be given—their husband's—it decreases their sense of being whole and important in and of themselves, with or without a husband. It signals women's selves and others' needs are incompatible and reinforces to their future children the idea that women are inferior to men.

None of us can live free from history, and when we change our names, we're celebrating, albeit symbolically, a tradition in which a woman was a man's property, which meant she didn't have a legal identity of her own and rape and most beatings weren't considered crimes within marriage. Today, taking a husband's name is seen as a choice. Yet, even among straight couples who share progressive gender politics, it's still only women who grapple with this "choice" and get treated like a disruptive teenage rebel if they don't.

The truth is, whatever name a woman uses will invite judgment, because we've set up a false dichotomy that says she must choose between herself and her family. She's either selfish, and doesn't really love him if she doesn't take his name, or aiding and abetting her own and other women's erasure if she does. The point is, if entering marriage on equal footing is important, then the decision shouldn't be based on gender. It might still mean taking your husband's last name like an old friend of mine who couldn't wait to get rid of her last name—Kuntz—or another friend whose husband took her last name because she was an only child and wanted to keep the family name going, whereas he had brothers who would do that. Other friends combined parts of their last names to create a new one, and still other friends created an entirely new name from the Hebrew word for voice. And yes, any of these name changes will also cause hassles, but at least they were made deliberately and not from a place of entrenched sexism.

The complication, I admit, can be the kids' last name. My husband and I each kept our own last names when we married because we were already professionally established. Throughout my first pregnancy my husband insisted he didn't mind our children having my last name. He assured me plenty of people have their mother's surname, including well-known people like Eric Clapton, Lauren Bacall, and Norah Jones. He understood the greater privileges men possess in almost every sphere and wanted our children to be born into as equal a world as we could offer. I wanted both of us represented in the kids, not just me, and suggested we do a hybrid of our names, one we could all take. "I'm too old to change my name," he complained. *Yes,* I thought, *changing your name as an adult is a funny thing, isn't it?* Even when his father expressed dismay, he insisted that giving our baby my surname was what he wanted.

And yet.

When he laid eyes on our firstborn, he broke the news to me: he wanted his name to be part of his son's name too. *Yes,* I thought, *it's odd for one's child not to have your name, isn't it?* My husband and I each kept our own long last names and hyphenated them for the (poor) kids, mimicking how it's done in Latin American countries. Those who disagreed showed their resistance to our choice by taking years in some cases to properly address mail to our kids. Others feigned indifference, but said (repeatedly) they don't understand what'll happen when the kids marry. Nevertheless, I'm glad my kids' names pave the way for pride in both their maternal and paternal lineages. And if they get married, they're likely to take a conscious approach to finding a mutually satisfying name with their partners, quietly dismantling power structures one generation at a time.

Undoing the Patriarchal Blueprint

Why do these traditions persist even among folks whose sexism detectors are pretty responsive? Maybe it's just a failure of imagination; we've been doing it this way for so long. Maybe, in order to see the world as fair, to counteract our cognitive dissonance, we have to buy into the myth of male privilege and the traditions that support that. Maybe we're choosing protective paternalism over hostile sexism. Whatever it is, we're not doing our daughters any favors to insist sexism has nothing to do with it. To quote Janine, "I just wish my mother had been real with me."

Rejecting long-standing traditions can feel like risking important relationships, viewed as rejecting the choices of people we know and love. Not rejecting these sexist trappings, however, can lead to accusations of being conformist. For these reasons, without realizing it, many of us jump through hoops to defend the sexism to which we've grown accustomed. We tell ourselves we're empowered women making a choice, which in and of itself is feminist. I'm not suggesting we criticize individual women's choices. Life is complicated, and none among us can live flawless feminist lives. We've been indoctrinated since birth, and even if we can clearly identify sexism, it's easier and, at times, safer to abide by social norms. But we need to have honest conversations with our kids about the choices we've made, and they're making, within a patriarchal system as just that: choices influenced by a system that doesn't have girls' and women's best interests in mind. If we take pleasure in certain sexist traditions, as I do polished toes and eyebrow threading, let's examine why rather than pretend it's as simple as something we choose to do for ourselves.

Women too often reach the top of the escalator with all the trappings and instead of enlightenment discover resentment and regret for sacrificing careers, intimacy, adventure, and self-growth. Not surprisingly, studies show women are less satisfied in their marriages than men and tend to be the initiators of divorce. They're also happier than men after the divorce. The path forward, for our daughters, for all of our children regardless of gender, is to cultivate intimate partnerships that celebrate self-expression, not at the expense of the relationship but in the service of it. Beyond examining relationship traditions, here are some other ways we can change the script.

⮕ *Encourage and Normalize Mixed-Gender Friendships*

Just as research shows promoting positive contact and cooperation between people of different ethnicities, races, and developmental abilities can improve attitudes and relationships, this is true of gender too. When adults support mixed-gender interaction, it leads to more collaborative play between genders. It communicates, too, that it's not only acceptable to play with another gender but also perfectly fine to play *like* them. Exposure to cross-gender experiences and activities can help cultivate more well-rounded people. These experiences liberate kids from restrictive gender scripts, helping boys feel freer to be emotional and girls freer to be competitive, for example. They provide opportunities to experience different communication and negotiation styles, which is important preparation for future romantic and professional relationships. Gender-diverse friendships are also found to reduce sexism and increase social competence. Boys are more likely to grow up viewing girls as equals rather than commodities. Such friendships help kids both understand the complexities of the other gender(s) and realize they're not actually different species, even if the Amazon and Netflix algorithms would like them to think they are.

When we allow for friendship rather than push romance, we set our kids up to expect equality. In a study of nine preschool classrooms, when two boys or two girls held hands, teachers talked about them being besties. But when it was a boy and girl, it was a budding romance. This was problematic not only because they were projecting adult intentions onto children's behavior but also because when the teachers perceived there to be a crush, they were more likely to interpret a boy's inappropriate behavior, such as hitting or kissing a girl, as affectionate instead of invoking the usual disciplinary instruction—even if the girl was upset. It's not hard to see how children grow up believing girls' consent isn't required, or at least is less important than boys' desires. Classroom rules like "keep your hands and bodies to yourself" should be applied equitably, across genders, to sexualized behaviors.

This whole cross-gender friendship thing came more easily to me with my son, Jonah, than with my daughter, Gabi. I'd made no differentiation in terms of gender when planning playdates and playgroups for him, intuitively understanding growing up with female friendships was as important for his development as having same-sex friendships. When the girls and boys began *naturally* segregating, I encouraged him to keep up with those girlfriends, sometimes inviting their families over for dinner to help maintain the connection.

Gabi, shier than Jonah, had a few close friends, all girls. I told myself I was respecting her reserved nature by not diversifying, but I think I was primed to encourage close female bonds. I knew the power of sisterhood and was thrilled she was learning it too. There was one boy—the son of close family friends—whom Gabi enjoyed being with when we got together. It's true at five she decided she wanted to marry him, but she also married several of her female friends that year. The obsession was weddings, not gender or the person she was marrying.

The marriage to this boy, or the memory of it anyway, didn't last, and soon they moved on to making up Harry Potter games together. But it's also possible she was in love for a time with one of these children. Even as we manufacture romance where there's none, we also tend to dismiss or mock the strong feelings of young romantic love. Falling in and out of love is relational practice, and legitimizing kids' emotions tells them there's something to learn here. Gabi's intense friendships with those girls continue to this day, but her social circle expanded in middle school to include more boys. When one ended up on our porch with her a couple of times, I had to stop myself from asking if they were dating. *Sheesh, boys and girls can just be friends, even in middle school,* I chided myself.

In her book *Beyond Birds and Bees,* Bonnie J. Rough expounds on the surprising lack of sexual shame and stereotyping found in Dutch culture. She describes girls and boys sitting together at school, playing together at the park, and having mixed-gender birthday parties. Cross-gender friendships start in toddlerhood and continue through childhood and adolescence into adulthood. Her adult experience in Amsterdam made me want to pack my bags. She writes,

> *I distinctly noticed the calming effect of life in a place largely unobsessed with sex and gender. Interacting as adults with neighbors and shopkeepers and strangers, it did seem that before we were men and women, we were people. There was no winky, teasing manner in which men spoke with women, no deferential or distrustful tone women generally took with men. With less attention on my gender, I simply felt happier in it.*

If American parents want to diminish power differentials in relationships, they should take a page from the Dutch playbook and create a sense of normalcy around gender-diverse friendships. We can buy children books and choose television shows that depict friendships between boys and girls, and we can model having friends of different genders. I chose to tell my children's beloved preschool teacher, who often called attention to her students' genders, about a study showing the power teachers have to shape cooperative cross-sex play. Just by positively commenting on cooperation a teacher notices between a boy and a girl, she could double the rates they play together. Think of the far-reaching effects, I said.

⮎ *Shatter the Glass Slipper, Endorse Love*
"First comes love. Then comes marriage. Then comes [Girl's Name] with a baby carriage." The order in which we're supposed to do things is the extent to which many of us have learned about relationships. The rest is what we've absorbed in our own homes and in the media. Based on the naïveté of the girls I work with, I propose we as parents address love concretely with kids in three related ways. First, we must dispel the romantic fantasy living in their unconscious, if not their consciousness, that says that a man's love (after sufficient tests of her own love and patience) will transform a girl from an invisible peasant into a princess beloved by all the kingdom (and her relationship will magically look different from her parents'). Second, we must ground love within an actual

definition. And third, we must address a common yet insidious dynamic in girls' lives: longing for the unavailable guy.

It's not that parents haven't tried to counteract the fantasy of being saved by a man in the last couple of generations. The soundtrack to my childhood was the iconic 1970s album *Free to Be . . . You and Me* about gender equality. On it was the story of Atalanta, the princess heroine who outran her suitors so she, rather than her father, the king, could choose whether and whom she'd marry someday. The story empowered little girls everywhere with the message they have the right to choose their futures. But that's where it ends. We didn't know once we chose—if that choice included marriage and kids—there'd be the double shift, the mental load, no paid maternity leave, expensive childcare, the need to trade pay for flexibility, the judgment we'd face for "leaning in" or "opting out." So our children have watched us get divorced in droves, or stay in relationships to "make it work for the kids" or to save face.

Today, we stress girls' independence and warn them against expecting anyone else to make them happy, encourage them to find fulfillment before entering a serious relationship, and tell them not to rely on a man for financial stability because "you never know." However, our expectation that they find happiness by following a script that ultimately has them supporting men's happiness with their bodies, their children, and their unpaid labor in exchange for economic support and social recognition hasn't changed much. Sure, there's been improvement. Now men cook and do bath time and, as long as women gush sufficiently, they're allowed to supplement their own dreams (just don't push it, girl).

Instead of helping them question romantic social norms and work through these fantasies, we've confused them; we've created cynicism and fear, and we might have inadvertently diminished the significance of relationships. We can no longer afford to let pop culture educate our children on relationships or to empower choice without also explaining the limitations. The good news is, kids tell us they want our help with loving and being loved. A project out of Harvard whose mission is to help caregivers and educators raise caring, ethical human beings found 70 percent of young adults reported wishing they'd received more information from their parents about romantic relationships.

We're in the tricky position of exposing the myth of romantic love for girls without belittling the fun of romance and the importance of deeply loving relationships, of making it clear our daughters are so much more than their romantic or sexual desirability without dismissing the real emotional turmoil that can come from unrequited crushes or badly matched relationships. Our wish to see our daughters find security, stability, and healthy partnerships can seem at odds with unmasking traditions that hurt them. But I've found that trusting girls with the dilemmas we face leads them to making better choices. They're already exposed to so many ideas and are forming more sophisticated opinions about the world and being a woman earlier than we ever did, thanks to the internet.

So, when you insist a guy won't magically bring her life into focus and make it matter, and finding personal fulfillment first is a good idea, also tell her there are actual ways she can and should expect to be fulfilled in her primary relationships. Tell her to pay attention to who *she* is with her paramour, not who he is on paper. I can tell when my teenage patients are in healthy relationships because they feel inspired by their partners to become the best version of themselves—better communicators, better students, more accepting people. They maintain their other friendships and develop personal interests, remaining individuals while being a couple. They feel supported in their personal aspirations.

One girl said to me, "I'm pretty amazed he thinks my yearbook work is as important as I do. Sometimes he'll spend hours with me at the office on a Saturday and never make me feel guilty." That's what we should tell our daughters to expect (and to provide). Without learning what they can expect, practically speaking, they risk spending years in a relationship that doesn't provide that, blaming themselves for not figuring out how to be fulfilled on their own. They should also hear from us that love includes both wonderful and disappointing moments; that it takes work in the way a hobby you're excited about takes work, which might be frustrating at times but isn't painful, exhausting work; and that conflict is normal, though intentionally inflicting pain is not.

We don't want to diminish the butterflies, fireworks, and heart thumping. In fact, we should encourage them to savor these things while also telling them that when the euphoria inevitably wears off is when love is tested. Enduring love is grounded, tangible, and stable. We can describe how being in a long-term, committed relationship—one that offers meaningful shared experiences, steady support, and opportunities to be supportive—is good for her well-being even after, or maybe especially after, the stomach churning stops. Perhaps most important, though, we need to drive home the message that nurturing those qualities is a choice. And it's a choice that's easier to make in the beginning of a relationship when their crush is little more than a projection of what could be. That's a very different message from the fairy-tale premise that we love instinctually.

I find it helpful to say something like "In the beginning, hormones are in the driver's seat and you get to coast along, carefree with the wind in your hair. But as the relationship grows, you'll have to take over the steering if you don't want to crash." It's far more difficult to continue in a relationship when it encompasses compromises, sacrifices, foibles and farts, expressing gratitude, listening empathically, forgiving. Those are skills that strengthen and sustain long-term social bonds, and we need to help kids understand this rather than hope maturity will make it clear eventually.

Perhaps the best way to explain love to our daughters—to all our children—is to invoke the renowned author bell hooks's words "Love is a verb." She argues, "Our confusion about what we mean when we use the word 'love' is the source of our difficulty in loving." We do our children no favors by having them enter adolescence believing romantic love is an indefinable and mystical thing. They don't know what to look for or how to know whether their intense feelings for someone else are likely to lead to healthy or unhealthy romantic relationships. When we help them understand that love is an action (which sometimes means "inaction, restraint, and self-control"), that love must be demonstrated and used to guide how people interact with each other—not just something someone says they feel—they'll be better able to assess their romantic relationships, alongside big feelings.

We can acknowledge that grand gestures are lovely while pointing out it's their beau's day-to-day actions that say the most. We can suggest they pay attention to what matters, giving our own examples: he gets my humor, she memorizes how much milk I take in my coffee, they put aside their phone to listen to what's upsetting me, he's not intimidated by my personal growth. Then we can explore what matters to them. Kids (and sometimes adults) need to be reminded that a healthy relationship inspires them to feel more hopeful, caring, generous, and self-respecting, not chronically desperate and self-doubting.

One evening as I drove Gabi, lover of animal facts, to her babysitting gig, she told me about a recent TikTok suggesting cats gravitate to those who give them the least attention. "Like people," I said. She looked at me, puzzled, and declared she's friends with the people who like her the most. "That's amazing; that's how it should be," I cooed. I'd been waiting for the moment to arise organically when I could discuss a destructive dynamic so many young women encounter: longing for the unavailable man. So I pulled out the old Groucho Marx quotation "I don't want to belong to any club that will accept me as a member" to explain how low self-esteem can cause us to reject people who like us romantically, and instead lead us to desire those who are incapable of answering our emotional needs. I asked her why she thought that might be, and she insightfully suggested some people feel powerful when they can fix other people. I added it might also make them feel special if they're the one whom this unavailable person finally opens his heart to, especially if they didn't feel especially seen by anyone as a child. Our early emotional attachments inform our future relationships. If those were deficient or abusive, we might transfer the early unmet wishes onto incompatible partners both to fulfill the infantile wish to change parents into proper caregivers and to overcome the sense of powerlessness we felt.

This is where the social meets the psychological. When we support dependence in girls and make any whiff of dependency humiliating for boys, we create a power differential that can stir up old wounds. Girls often express frustration because they sense a boy has feelings for them but is afraid of getting close. Their ability to empathize with how the boy got to be like that can make it harder for them to get angry and walk away. Instead, they're spurred to want to prove their love in order to help him feel safer so they can finally have the love story they're meant to.

Girls don't always appreciate that for a relationship to thrive, it must be a mutual project consciously tended to by both partners. "You should never have to grovel for love," I told Gabi. "The person you choose should choose you back." This is where "Love is a verb" comes in handy.

"It doesn't matter if he feels it if he can't show it most of the time. It doesn't matter, even if you understand his trauma," I said, and added, "You can't teach someone intimacy; they have to learn to tolerate it for themselves." The concept behind these words is you can't love a man into examining his pain, no matter how beautiful, smart, or caring you are, because you can't compete with the social rewards he otherwise reaps from stoicism and an unequal stratification of power. Then I gave Gabi some examples from my young dating life. There's no guarantee that will save her from similar heartbreaks, but oh, how I wish I'd understood that concept as a teen.

With girls it's also important to address abusive relationships, which often start in adolescence and run the gamut from being painfully strung along, sometimes for years, to psychological, physical, and sexual abuse. While understanding the dynamics of a relationship and our role in it gives us a better chance of creating something healthy, our girls need to hear that when it comes to abuse, nothing they bring to the relationship warrants it. You can borrow another line from bell hooks and tell them that "love and abuse cannot coexist," while also explaining to them people who've been hurt by parents or others who were supposed to love them can form an unconscious connection between love and suffering, believing they go hand in hand.

You might be thinking no matter how well we educate our children to assess a love interest, love cares little for our left-brain logic. As the novelist-philosopher Alain de Botton writes in his book *On Love,* "There is a great difference . . . between wisdom and the wise life." While love may indeed oppose reason, and attraction can't easily be suspended, I believe the seeds we've planted will sprout before our daughters establish dysfunctional patterns that are difficult to break. There's plenty of research that shows children who have a healthy relationship with their parents or whose parents modeled a warm relationship are more likely to develop positive romantic relationships, but I couldn't find any that tested the benefits of teaching kids about relationships. Anecdotally, though, I see it all the time. A fifteen-year-old named Alyssa, for example, recently said to me after she decided to stop pursuing her elusive, sometimes mean boyfriend, "I kept hearing my dad's voice saying, 'If a boy's not being nice, they're just not into you or not mature enough to be dating' and remembering you saying, 'I'm not sure that's what "like" looks like.'" I'd said that empathically, without judgment, in response to her insisting she knew he liked her, even though he ignored her at school, because he'd show up at her house later to make out. It's worth adding, I've found fathers have an enormous influence on their daughters' approach to love.

BY QUESTIONING TRADITION and gendered relationship patterns, we can better resist passing on sexist conventions to girls. I don't want my daughter to wake up in twenty-five years and wonder why she made a life that doesn't suit her. I don't want her, like so many women today, isolated in a nuclear family, caught in a shame spiral because she's facing the impossible combination of society's unachievable parenting standards and its almost total lack of support for mothers. I already fantasize about my future grandchildren and helping my kids with that unending, decimating, transcendent thing that is childcare. But that doesn't mean I want my daughter blindly following a life script of marriage and kids that asks more of her than she has to give. Nor do I want my son to reap benefits that tax his partner. It's not always easy to admit this to myself, because it means a reckoning of what I did to follow that script while also desperately holding on to at least a piece of myself. We may not have a magic wand that ensures our girls get the respect and assistance they deserve, but we do have the ability to guide them in matters of love and equality as best we can and be open to where they're taking their lives.

CHAPTER 3

Stereotypes and the Gender Binary

Reimagining Gender

"I can't keep up anymore," Melissa said breathlessly into my voicemail when she called to set up an appointment for therapy for her and her fourteen-year-old, Maddie. "Until a few months ago she, I mean they, were my daughter, who had crushes on boys. And now they're my non-binary child dating girls, but they say they're not a lesbian because they're not a girl. I don't mind it, I swear, I just want to understand her better. I mean them."

While gender terminology today may baffle many parents, plenty of us, including Melissa, are aware of the limits that come with rigid gender norms. But a binary structure is easy. It's shorthand for what clothing or toys to buy and what to expect, which for girls stereotypically means being demure, nurturing, agreeable, and sexually naive; for boys, it means being active, aggressive, in charge, and sexually experienced. When someone crosses the divide, it challenges our ingrained, generations-old conviction of well-defined gender roles.

We've come to believe these gender roles always existed and so must be biologically driven. But the broader, more creative world of gender isn't a twenty-first-century creation, though it's more mainstream than at any other time in history. Many indigenous cultures held more fluid and dynamic understandings of gender, recognizing at least four genders (feminine female, masculine female, feminine male, masculine male) before being subjected to European theories of gender. Today, "Two Spirit" refers to the concept that people possess both a male and a female spirit, and their identity is determined by the spirit most dominant within them, not by their bodily form. What if our most fundamental way of perceiving others is an illusion?

Even if we don't believe in biological essentialism, puberty tends to heighten gender expectations as parents scramble to manage or prevent sex and all the risks and complications that come with it. We're parenting from a pattern cut from the dominant culture—the one most of us grew up with, where only boys and girls appeared to exist and they mostly dated the "opposite" sex—and we're wildly searching for a freer and more inclusive way of seeing our own kids.

Kids of all genders, including those who are cisgender, tell us understanding gender as a spectrum is liberating and truer to their experience. Indeed, a majority of the Gen Z set believes there are more than two genders, and one out of eighteen young adults identify as something other than male or female. Even though heterosexuality and a binary gender identity are what we've decided is "normal" in the larger population, most kids given the space to explore will fall somewhere along these continuums and not at either end. Yet everything—behavior, clothing, relationships, and identities—is measured against that of the cisgender straight person who embodies one end of the binary; kids who aren't heteronormative are often forced to explain themselves.

Just as we don't want our daughters devoting their mental energy to their appearance, we don't want gender-fluid kids spending their time explaining themselves, correcting people on their name, pronouns, and identity, and metabolizing the confusion, hurt, and anger others throw their way because of bias. Even cisgender heterosexual kids who don't fit stereotypes or who want to explore wearing something different face pushback. Embracing gender as a continuum reduces stereotypes, and that's a good thing for everyone, particularly our girls.

. . .

IN OUR FIRST session Melissa explained why she wanted to learn her baby's sex during pregnancy. "Ever since I was a little girl, I wanted a daughter, and gender reveal parties had just become a big thing. I didn't need mine to go viral or anything. I was doing it more because I wanted to be held accountable for what's important if it was a boy—his health, not gender—and to celebrate mightily if it was a girl. When I cut into that cake and saw pink frosting, I was elated for weeks." In that sentence, Melissa did what most of us do: she conflated sex and gender.

Sex is about body parts, and gender is how you're expected to act because of those parts. Actually, it's more complicated than that. As kids blow up the binary, researchers are scrambling to better understand what besides socialization contributes to gender identity, such as genes, hormones, and trauma. Still, gendered socialization is arguably more common than ever before, driven by its profitability and the cultural embrace of girls' sexualization. A gender reveal party then is really more a *genital* reveal, but friends and family gather at these events as if in collective agreement that biology is destiny and the fate of this little human rests on the pink or blue confetti that will spring from a popped balloon.

The Making of a Two-Gendered World

When I grumbled about stereotypes growing up, I was often dismissed with the insistence that boys and girls are just different, a lazy shrug indicating we're at nature's mercy. But it's now widely accepted that nature *and* nurture—biological *and* social processes—create differences among the sexes. In other words, our social, cultural world heavily interacts with our genes and hormones to amplify differences between boys and girls. Nurture, however, is the only part we have any control over.

Many of the characteristic differences seen as distinctly male or female, such as activity levels, emotional reactions, interests, and intellectual abilities, are far less significant than we think. Most differences are only obvious if you look at extreme examples—the most fidgety boys compared with the most fidgety girls or the most skilled readers from each group. The average (or typical) boy and girl show only minor differences, and most of us fall in the average range. In fact, boys' and girls' brains are remarkably alike.

The brain's sex differences—most of which have been found in adults only—are innate, but that doesn't necessarily mean born that way. The brain has what's called plasticity; it can be and is molded by its environment. As the neuroscientist Lise Eliot put it in *Pink Brain, Blue Brain*, your brain is what you do with it. "Every task you spend time on— reading, running, laughing, calculating, debating, watching TV, folding laundry, mowing grass, singing, crying, kissing, and so on—reinforces active brain circuits at the expense of other inactive ones. Learning and practice rewire the human brain." Or, as the neuropsychologist Donald Hebb famously said, "Neurons that fire together wire together."

Children themselves intensify the disparities by playing to their modest strengths. As Eliot says, "They constantly exercise those 'ball-throwing,' 'doll-cuddling' circuits." Instead of encouraging kids to stray from their comfort zones and develop more fully, we too often assume their comfort zones are a delineation of their skills, and we behave in ways that motivate them to remain in that initially pleasant but ultimately constricting box. Then we insist those differences are "natural," "essential," and "biological."

So why, then, if science shows the innate differences between the vast majority of boys and girls are so small, do we hear a maddening amount about them? Stereotyping is our brain's way of simplifying the complexities we encounter every day so we can make sense of the world and recall things more quickly. So the small differences we see at birth get magnified by parents, teachers, and others in how they talk to and play with their children. The media loves to hype up the differences we've inflated with our binary-constructing impulse. Boys have trouble learning! Girls can't do math! Girls are nurturers; boys leaders! The more adults harp on those differences, believing they're immutable, the more these stereotypes materialize into children's self-fulfilling prophecies.

Actually, we start constructing boxes for our babies even before birth. Mothers who know they're having a boy are more likely to describe their babies' movements as "strong" and "vigorous," but mothers who don't know the sex describe no such differences. Once born, infant daughters are described as little and beautiful and are rated as finer-featured, less strong, more delicate, and more feminine than infant sons, even when there's no objective differences in birth length, weight, or Apgar scores. Consistently, in experiments where babies are randomly assigned labels of female or male, they're perceived differently regardless of their actual sex. Those labeled boys (even if they're girls) are described as stronger and more masculine. Adults interpret behavior through a gendered lens, as in crying means a girl is sad but a boy is angry, and they give them stereotyped toys based on their hypothetical sex. These stereotypes are the foundation on which sexism is built.

I DESPISED THE mandate to be "feminine" growing up because, even if I couldn't have articulated it at the time, it connoted an artificial binary that left me with the short end of the stick. It required a performative softness, a quiet Goody Two-Shoes who relinquished her own will and followed the boys. I made note of the women in my life passively watching while the men did, worked, and played. The women were more active in the domestic sphere, cooking, cleaning, and often putting together elaborate dinners, but when the guests arrived, the men took their seats at the head of the table, leading whatever party or religious ritual was going on while the women served quietly in the background. Judith Butler's theory of gender eventually confirmed the sense lodged deep in my psyche, despite my resistance, that I had to "perform gender" properly in order to be liked. It seemed then and still seems today as if femininity must be devoid of anything "too" interesting. Being interesting comes in a distant second to mastering the waifish, passive, pleasant persona that, in part, is signaled by spending a good deal of time grooming. Just being human can be unfeminine, a lesson my friend's infant daughter was privy to at just two weeks old. After having an explosive bowel movement that leaked out of her diaper and all over her, her mom, and the exam table at the doctor's office, the poor nurse had to clean it up and as she did, clucked, "Not very ladylike, missy. Not ladylike at all."

Because being feminine has historically required girls and women to let go of so much of themselves and reduced their power to their appearance, second-wave feminists shunned femininity. They wanted girls to be recognized as more than just good-looking property. They wanted them to forgo the two-dimensional nature demanded of girls that crushed their spirits and was used against them as proof of incompetence. They wanted girls to have the freedom to develop all of their skills and talents rather than direct the bulk of their energy into their appearance. But feminism has evolved, and we know people can be many things. We know femininity no longer equates to pretty and coquettish and a woman who shaves or wears stilettos can also be a badass. The problem isn't wholly with traditional femininity itself. It lies also in the male-centric value system that considers all things feminine vapid and superficial. Masculine interests get the respect, so economic power is valued over intimacy, baseball over fashion.

Femininity is problematic when it becomes prescriptive and is foisted on girls who don't find specific clothing, activities, or personality traits associated with femininity appealing. Using biological sex to determine gender places a forced inhibition on one's identity. Like a domino toppling all other dominoes in its path, if we expect a vulva to mean innocence, glitter, and ballet, we risk toppling someone's identity formation. "Girl" is only one characteristic—arguably the least interesting—of many, and to emphasize it above all others is to miss out on who the person in front of you really is.

LIKE MELISSA, I'D wanted a daughter for as long as I could remember, something I've never been totally able to square with my disdain for the emphasis this culture places on gender. I'd read the meta-analyses and knew most differences hyped by the media were unfounded. If the two sexes are mostly similar, why did it matter to me? I'd like to say it was all about giving her the freedom to be herself without the constrictions of femininity, but that would be only partially true. Like many people, I imagined a sweet, helpful daughter who would borrow my clothes, have similar interests, talk long into the night with me, and be deeply connected forever. I'd heard many times the Irish saying "A son is a son until he takes a wife; a daughter's a daughter all of her life." Was I already excusing my son, not yet conceived, from being helpful and remembering to call? When I was pregnant with him, I joked I could practically feel the fire trucks ramming against my insides. And guess who became obsessed with fire trucks by the time he was two? I mention these things because I want you to know no one, not even people who write books about gender bias and sexism, is immune to stereotyping.

In the Western world, we over-assign gendered meanings to anatomical sex, and we've relied on a long history of stereotypes to determine what's right and wrong for each sex. But gender norms have always been dependent on place and time; little more than a social construct shaped by years of history and evolving fashions. Dresses, heels, wigs, makeup, and the color pink, for example, were all once worn by boys or men. It seems absurd how adamantly we argue now these things are for girls only.

Beyond the Binary—a Gender Revolution

Despite major backlash in recent years, U.S. culture is increasingly less tolerant of the hierarchies that disadvantage gender-nonconforming people like Melissa's daughter, Maddie, and kids are leading the charge. They're a generation more open to recognizing the complexities of sex, sexuality, and gender. They're fluent in gender diversity and alternative pronouns. They're tired of men being valued more than women, heterosexual folks more than LGBTQ+ people, and those who conform to gender stereotypes more than those who don't. They see more clearly than prior generations that masculinity's status is maintained by the deprecation of femininity and homosexuality and that girls are sexualized as a means of putting them in their place. They're in the midst of a revolution, trying to escape the carefully drawn lines that keep boys and girls in their respective lanes. One-quarter of Gen Z kids across the world expect to change their gender identity at least once during their lifetime. Their younger brains do not fight fluidity the way ours do.

While some see the explosion of diverse gender identities and expressions as a trend that will fade, I take its wide embrace by kids today as a sign that our hypergendered world has been a hindrance to youths doing the developmentally important work of figuring out who they are.

There's great freedom and relief in not being required to make choices about your identity, your likes and dislikes, and your presentation to the world before you really get to experience who you are. For girls, it's a respite from the sexualized, commercialized, heteroeroticized femininity that provides little appreciation for other ways to be a girl.

When kids first become aware of their sex, they don't understand it's a permanent state. Instead, as astute observers with a biological need to belong, toddlers take note of what makes girls and boys, women and men, different from each other. Then they conflate these observable differences—who cooks, who mows the lawn, who wears makeup and dresses (that is, gender stereotypes)—with biological sex. The lucrative rise of color coding and Disney's far-reaching princess campaign have translated for little girls into their insistence on "PFD," the acronym for "pink frilly dresses" coined by researchers who study gender development. Kids also police their own and others' gender expression. When my friend Gillian asked her three-year-old to help her put windshield washer fluid in her car, he declared, "Only daddies fix cars," even though he'd helped her under the hood just months before. While we don't have to contradict toddlers who insist they aren't the sex we told them they were, we also don't need to make a whole lot of meaning out of their proclamations. If we impose our own ideas of gender on our children, whether that means refusing to accept a girl's love of suits or rushing to label that child a boy, we risk unwittingly calcifying traditional categories.

AFTER HER ANXIOUS voicemail about Maddie, Melissa came in with a tangle of feelings about her only child's emerging identity. She wasn't in the difficult position of having to make medical decisions for Maddie, because Maddie wasn't asking to change their body, but she still worried constantly that the wrong parenting choice might negatively affect their social-emotional well-being. Part of this was that, despite her efforts to make it unimportant, Maddie's gender identity made a big difference to Melissa's sense of who her child was. Her understanding of gender, like many of ours, was based on a binary system rife with stereotypes. An administrative assistant at a hospital who'd married at twenty-five, she described having grown up as "girlie and unquestioning." When her husband left her when Maddie was eighteen months old, Melissa's world was upended. "I was like a 1950s housewife. I mean I worked, but I didn't know anything about how a house works . . . about plumbing and electrical. I barely knew how to use a thermostat, I swear. And I had no idea about our finances, which he tried to keep that way. I swore I would never let anything like that happen to Maddie. I taught her to use power tools when she was eight after I took a woodworking class." She also took finance and car repair classes. Melissa's story serves as a cautionary tale for girls who grow up learning only "girl things." Melissa had worked hard to figure out who she was as a person, apart from being a woman, so her reaction to Maddie confused her. "I felt secure in my values when it was all just theoretical. I'd learned to let go of judging other women and keeping them in the same boxes I'd been put in. I really believe people should get to be whoever they are. But when it's your own kid, it really tests those values."

Melissa worried Maddie wouldn't fit in. How, she wondered, could she both support Maddie and keep them safe in a world unkind to minority groups? She wondered if she caused them to become nonbinary by, she joked, "embracing my own inner man." It's worth noting Melissa was always impeccably dressed in a skirt, blouse, and pumps, and she and Maddie had a standing manicure date one Saturday a month (Maddie's fingernails usually sported skulls and crossbones or had "they"/"them" written on them). Melissa also felt as if she were losing her daughter, her only child, who was considering changing their name. Maddie was in most of our sessions, and in one such session Melissa told me ruefully, "I named Maddie after two women—my grandmothers, Margaret and Marjorie. They're just becoming someone I hadn't imagined for them." Taking a break from their usual exasperation with their mom, Maddie responded kindly, "Mom, this is who I always was but with longer hair. I just didn't have the words to describe it." They reminded their mom that they'd been the one who begged to learn how to use a drill, that they'd cried for hours when it was time to wear a bra, and that their favorite character in *Little Women* was Jo, the outspoken tomboy. They also took this moment to tell their mother they were leaning toward changing just the spelling of their name from Maddie to

Mattie. Melissa smiled through her tears and said, "Well, I do like it better than Cloud, but I know you have to do you."

The "new" Maddie also stirred up feelings of rejection in Melissa. When teenagers begin claiming identities and values that diverge from our own, it can feel like criticism of us, in part because teens make it known they're different from (read: better than) their lame parents. Sometimes cruelty is a teen's only leverage. Though Maddie wasn't intentionally using their identity as a form of criticism, it unearthed Melissa's own insecurities about the choices she'd made in her own life. It felt like a rejection both of girls in general and of Melissa's way of being female.

Finally, Melissa found herself experiencing envy. Envying our kids, especially as we're trying to provide them with more opportunities than we had, is uncomfortable, but it's also common and normal. We envy them for their youthful bodies, the world of opportunities still in front of them, and the expanded options they (especially girls) have outside the binary. Melissa told me, "I never had any of these choices. Who knows if I would've taken them, but I have no doubt I would've been happier and more well rounded as an adult if I hadn't been so girlified."

Melissa may be right. There's research showing that kids who reject strict gender norms and are more psychologically androgynous—meaning they possess personality characteristics of both genders—tend to have higher self-esteem and fewer sexist beliefs, feel less pressure to conform, and do better academically and psychologically. They also tend to show more creativity and cognitive flexibility, have fewer mental health symptoms, and report more life satisfaction. These are all good reasons to eliminate gender restrictions and encourage our children to draw from the whole spectrum of human characteristics.

Maddie said they didn't feel like a girl or a boy, though some days they felt more like embracing the things we think of as girlish like heels and makeup, while other days they cherished baseball caps and skateboards. I never saw them without a large, fun pair of earrings. Mostly, they liked to think of themselves as a feminine boy. To someone like Melissa who'd grown up with the neat classifications of boy and girl, this made her head spin. She'd actually hold her head in her hands at times when Maddie would talk about various friends' identities. Melissa once said it might be easier if Maddie wanted to be male; identifying as both to different degrees and sometimes neither "gives me nothing to hold on to."

Why not, Melissa asked Maddie, just embrace the things you like and feel but still be a girl? I hear a version of this over and over from parents with genderqueer children who would like society to drop its stereotypes so their daughter (or son) can just be "she" (or "he") with no expectations for behavior and dress. Isn't that what second-wave feminists were fighting for? Of course, many kids who don't conform to traditional norms maintain the gender and pronouns assigned them at birth. But for Maddie and other gender-fluid kids, "girl" and "boy" are too fraught with meaning at this point, and the terminology doesn't reflect who they are on the inside. "By separating my identity from my body, I can be who I truly am, not who society wants me to be," Maddie explained, sounding almost giddy. But it's also more complicated than rejecting stereotypes. Maddie struggled to reconcile the idea that anatomy is irrelevant with their occasional wish for top surgery. We may one day exchange the concept of what it means to be a man or woman with what it means to be human, but for now nuanced labels like bigender, agender, and demigirl allow kids to use vocabulary that characterizes them and find others like themselves who aren't reflected in the culture at large.

Melissa also asked Maddie if she were born a girl and is dating a girl, why not just call herself a lesbian? Tearfully, Melissa turned to me and said, "A mother is supposed to help their kid become whatever she wants to be. How on earth can I do that if I don't know what that is?" Maddie didn't use a label for their sexuality. Their girlfriend identified as female, and they alternated between calling her "my girlfriend" and "my partner," whereas their girlfriend only ever referred to Maddie as her partner. "Gotta give up the labels, Ma," Maddie quipped, somewhat paradoxically, more than once.

I began to understand that much of the tension between them arose from Melissa's wish to know where to place Maddie—having labels can diminish anxiety—as well as from Maddie's not yet having the language or the answers both of them were seeking. Both, I pointed out, wanted labels, but the labels they wanted sometimes differed. Melissa tried to be supportive but couldn't help but long for the simplicity of the binary.

Maddie felt pressure to hide their confusion, sometimes even from themselves, so they wouldn't be dismissed or talked out of their identity. They explored with me privately the possible connection between "sort of becoming the man of the house" after their father left, and feeling nonbinary. If they revealed any ambivalence to Melissa, they worried their identity would be interpreted as inauthentic or merely a phase. Like most teens, they wanted to be the one to define themselves.

Maddie eventually disclosed they were pansexual, meaning gender and sexuality weren't determining factors in whom they were attracted to. Like gender, sexual orientation is viewed by researchers as a range on a continuum, from exclusive attraction to the opposite sex/gender to exclusive attraction to the same sex/gender. But Maddie was also confused about what their labels might be depending on the relationship. They told me in confidence they'd asked the question anonymously online, "Am I a lesbian if I was born female but identify as nonbinary and am dating a girl?" There was no single answer. Some people said yes, because lesbian is a sexual preference, not a gender preference, while others said if they considered themselves more "femme" (referring to their gender identity), then they could go with lesbian. Other people disagreed, because lesbian doesn't honor their gender identity as being neither girl nor boy. Many repeated the invitation to give up the labels.

As we slowed things down in therapy so Melissa and Maddie could actually hear each other, they realized they were seeking similar knowledge and that they both vacillated between clarity and confusion. This allowed them to stop butting heads. They came to understand that like many parts of growing up, this was a process. Melissa was able to back off and stop demanding answers from Maddie, and Maddie was able to empathize with their mom's disorientation and disclose some of their own.

AS FOR GENDER reveal parties, even Jenna Karvunidis, who inadvertently started the trend in 2008, now finds the parties problematic, and not just because they've resulted in plane crashes and natural disasters in people's efforts to outdo each other. In a 2019 Facebook post she wrote, "Who cares what gender the baby is? Assigning focus on gender at birth leaves out so much of their potential and talents that have nothing to do with what's between their legs." Her post was accompanied by a photo of her short-haired daughter wearing a pale blue blazer and matching pants. "PLOT TWIST," Karvunidis wrote. "The world's first gender-reveal party baby is a girl who wears suits!"

What can we do, as parents, to ensure our children feel seen far beyond their genitalia and are allowed to develop into the complex people they are?

➜ Don't Believe the Stereotype Hype

Sex differences, amplified by a thicket of pseudoscience, are nearly always exaggerated and used to justify low expectations or unfair treatment of girls and women. By embracing gender as a spectrum, we withdraw the boundaries placed by stereotypes, freeing kids to be themselves. Most sex differences are not either-or traits but a continuum that can be strengthened or weakened. Intelligence, athleticism, creativity, and self-control are all eminently improvable skills. No matter what skill we're talking about, persistence, effort, and experience matter a lot. When girls are given the opportunity to practice their spatial skills, the small gender differences disappear. And children who play with spatial toys (usually marketed to boys) have been shown to participate more as teenagers in spatial activities like basketball and soccer. This relationship is particularly strong for girls.

By intervening early in kids' lives, we better their chances of having a well-balanced set of cognitive and emotional skills. Strengthening weaknesses and embracing the expression of less typical or gendered strengths makes a profound difference in a child's life. Not only does categorizing children by gender potentially rob them of expressing what's nuanced and interesting about them, but it can muddy their grasp of who they are. The development of "cross-gender" abilities and less stereotypical gender roles, however, is associated with intelligence and academic excellence.

Because bias is so often unconscious, it's impossible to eliminate it completely. But we can cultivate self-awareness to catch ourselves when we're employing destructive biases with our kids. For starters, try not to magnify gender differences, remembering that most are so subtle as to be meaningless, or they narrow over the years, belying the notion of a fixed differentiating factor. Frequently ask yourself if your response or action might differ if your child had different genitalia. Allow and encourage your daughters to be physical and resist telling them to be careful. Attend to your sons' feelings and pain, picking them up when they cry and looking them in the eyes.

When my son was two, and crazy about other kids, we registered him for a Montessori toddler class, where he and other toddlers spent two hours each day learning to cook, bake, make knots, arrange flowers, sew, build, garden, and keep "the community" clean and organized. They learned how to greet someone they haven't met before and to politely decline an offer. No activity was gender-specific because they were learning to be thoughtful, engaged members of society, not how to be boys or girls. Their work and play were self-directed, and the materials and books available were carefully chosen not to promote stereotypes. I tried to learn from this intentional community, but I'm not that organized, and donating the onesies we were gifted that said "Macho man" for him and "Daddy's princess" for his sister was but one small drop in an ocean of cultural gender bombing. Which brings us to gendered toys and activities.

➲ Encourage Ungendered Play

Toys and activities are notoriously stereotyped and offer another place to get ahead of bias. We know kids' brains are malleable, so what they play with can encourage a host of abilities—literacy, gross and fine motor skills, social skills, and occupational aspirations—or foreclose them. The gifts my newborn babies received were not just color coded. They were also different in the level of engagement they required despite boys and girls playing in roughly the same ways before gender awareness begins. Gabi got mostly passive toys like rattles and stuffies, while Jonah got active toys—trains and gadgets that required figuring out how to make them spin, roll, or fit together—toys that encouraged him to flex his emerging spatial and mechanical skills.

Their shared room was white with a slanted ceiling delightfully hand painted with blue sky and large velvety clouds that were there when we moved in. I was pleased it was gender neutral. But most nurseries aren't. Boys' nursery decor and clothing generally convey action and toughness—sports, action figures, dinosaurs, and trucks. They say: *See, little man, you're a fearless defender capable of venturing out into this dangerous, action-packed world.* They may also imply *little man* must check his vulnerability at the birth canal if he's to face down dinosaurs and bad guys. Girls' rooms, with their fairies and butterflies, promote grace and softness, and their closets are filled with pretty dresses, dolls, and tea sets. *See, my lady, you'll be a wonderful, well-dressed hostess and mother.*

Tea sets and dolls, like the color pink, aren't inherently bad. I never tired of Gabi's elaborate tea parties created for her baby dolls, and I couldn't wait for her to get old enough to be interested in the dollhouse (complete with electricity!) I'd saved from my youth. She wasn't interested in my wooden toy kitchen that I'd also kept, though Jonah played with it incessantly. But if toys are part of what prepare children for their futures, then most boys are learning to build and solve problems, while most girls are learning to dress babies, bake, and make their own (usually pink) soap/jewelry/lip gloss and other appearance-focused creations.

When we decide what's "boy" and "girl," we place unnecessary limits on our children's imaginations and inclinations. Most kids will go back and forth between the toy kitchen and the toy car if given free rein. Though if your son is hooked on baby dolls and all your daughter wants to do is play cops and robbers, that's not a bad thing. Boys need opportunities to learn to be nurturing as much as girls do, and girls need to run around and feel empowered as much as boys. This is true for the extracurricular activities they participate in too. The younger they are, the more likely it is they'll be open to trying less "gender-typical" things, whether it's dance, hockey, or martial arts.

We can help our kids spot the sexist images and ideas they're absorbing by pointing them out in everyday life. Toy manufacturers have been peddling objectification and the erasure of girls for financial gain for decades. Barbie is, perhaps, the most debated toy in feminist history. As we learned in the *Barbie* movie, the concept (if not the representation) of Barbie was revolutionary, designed by a woman to show girls they could aspire to more than motherhood. She's certainly come a long way since the 1960s, when Babysitter Barbie's book titled *How to Lose Weight* had one simple phrase, "Don't eat," and 1990s Teen Talk Barbie, who said, "Math class is tough. Want to go shopping?" The last decade has produced Barbie Career Dolls, featuring her in some male-dominated positions such as astronaut, and the Role Models collection with feminist icons such as Amelia Earhart and Frida Kahlo. But despite being a multibillion-dollar company that presumably could hire consultants trained in sensitivity and inclusivity or, say, a real female astronaut, Mattel has had a rough road avoiding stereotypes. In 2017, when Gabi was nine, she came home clutching Engineer Barbie, a purchase she made with her own money from a neighbor's yard sale. Eyeing her lab coat, I said to my husband, "Well, that's a step up." But then he pulled out an array of all-pink plastic pieces meant for Engineer Barbie to build a revolving closet, a washing machine, a jewelry holder, and a rack for shoes. Seriously?

Rather than banning these toys outright, I try to use them as educational opportunities. Gabi already knew my stance on Barbie's shopping obsession and unrealistic body proportions. We'd laughed that if Barbie were a real girl, she'd have to walk on all fours because her ankles wouldn't be able to hold her up, so I said, "I can see the people who make Barbie are trying to be less sexist. I wonder why, then, they decided she could only build things in pink that have to do with fashion and household chores and not, say, a green bridge or an orange airplane." "Maybe she doesn't want to build an airplane," my girl responded. I said, "Maybe not. But I want you to know you can build an airplane one day if you want to, and it's hard to know that's true if even your dolls don't have that option."

Gendered play and activities also apprise children of who they are in relation to each other and have negative long-term effects on their potential, attitudes, and ambition. If girls are the known nurturers, why should boys care about helping raise babies someday? If boys are the mini engineers, why should girls think they can put together a crib? Girls who've been given opportunities for "cross-gender" play are less likely to tolerate being told something they want to do or wear is for boys. Their sexism detectors will beep, letting them know that something is awry and that it isn't them.

➲ *Create Gender-Inclusive Environments*

Being gender inclusive, whether for your genderqueer child or simply to remove the stigma of not tucking neatly into a stereotype, requires confronting our own anxieties about gender. The single most helpful thing we can do as parents is to examine our own biases so we aren't parenting from a place of fear. There are some concrete things we can do too: Don't assume someone's gender identity based on their appearance. Adolescence is a fluid time when kids are trying on various identities, so assuming we know their or their friends' gender identity or sexual orientation may prevent them from being open with us. Consider using "they" and "them" before you know people's pronouns. We tend to do that naturally when someone isn't in front of us and it's unclear. If you're dying to know their friend Gray's gender, just ask what pronouns they use, but asking what gender they were assigned at birth is equivalent to asking about their genitals.

We need to be conscious too of not reinforcing a binary by, say, dividing kids into girl and boy groups. Instead, we (and their teachers) can use first initials, birth dates, dogs and cats, winter and summer. Putting up signs that recognize gender diversity like "All genders welcome" and hiring a male babysitter, a female handywoman, or a nonbinary tutor reject stereotypes and normalize differences. Getting to know other families with gender-nonconforming kids will serve to normalize gender expansiveness and teach kids that different, in all its iterations, is good, beautiful, and often brave.

If your child is questioning their gender or considering transitioning, focus on the process rather than the outcome, even if the child is outcome focused. A child who wishes to transition or is experiencing emotional pain because of the body they're in can seek therapy with an experienced therapist, one who treats those in gender distress as complex human beings rather than simple cases of gender dysphoria and will do the crucial work of helping the child assess whether their dysphoria is a cause or symptom of other problems. The wish to transition may dissipate as kids age, or come instead to signify being attracted to someone of the same sex, or suggest they just don't fit traditional stereotypes. Gender nonconformity and gender identity aren't the same thing, even if they sometimes overlap. Or their wish may be indicative of a transgender identity. Remaining open and curious, seeking education and support, are key for both parents and kids so they don't foreclose on their identity.

The single most helpful thing we can do as parents is to examine our own biases so we aren't parenting from a place of fear.

Part II

The Cultural Forces
We're Up Against

CHAPTER 4

Beauty Is the Beast

Arming Girls for Battle

When Geneva walked into my office at age seventeen, she was an underage exotic dancer who was failing out of school and struggling with bulimia. She was also a kind soul whose big, pleading eyes revealed a naïveté incommensurate with her experience in the adult world. She was on a quest to leave an industry that made her feel increasingly empty, but she found the "easy money" too difficult to give up. As time went on, she started recognizing the money wasn't so easy; the job kept her preoccupied with her body and took a toll on everything from her ability to function in school to her relationship with her mother, who sensed she was covering something up.

These realizations increased her motivation to leave exotic dancing behind, but it would take a couple more years for her to do so. The money gave her the independence from her family that she craved, and she was saving up for breast augmentation surgery, something she'd wanted "before I even had boobs." Geneva realized she'd gravitated to exotic dancing because she'd internalized the idea that the only thing she had to offer was her sex appeal. "I can't tell you how many times people said to my mom, 'She's gonna turn heads,' which my mom loved. I started feeling pressure to make it happen." She'd learned to emphasize her appearance and was rewarded with what felt like the holy grail of adolescence: compliments, boyfriends, and her mother's approval. But with puberty comes body fat, and Geneva attended to her weight as if it were her job (which, by the time I met her, it was). My heart broke for Geneva as it does for those millions of smart, funny, interesting girls who are encouraged to focus on their appearances at the expense of everything else they have to offer.

Of course, not all of our daughters become exotic dancers, but they all face pressures similar to Geneva's. They're in formative stages of identity and expected to be something they can't ever be—flawless. The unabated focus on their appearance is a constant reminder they're falling short, and the ubiquity in every type of media of the tall, slim, angular woman with radiant skin and cartoonish eyelashes makes these uncommon appearances seem normal, real, and attainable. Inundated with "solutions," girls plunge their financial, emotional, and intellectual resources along with oodles of time into their appearances. To wit, teen girls spend 7.7 hours per week on their appearance, nearly double that of boys, who have permission to get on with their lives with a quick shower and comfy clothes. If a girl spends an extra hour getting ready while a boy is, say, practicing his instrument, that's another barrier to gender equality. It's also the equivalent of a two-week vacation lost to trying to flatten human diversity into sameness.

Beauty is a mysterious blend of measurable factors like proportion, symmetry, and complexity with our own idiosyncratic, involuntary responses thrown in. But modern beauty culture has crowded out personal response with a stubbornly narrow definition of beauty, unrealistic for most women. By making girls of all shapes and colors, including those who meet the ideal, regularly feel like shit about themselves, beauty culture keeps them scrambling to get closer to its archetype, even as achieving it is itself used as proof of vanity, brainlessness, or the reason for their success.

It's true, the world is moving incrementally toward more inclusive advertising and media, but just barely. As Renee Engeln writes in her book, *Beauty Sick: How the Cultural Obsession with Appearance Hurts Girls and Women,* "It's hard to change the world when you're so busy trying to change your body, your skin, your hair, and your clothes." We can help our daughters understand that what feels like freely chosen beauty behaviors to them is actually coercion by the forces of a beauty sick culture.

Beauty's a beast, but by getting to know the beast intimately—what motivates it, its shape-shifting nature, and the various limbs of its anatomy—our daughters will be better armed to defeat it.

What Motivates the Beast

The beast of beauty culture is arguably the patriarchy's greatest tool for maintaining the status quo. The relentless push for girls to meet an impossible standard of beauty lines the pockets of the beast by satisfying his appetite for gender stereotypes, racism, and classism, all of which reinforce ideas about who matters.

Capitalism and Corporate Profits

Geneva was clear from the start she wanted breast implants, but over time her idealization of the thin, cisgender white girl waned and was replaced with the slim-thick ideal, making a boob job feel even more urgent. Made popular by Kim Kardashian, slim-thick is a blend of the curvy and thin body types that requires or "allows for" prominent booty, breasts, and thighs paired with a tiny waist. Slim-thick is generally made possible by genetics or personal trainers, waist trainers (a modern-day corset), and cosmetic procedures. *Cha-ching.*

The beauty industry, worth $579 billion globally in 2023, is booming. The United States alone made up 20 percent of that revenue. Total revenue from surgical and nonsurgical cosmetic procedures in the United States was $14.6 billion. On skin care alone, the average American woman spends $15,000 in her lifetime—enough for a down payment on a house—and is walking around with an average of eight dollars' worth of products on her face. Women who say they routinely spend money on their appearance spend more than $300 a month or a quarter of a million dollars over their lifetime—enough for an entire house. Corporate America today has tapped wholeheartedly into the tween- and teen-girl markets and sees girls as consumers and sex objects to whom it can sell crop tops and heels. It doesn't care that girls are in the midst of the important and intricate task of forming identities. In fact, it behooves them to interrupt that process by making girls feel bad about themselves so they'll buy things to feel better. The fashion and beauty industries in particular target children, pushing beauty as sexiness and a generic sameness at younger and younger ages. This provides the opportunity to build brand loyalty, and the earlier girls buy into a monolithic definition of beauty, the greater number of products and services they'll be convinced they need. Credibility and confidence are just one new dress or makeup trick away.

As women have gotten savvier, calling out the beauty industry for its destructive messaging, so too has the beast. Rather than focus on women's flaws, beauty in recent years has been wrapped in the language of wellness and self-empowerment. The former Disney star Selena Gomez's beauty line boasts makeup with monikers like "Ascend," "Daring," "Heroic," and "True to Myself." The brand's website states, "Rare Beauty is breaking down unrealistic standards of perfection. This is makeup made to feel good in, without hiding what makes you unique—because Rare Beauty is not about being someone else, but being who you are." How then to explain their concealers and foundations? Reframing beauty as self-care bypasses the reason such self-care is required in the first place: "flaws" and aging are punishable offenses.

In a clever yet disheartening way, beauty has co-opted feminist rhetoric, recasting conformity to beauty standards as a woman's "choice" to make room for herself in a world that doesn't. Women should have not only the right to choose abortion but the right to choose feminine actualization. Rather than capitulating to the male gaze, women are exercising their right to a flawless body. Of course, women should be able to primp in any manner they want, but using feminist sensibilities to drive consumption while pretending they're not profiting off women's insecurities is disingenuous. The UK professors Rosalind Gill and Ana Sofia Elias critique the proliferation of what they call the "Love Your Body" discourse in advertising. Increasingly, as we pop open new boxes of scented candles, lotions, or highlighters, we find seemingly uplifting messages like "celebrate yourself" written on the inside. While this certainly seems like an improvement on more blatant articulations of sexism, Gill and Elias believe it's actually a "more pernicious regulation of women that has shifted from bodily to psychic regulation," because it takes culturally induced insecurities and renders them as the issues of individual women who need a simple mindset change.

Promisingly, younger consumers have tired of the airbrushed imagery and narrow representation in the beauty industry, and teen girls especially prefer relatable spokespeople who look like them. For better and worse, this preference has become a reality with the growth in influencer marketing and 24/7 access to the internet. The benefit is a more inclusive beauty with regular people of all genders, sizes, races, and ethnicities becoming role models. Geneva would get lost in makeup tutorials and "haul videos" in which vloggers shop for, demonstrate, and review their haul of new beauty items. These innocuous-seeming videos can be lucrative operations that make money through ads, sponsorships (in which companies pay users for posts that include their products), and affiliate codes (commissions to the content creator and discounts for the buyer). It can be mesmerizing and helpful to watch someone who looks like you apply makeup, express themselves creatively, and tell you why they like a product.

But the insidious persuasion is powerful because it feels real, and to an extent it is. Influencers talk in a familiar way to their followers about their daily lives, families, and intimate feelings and end videos with "I love you" or "I can't wait to see you again." They come to feel like trusted friends whose glamorous lifestyles and infinite time and money are aspirational. Of course, they aren't attainable for the ordinary girl, but what is attainable are the moments of pleasure she gets from that lash-elongating mascara. These videos have her eating right out of the beast's hand, convinced her transformation is possible with the right makeover, dieting plan, purchase, or in-office treatment. Botox injections, eyelash lifts, and dermal fillers are on the rise, putting the fallacy of "effortless beauty" within reach for those with disposable hours and dollars. Capitalism fuels our fantasies of the good life even as the conditions of capitalism block that path for most Americans and women in particular. It's not surprising kids today experience deeper feelings of emptiness than those in previous generations.

Gender Policing

Both culture and the beauty industry establish "proper" gender expression for girls and then set out to police their bodies, creating police officers out of us. To the industry, the motivation is simple: selling more beauty products. But culturally, performing beauty is framed as a moral imperative, and girls mistake fulfilling this duty for both goodness and pleasure. Why wouldn't they seek traditional beauty? As mini social detectives, they yearn to meet expectations but come to learn those expectations are moving targets. One year having the body of a prepubescent boy, accented with sleek, straight hair and smoky eyes, is in. The next it's having a big booty, curly locks, and the no-makeup makeup look.

The one constant is thinness; no flab or cellulite allowed, or you risk having your character called into question and being deemed lazy, unhealthy, and gluttonous. Girls as young as three associate meanness and other negative qualities with bigger bodies. Being the fat girl, especially in high school, can mean being outcast: the uncool kid who obviously doesn't want friends because if she did, she'd control herself, as if being larger-bodied were a character failure rather than the often unavoidable outcome of genetics. But maybe worse than how other kids see a fat kid is how that fat kid sees herself: she's internalized the beast and its fatphobic, body-blaming ideas, so she too believes herself unworthy. It starts with food, but the message to girls is they must control all of their appetites—for food, for pleasure, for power—because too much of anything but self-restraint and deprivation is unfeminine.

It starts with food, but the message to girls is they must control all of their appetites—for food, for pleasure, for power—because too much of anything but self-restraint and deprivation is unfeminine.

The World Health Organization published a study in 2016 called *Growing Up Unequal*, which surveyed the health and well-being of

220,000 eleven-, thirteen-, and fifteen-year-old boys and girls in forty-two countries in Europe and North America over a period of thirty years. In every single country in every age-group except for four countries in the youngest age-group, girls more than boys reported being "too fat." Here's the kicker: in nearly every single country and region the boys were plumper than the girls. In other words, feeling fat is a product of being a girl, not of actual body size.

If the game is rigged, why don't girls stop playing? Because not playing by the conventional rules of attractiveness isn't a viable alternative. It closes doors they sense are only partially opened to them anyway. Being attractive allows us to be part of the cultural conversation, to be acknowledged, desired, given a job another female applicant perceived as less attractive won't get. Decades of research show we assume attractive people are kinder, smarter, and more trustworthy and generous than those we consider less attractive. In court, attractive people are less likely to be found guilty and are given lighter sentences. We actually believe pretty people are intrinsically better and more deserving humans, so the climb to pretty seems worth it.

Whether they are conventionally pretty or not, ugly is what we call women when we want to silence them and trivialize their achievements, especially those who have the audacity to put themselves in the public eye. There's a long history of denigrating public women by focusing on what their looks and clothing say about them more than the substance of their ideas or skills. Hillary Clinton's hair and laugh have been the subjects of derision for decades. Serena Williams, one of the all-time tennis greats and a rare Black woman in tennis, was frequently criticized for her muscularity, and her success was questioned with implications she must've been born male. Girls who heard the "Princess of Pop" Britney Spears's body being torn apart by the media when they were seven are now the fourteen-year-olds who are critiquing their own bodies part by part.

Being thin doesn't always get you a pass either. Angelina Jolie lost weight while grieving the loss of her mother, and the body-shamers complained she was too skinny. It's not really about how girls and women look; it's about keeping them feeling less secure and powerful than they might if they weren't scrutinized. When women avoid writing or saying things publicly to escape their appearance being mauled or facing rape threats, it's another obstacle to gender equality. Men in the public eye don't contend with the vicious attacks on their bodies that women do, and girls take note of this. Gender policing has reverberating effects: studies show girls are wary of pursuing leadership roles because of the harassment and discrimination they see women leaders endure. If girls shy away from leadership positions, then women in decision-making roles will continue to be a minority.

More than ever girls are successful scholastically and professionally, so you'd think perfecting the ideal look would've gone out with the corset. It hasn't. In fact, the time and cost sunk into beauty has only increased over time. Research supports this, showing when people are primed to think women have a chance at attaining equal status with men, they're more likely to indicate women should spend more time on beauty. This is reminiscent of the 1980s, when women began flooding the workforce and we added the "Good Mother" trope that included an exponential rise in expectations for mothers, ensuring they'll constantly fall short and be self-critical. The author Peggy Orenstein suggests the teen version of this is the rise of hookup culture and the centrality of male pleasure just as girls began outperforming and outnumbering boys in school. In other words, the greater the threat to the gender hierarchy, the more women are externally and internally pressured to accommodate men. It's exhausting to try to be everything. Something has to give and, as with Geneva, too often it's mental health.

Bingeing and purging offered Geneva a diversion from the underlying pain and feelings of worthlessness. She felt "jittery" when she couldn't binge and often stayed up late into the night to have the kitchen to herself. She was exhausted from sleeplessness, crash dieting, and late nights at her job. Her preoccupation with food, weight, and periodic purging was disrupting her life and draining her of pleasure. She felt anxious around food, so she avoided friends and parties. She saw her boyfriend regularly but said, "I paste on a smile and pretend I'm there but mostly I'm just thinking about food," which she thought was a problem but is really a normal way to experience hunger. And she hid the burning pain in her esophagus caused by vomiting. No surprise, her secretive behavior was putting a strain on her relationships.

Racism and Classism

I was hoping I could help Geneva broaden her view of herself so she could see she was more than just a body. She didn't view the time, energy, and money that went into reaching for perfection as a sacrifice, even though it meant slipping grades, health, and friendships, and a self-confidence that was dependent on the one-to-ten rating she gave her appearance each day (she was usually between a one and a five). At the same time, I understood the social costs of giving those up, especially for a girl of color, who's already likelier to be scrutinized.

Geneva identified as "mixed" because she had a Black mom and a white dad, but most people thought of her as Black because she had "Black girl hair," which she described with air quotes. She'd begged her mother from the time she was six for straight hair after a white boy in her class started calling her "Afro head," but because the chemicals in hair relaxers are harsh, her mother resisted her pleas until her tenth birthday. Geneva had adored the straight shiny look, but now the chemicals had damaged it and she despised her hair.

Geneva had a complicated relationship with her weight. She'd worked out every day and twice on the weekends and was feeling all right about her body until her mother's family came to visit from New Orleans. The first thing her aunt said was, "Genny, we've got to get some meat on you." She felt out of place all weekend because she noticed she was significantly thinner than her beloved cousins. That confused her, because she'd spent the last few years feeling fat. Her aunt's comment was playful, but Geneva heard it as an insinuation that by rejecting thickness, she lacked appropriate racial pride, echoing some comments she'd heard from Black kids at school. That was the first weekend Geneva binged and purged. "I remember thinking, 'I can't please everyone, so screw it.' Like I was sort of aware the world wasn't fair but I couldn't see a solution, so I binged as a kind of ef-you to everyone and then I felt gross, so I threw it all up. But then . . ." She paused, considering her words, and said, "I felt like a badass with superpowers." She could have her cake and throw it up too. Like other girls with eating disorders, Geneva felt she'd found a secret answer to the culture's chronic double binds, and it made her feel powerful, at least until shame overcame her. She told me she wished her strength had looked like saying, "Screw everyone else, I'm going to please myself," and then added, "But that would've meant knowing what I wanted and I had no clue."

The ideal beauty in Western culture excludes most of the actual body shapes, skin, and hair real people of *any* color possess. It also creates a vicious cycle for people in poverty who can't afford braces, teeth whitening, dermatologists, and fancy beauty salons. This Eurocentric ideal is pointedly not meant for women of color and was actually codified by the Miss America pageant, whose rules before 1950 stipulated all the contestants had to be "of good health and of the white race." Though every day can feel like a beauty pageant no matter your race, girls of color are held hostage to colonial beauty standards, ensuring there's no way to win. That doesn't mean they won't try. Who doesn't want to be beautiful? Which is another way of asking, who doesn't want to matter, fit in, be respected?

In her book *So You Want to Talk About Race,* Ijeoma Oluo writes that the perceptions of who we see as smart and beautiful "are determined by our proximity to the cultural values of the majority." Children of color see that those with power—their teachers and government leaders—are white. They're also the ones with "good hair" in shampoo commercials and with the "right bodies" in fashion magazines. The message is white features are the default and those of people of color are deviant. "For young people of color with developing bodies that can never actually assimilate into the mythical monochrome of middle America," explains Mikki Kendall in her book *Hood Feminism,* "there's very little validation available in media or anywhere else." Embody whiteness and you'll be rewarded. And so dark-skinned girls consider skin bleaching and Asian girls contemplate double eyelid surgery. White reigns supreme not because the KKK is burning a cross but because, whether we're conscious of it or not, white bodies are perceived as better, normal, natural.

Geneva noticed other Black girls in her predominantly white school wearing their hair natural and went down a months-long rabbit hole of natural hair videos. The natural hair movement, which grew out of the Black Is Beautiful movement of the 1960s, has become popular again in the last twenty years and encourages people of African descent to embrace cornrows, locs, and Afros, connecting to their roots and rejecting being shamed for their natural beauty. Geneva was toying with the idea of giving up hair relaxers but worried her white boss wouldn't give her shifts if she did. She had reason to worry. Black girls and women routinely face discrimination in racially biased educational and professional settings for having hair that looks different from a white woman's and can be policed by people in their own group for appearing in the world in a way that reflects badly on them. If they haven't internalized the idea that straight hair is better, then they're put in the position of choosing between their own hair wishes and social acceptance. When Geneva finally decided to leave relaxers behind, she went through months of self-loathing and threats from her boss to fire her if she didn't "take care of" herself.

Even when she got her hair to a state she loved, she wasn't prepared for all the attention and microaggressions it brought. People touched her hair without permission. Others assumed she was making a political statement or ascribed personality characteristics to her like angry, brave, and hip. Almost every day brought at least one comment or question about her versatile hair and style, reminding her she was different and didn't belong. Initially she tried to be understanding and recognize when comments were well meaning, but one day she'd had enough. "I feel like a circus animal. I'm not 'brave'; I just got tired of having an inflamed scalp. I need my hair to not be a topic of conversation ever again!" The times Geneva did try to address the hurt, she was met with defensiveness or faux apologies that boxed her into the sexist/racist tropes of Dramatic Girl or Angry Black Woman, leaving her alone to deal with feeling undermined.

The Beast's Shape-Shifting Nature

Now let's consider some of the thornier beauty issues girls face—weight, hair removal, and makeup—that often bring up conflict with and for their parents. Girls can be tenacious when it comes to beauty choices because they're the ones both at the vanguard of fashion and in the sight line of bullies. Stereotypical feminine trappings can create tension between those who have them and those who don't. The ten-year-old girls who wear lip gloss or wax their upper lips are more likely to find the bare- or hairy-lipped girls unfeminine or unsophisticated. Girls have been sold a lifestyle of resplendence, so it's no wonder they don't tolerate peers with so-called mustaches or nails that don't shimmer from a fresh mani. What girls find beautiful feels deeply personal; they don't realize it's wholly entwined with larger forces and circumstances. If they are going to reject certain beauty standards that reward them with intoxicating attention but little else, let's help them grasp the socially constructed, shape-shifting nature of them.

When Did Thin Become In: The Skinny on Skinny

When girls hit puberty, they typically develop more body fat, a reality we've come to pathologize. Thin and conventionally pretty girls are popular, yet here's the rub: no matter what size a girl is, no matter how popular, she's likely to hate her body at some point. If she's lucky enough to escape hating her body and fretting over it forever, she'll go through at least one—but likely many—phases of picking on her body. Bodies bloom into a million different shapes, but basically only one is acceptable.

The naked truth is you get treated better when you're thin, so it's no wonder teenage girls everywhere are dieting, throwing up their food, starving themselves, overexercising, and/or preoccupied with every calorie they put in their mouths. Boys are given more leeway when it comes to weight, but girls who don't have a thigh gap are fat. At increasingly tender ages, girls begin to wonder if their thighs are too chunky, hips too wide, breasts too small, rear too large, torso and/or legs too short, knees too dimpled or knobby, nose too pointy, lips too thin, eyes too small, hair too stringy. In other words, girls as young as nine stop inhabiting their bodies and instead stand outside them, cleaving them into disparate parts and evaluating them in all their minutiae.

America wasn't always obsessed with thinness. "Plump as a partridge" used to be a compliment. It wasn't until the late nineteenth century that weight became a part of the national conversation. As the corset—meant to redistribute fat based on the fashion trends of the time, not to make women look thinner—became a health concern and lost popularity, the Industrial Revolution brought both standardized dress sizes (in lieu of seamstresses) and more sedentary jobs. Eventually, too, the science of food advanced, giving us the calorie and a way to quantify our intake. Once the scale was invented, we had an accurate and objective measure of our weight by which to compare ourselves with others. When unnatural thinness is revered, girls do unnatural things to be thin. An eight-year longitudinal study found 12 percent of girls experienced some form of eating disorder. Eating disorders are among the deadliest mental illnesses, second only to opioid overdose.

The trend toward thinness isn't linear, though, and ideal body weights shift with the social, political, and economic realities of the time. Ads for weight loss were plentiful during the prosperous 1920s, when plumpness could signal a lack of self-control, but during the Great Depression of the 1930s, when thinness could reflect poverty, ads for gaining weight were common. Even the size of Playboy Playmates of the Year between 1960 and 2000 varied according to economic conditions. The tougher the times, the larger-bodied the Playmate. Many non-Western societies see a robust female physique as a marker of well-being, and before the economic boom of the nineteenth century, Americans did too. Now most American women are on a diet or feeling guilty about not dieting.

When (and Why) Did Hair Removal Become a Thing?

So many parents walk a tightrope between encouraging self-acceptance and not leaving their children to suffer teasing. "If I let her shave her legs at eight, where does it stop?" asked the mother of Darya, an Iranian American girl who was given the unfortunate nickname Chewbacca the first time she wore shorts to school. Darya refused to wear shorts all summer, no matter the weather, when she was surrounded by her fair-haired friends. "I want her to know she's beautiful as is," her mother added.

But sometimes it's us parents that long for an "improved" presentation in our kids. The mother of a nine-year-old white girl in my daughter's violin class said she'd bribed her daughter to perform in front of us with the promise she could wax her eyebrows, whispering, "Honestly, she's needed it from birth." Knee-jerk vanity reactions to our kids come from years of conditioning on which appearances are acceptable. While my hope is that we all start questioning beauty norms more, I know beneath that mom's comment was the knowledge that her daughter's unibrow would likely come to haunt her daughter someday. All mothers understand a girl's appearance can be a matter of survival and social status.

When my own daughter wanted to shave, we wondered together why body hair on women was considered gross and required removal. We decided we could sort of understand it for men, since hair on the face can become unruly, cover the mouth, and be a nuisance with food. Yet for men shaving is usually a style choice, not an obligation, and their leg, armpit, and chest hair remains intact. Body hair isn't difficult to main-tain or keep clean, and if everyone had it, it wouldn't get a bad rap, so why do we bother? There are plenty of Reddit posts arguing men are biologically programmed to like shaved women because shaving exag-gerates the sexual dimorphic trait that already exists (women having less hair). Yet our obsession with sleek, hairless women is a modern phe-nomenon, and I can assure you men and women have been hooking up for millennia.

As Gabi and I researched, we learned it all started in 1915 with a *Harp-er's Bazaar* ad showing a young model in a sleeveless dress posing with both arms over her head, exposing her hairless armpits. The accompany-ing words read, "Summer dress and modern dancing combine to make necessary the removal of objectionable hair." Poof, just like that, the bare underarm campaign was launched. To think that literally days before girls had no idea this "problem" even existed. Marketers jumped on board the humiliating-armpit-hair train with ads like "The fastidious woman today must have immaculate armpits if she is to be unembarrassed," and the rest is history. As hemlines got shorter, body hair removal crept upward (think the miniskirt of the 1960s). Writes Sarah Hildebrandt in *The EmBodyment of American Culture,* "The more clothes women were 'allowed' (or expected) to remove, the more hair they were also expected to remove." Had we never started shaving, we'd never think hair was vul-gar. Sure, we may feel sexy after we shave, but we have to ask *why* we have to be hairless in order to be sexy. In many other countries, body hair is just part of being an adult.

While leg hair has remained staunchly unwelcome, armpit hair seems to be making a comeback, with some young women growing and even dying their armpit hair. Hashtags like #armpithair and #pithairissexy on Instagram are used by mostly women displaying their pit hair. @lindsaysyum posted a selfie by the ocean, her arm slung happily around her boyfriend's neck, revealing her underarm hair. She'd stopped shaving because she wasn't a fan of razor burn and ingrown hairs. "It wasn't this big rah rah feminist decision or movement. It was a reclamation of my body and simply choosing what felt more accessible and comfortable to me." She gets to choose whether she identifies as a feminist, but I'd argue showing people that you can, in fact, not conform to traditional beauty standards and still be desirable to someone gives other women permission to do the same, making it a pretty feminist move.

Beating Around the Bush

With the introduction of the bikini in 1946, the stage was set for women to start fretting about pubic hair too. The trend has moved from trimming of bikini lines to the whole enchilada, naked as a baby's, except for a short stint in the 1970s when even porn stars sported full bushes. Sixty-two percent of all women have opted for complete removal of their pubic hair at some point, with higher percentages among younger women aged eighteen to thirty-four. Until *Sex and the City*'s infamous Brazilian wax episode in 2000 started a movement, this was the stuff of fetishes. Girls today tell me that preparing their genitals is serious business. Do I want a skinny landing strip or a thicker Mohawk? Postage stamp or Bermuda Triangle? One college-age patient explained vajazzling to me after the crystals glued to her shaved mons pubis cut her up during sex. The landscaping that goes on down there can be added to the category of time-, money-, and energy-sucking beauty regimens. Like shaving our legs and armpits, full frontal waxing is now a rite of passage to adulthood (ironically so, given hair growth is a sign of maturity). Girls say they think it's prettier, cleaner, and what boys want. In this case, I think pretty is what you're used to.

As for cleaner, prepubescent girls have higher incidents of vaginal irritation because they don't have hair to trap bacteria and stop it from entering the vagina. Those who remove hair can also have grooming-related infections, lacerations, and allergic reactions. Some researchers believe a bare vulva may also make girls more susceptible to STIs (sexually transmitted infections). No matter how you cut it (so to speak), hair removal leaves microscopic wounds. Doctors suggest leaving a little bit of hair around the vaginal opening because the skin there is sensitive and hair helps wick away sweat and bacteria from our bodies.

It's true that some boys do expect the so-called bearded clam to be unbearded. They might never have witnessed a vulva with hair due both to porn and to previous sexual experience with fully shaved vulvas. So, the unexpected is "disgusting," and girls don't want to risk humiliation. The hypocrisy that pubic hair on girls is dirty and gross, but on boys it's totally normal, doesn't seem to register. Manscaping is becoming more popular, but it's still personal preference. Ultimately, hair removal seems like yet another double standard and a way to make girls feel their bodies need overhauling.

The circumscribed beauty we chase requires maddening replicability, and vulvas are no exception. Without pubic hair, girls are better able to see and evaluate how closely their vulvas match their perceptions of normal vulvas. The airbrushed images girls see online don't represent the variations of shape, color, size, and asymmetry of normal vulvas. Instead, girls believe, not unlike the rest of their bodies, their vulvas should appear prepubescent and take up as little space as possible. Enter designer vagina surgery or vaginal rejuvenation (sounds like a yoga retreat for your vagina without the radical self-acceptance). Cosmetic vaginal surgery increased 262 percent between 2012 and 2018. A huge spike among teens prompted the American College of Obstetricians and Gynecologists in 2016 to issue guidelines to doctors urging them to educate and reassure patients, suggest nonsurgical alternatives for comfort and appearance, and screen them for body dysmorphic disorder.

It's heartbreaking that the organs of the vulva, which allow for something as basic as urinating, as vital as reproduction, and as fundamental as pleasure, are tethered to shame and scrutinized so uncharitably. (Perhaps it's not surprising that the anatomical term for vulva is *pudenda membra*, from the Latin word *pudere*, meaning "to be ashamed.") When people ask my opinion about hair removal, though, I generally say I don't have one. I only care that girls and women have a choice. Do what makes you happy, but be mindful of the forces at work.

Makeup: Vanity or Self-Expression?

Daily makeup use was unheard of before the birth of photography, mirrors, and motion pictures in the late nineteenth century. In the age of internet tutorials, today's teenage girls regularly apply contour and enhance their Cupid's bows. Does using makeup mean our daughters are controlled by the machinations of patriarchy, attempting to mask their every "imperfection," or is it a tool of empowerment and self-expression? Makeup is a frequent struggle between the mothers and daughters I see. Personal choice is important to most of these mothers, who believe women should be able to decide whether to adorn themselves without being judged either way. Yet many are also troubled by the obsession with youth and beauty being sold to girls, who are then ridiculed for putting effort toward those values by wearing makeup or derided when they don't.

When Gabi started experimenting with makeup, I was concerned she was learning to reject her natural self. The little makeup I wear is, without question, an acquiescence to social norms, and I'm aware I'm influencing her and contributing to a culture that views women as ugly when they don't wear it. My concerns, though, were met with eye rolls. When I backed off and became curious, I learned she felt I was undermining her individuality and creativity. If I'd blurted, "Makeup is the tool of the patriarchy and you're its pawn," I would've missed the opportunity to hear that she believed girls were luckier than boys because they can play with their appearance in a way boys aren't culturally guided or "allowed" to do. It showed me she understood the pressures of gender norms. She assured me she was having fun experimenting, not trying to fix something "wrong" with her. She's become quite the impressive makeup artist, though many days she wears none. Because I listened to her, she was more willing to consider where focusing on her body and altering her appearance fit into the larger message about what girls have to do to be pretty.

Makeup is a nuanced beast, used because it's fun, theatrical, allows you to gender bend, feel spunky, and a hundred other reasons including, most often, because girls think they look better with it. In a sexist world it's hard to see themselves any other way, or maybe it's just easier (and safer) to reconcile themselves to certain norms. So when Gabi asks, I admire her 1960s makeup look or cat eyes, but I still occasionally squeeze in that my favorite look is the one she was born with. I'm willing to be "cringey" in service of this mission.

How the Beast Seizes Control

Beauty is a cunning beast whose far-reaching arms—objectification and self-objectification—encircle girls and hold them in place.

Objectification

We bandy about the term "objectification" so much it can start to feel overused and meaningless. What does it really mean when someone says women are sexually objectified? In a nutshell, it means they're viewed more as things to be used or instruments of pleasure than as people with thoughts, feelings, and abilities. The media's a major culprit in separating women's bodies, body parts, or sexual functions from their humanity and wholeness. Female sexuality is used to sell cologne, cars, beer, and anything else you can think of that has absolutely nothing to do with a woman's body. Take Burger King's ad showing a close-up of a woman's profile, her mouth open, and its "Super Seven Incher" sandwich hovering in front of it. The tagline: "It'll blow your mind away. Fill your desire for something long, juicy, and flame-grilled."

Objectification is inescapable, even beyond the media. It's at the mall when the lady behind the counter tells you she likes your curls; it's at the beach when a group of boys comments on your legs or your love handles; it's at school when your friend tells you your boobs look big today. When the focus is on the size of our thighs or the height of our cheekbones, nobody cares about our intellect or our dreams and ambitions. Once girls realize their outside is more important than what's inside, beauty becomes the goal, and the beast has seized control.

When Gabi turned thirteen, we had a small bat mitzvah for her in our backyard and were elated when friends and family received their COVID-19 vaccinations just in time to come after an eighteen-month separation. While it's been crystal clear to me for a long time that a girl's appearance is of great and constant importance, it was uncomfortably explicit in this context. It took me back to being Gabi's age when my own body was changing and suddenly my appearance was the most central thing about me. Unsolicited comments about my freckles (cute or needed bleaching), my thinness (lucky or bony), and *almost* having the perfect nose (if only the tip were slanted up a centimeter) made me increasingly self-conscious. I watched in real time as Gabi's body became an open topic for discussion. Family and friends commented on her long legs, her slender fingers, her lovely curls, her cute skirt, her feminine lips, her *un*feminine Doc Martens boots. Give them a break, right? They hadn't seen her for way too long and they were taking in her changes. Yet my son, two years older but at a similar point in puberty, got a total of two comments: you've gotten tall, and your voice has gotten deep. Nothing about individual body parts, clothing, or his new haircut. One night, when I asked my kids if they'd had enough to eat, my father turned to Gabi and, poking her belly jovially, said, "Glad you had enough because you're so fat already." Because she's an obviously slender child, and because he's an incredibly loving grandfather who's notorious for bad dad jokes, no one thought twice about this comment. But I don't want my daughter associating dinner with her weight. I don't want her to think of her weight at all. And I don't want her thinking "fat" is a bad word. I want her unencumbered to grow into whatever nature has in store for her body. Undoubtedly, these comments were meant as compliments (well, except for the "unfeminine" boots. "Unfeminine" is never a compliment, even as femininity is roundly devalued in our society). But even compliments are an evaluation. I don't want her worth tied to her body, because, as she fills out, she'll be evaluating herself based on the many freely offered critiques she's absorbed along the way.

None of these comments were lost on Gabi. Each time someone commented, she was either shocked or embarrassed, and we'd silently lock eyes—big, round, laughing eyes. My husband and I rarely comment on her appearance (though the temptation is great), and she's growing up in a generation in a part of the country that's more aware of bodily autonomy and women's rights. Friends of mine wanted to give her a gift certificate as a present, and when I suggested a popular teen clothing store,

Gabi said, "No way. They're fatphobic: they only sell two teeny sizes. And they treat their employees terribly." She's definitely been armed to think critically, but that doesn't mean the gale-force winds of lookism and sexism don't make their way through the layers of wicking we've wrapped her in. After the final guests left, we sat down to look at some bat mitzvah pictures. "Ew! My hair's frizzy," she blurted of her long locks. Which brings us to self-objectification.

Self-Objectification

Sometime around age twelve I stopped being the kid who vigorously raced my best friend down the hill to her house, unaware of the tangled web it created of my thick hair, and became the girl who stood in the mirror wishing for thinner hair and pushing my nose up a centimeter. I was sure that if I could make myself attractive enough to fit in but not so attractive as to draw unwanted attention and envy, I'd be whole and lovable. Growing distant from a felt sense of myself, I stopped being and started seeming, just as Simone de Beauvoir described girls coming-of-age.

Being constantly on display takes its toll on girls' psyches as they gradually internalize the objectifying gazes, evaluating their external physical selves as an observer might. Research suggests such "self-objectification" leads to habitual self-monitoring, with girls taking note approximately every thirty seconds of whether their hair's in place, their legs are in proper position, their shirt is sitting right. Joining the chorus of other girls in asking, "Do I look okay?" they focus on how others perceive their bodies' appearance, scent, and feel, rather than how it feels for them to be in their own bodies. This leads to a host of negative mental health outcomes. Girls who self-objectify increasingly experience shame and anxiety about their bodies, putting them at risk for eating disorders, depression, and sexual dysfunction. Despite the early and persistent emphasis on becoming sex objects, by the time they're ready for sex, they're too preoccupied with how their angles, belly rolls, cellulite, and smells are being perceived to enjoy it. Looking desirable has replaced feeling desire.

Before looks and femininity become prioritized, research shows girls are more confident, outspoken, and passionate. They're budding scientists making homegrown volcanoes, architectural wizards building pillow forts, mini Katie Ledeckys testing out how fast they can swim, and uninhibited artists putting their quiet or chaotic feelings on the page. But as puberty hits and objectification ramps up, we watch helplessly as our daughters' creative energy is redirected to obsessing over perceived flaws, concealing blemishes, evaluating various body parts that "need" perfecting. The superficial standards of others supplant the once genuine delight they saw in themselves. They spend countless hours trying to create the perfect selfie rather than, say, perfect pitch. But even if they don't sacrifice skill-building activities, they often become hypercritical of them. Their confidence plummets, and they believe nothing they do is good enough. This is what the psychologist Renee Engeln means by "beauty sick."

Geneva was one such beauty sick kid who continually talked herself out of doing things she enjoyed—the end-of-school barbecue, the school play, the soccer team—because she didn't want to draw attention to her "ugliness," which she equated with lack of skill. Her job was different, she said, "because I know I can dance and it's not really me up there. I'm a character hiding behind a ton of makeup." Many girls describe a similar performative femininity. Some nights Geneva lay awake panicked she'd sleep poorly and have to go to school with bags under her eyes, which exacerbated her fear other girls were prettier than her.

Self-objectification disrupts the powerful intimacy girls once found in shared secrets, giggles, and hair braiding. It dawns on them their appearance is currency, and they're in competition for the title of Hottest Girl. Their power lies, instead, in dissing other girls. And instead of making style choices based on self-expression and comfort, they focus on choices that might generate desire and jealousy in others. The resulting rifts among bosom buddies are heartbreaking.

Perhaps the greatest resource exploited by a beauty-obsessed culture is our minds. Girls who self-objectify have more difficulty with cognitive tasks. Research shows self-objectification usurps our cognitive resources, making it difficult to get into the flow states necessary for performance and achievement. Similarly, if you compliment a girl, you'll improve her mood but impair her mental capacity. It's worth wondering how often girls receive a body comment right before an important test or piano recital. Even saying nothing about her body but putting her in a situation to think about it while taking a math test means she'll do worse than others not primed to think about their bodies. That was the finding in a study, cleverly titled "That Swimsuit Becomes You," that induced self-objectification in college students by having them try on a one-piece swimsuit or a sweater. Students were told they were participating in a study on "emotions and consumer behavior" and asked to keep the garment on in the dressing room with a full-length mirror for fifteen minutes before rating it. While they were waiting, they were asked, as a ruse, to complete a math test for an experimenter from another department. The women wearing swimsuits performed worse than the women wearing sweaters. Additionally, when later asked to "evaluate" cookies and a drink for the study, women in the swimsuit group were more likely to restrain their eating. Men's cognitive abilities and eating behavior were not affected by what they'd been wearing, perhaps because men typically receive compliments on skills and tend to think about what their bodies can do. Every man interviewed for another study of body image concerns talked about his body's abilities, but not a single woman did.

Relationships and meaningful pursuits bring us far more lasting happiness than beauty does, yet our daughters' growth in these areas is stunted by the magnetic pursuit of unattainable beauty standards. And in a maddening patriarchal catch-22, a study called "Objects Don't Object" finds self-objectification motivates women to increase their support for the gender status quo and reduces their willingness to participate in social action that would challenge inequality. It's therefore pressing that parents lift the veil of sexism through which girls see themselves before they're lulled into complacency and can't battle the beast themselves.

Battling the Beast

I want my daughter to like her appearance, which is why I embarked on "Operation Love Your Curls" when she started wishing her hair were straight. After a special salon appointment with a "curly girl specialist" and new products, it worked! Caring about how we look is a normal part of being human, but putting too much stock in our own attractiveness outsources our self-worth to others' opinions. Thanks to social media, our girls are chronically subject to others' visual inspection, making it critical for us to raise girls who don't overvalue their appearance.

One way to do that is to help our kids reorient to what's beautiful and why, not only to see beauty in a wider array of appearances, but, more important, to know beauty encompasses more than aesthetic pleasure. If notions of beauty swelled to embrace an open heart, an emanating warmth, a moral sensibility, an analytic mind, an acerbic wit, kind eyes, deep empathic listening, a willingness to compromise, a willingness to be direct about one's needs, an ease in one's body, or the capacity to accommodate new information even when we thought we knew the answer, we'd live in a more inclusive world.

How, then, can we keep our eye on the prize of self-esteem and inner beauty and teach our kids to do the same? We need to decouple a girl's appreciation of her body from society's appreciation of it. I don't think there's anything more radical in the fight against sexism than to teach our girls not only to love their expanding hips and developing curves but to view themselves as embodied and whole, rather than as a collection of parts. When the beast can no longer drive cracks in their self-esteem, it'll lose its power to make girls' bodies a cultural battleground.

Contrary to what some people think, body positivity isn't pretending aesthetic preferences don't exist. It's about knowing that what matters is how your body feels to you, not how it looks to other people. It's knowing, too, that how you appraise your or someone else's body has been largely decided by the culture you inhabit. It's recognizing that limiting what's beautiful to one particular physical type inevitably excludes most women. When we can appreciate beauty beyond its current narrow confines, it no longer seems far-fetched that fleshy, disabled, and old bodies can be beautiful, that pockmarks, wrinkles, and scars can be beautiful. It might mean loving those qualities or just being gentle with yourself and avoiding expensive or painful "beauty" regimens. It's knowing you should be treated with respect and autonomy whether or not you're considered beautiful.

Body positivity isn't pretending aesthetic preferences don't exist. It's about knowing that what matters is how your body feels to you, not how it looks to other people.

In my kitchen is a linoleum print that says, "Perfect is the enemy of great." And, I'd add, perfect is the enemy of spending time well. Perfectionism inhibits creativity. Rather than tuning in to ourselves and allowing what we find to flow outward, we get mired in details, trying to produce what we think others would deem perfect. But we're not as helpless as we sometimes feel in the face of our kids' body image. I'm heartened by a recent study that found body dissatisfaction across cohorts and time may be on the decline, an indication the sociocultural shifts in body acceptance and diversity may be working. Here are six ways you can help your daughters achieve positive body image.

➲ *Practice Body Neutrality: Focus on Their (and Your) Achievements and Character*

I've found the easiest way to remove focus from girls' bodies is, well, not to focus on them. Teach them to care for their bodies, but don't nitpick. Every time you smooth the baby hairs away from her forehead or straighten her clothes, she's reminded her presentation is being evaluated. Ask yourself first if it matters at that moment. Would you rather she spend time writing in her journal or preening in front of a mirror? If she's going to her BFF's house, does it matter if her hair is messy or there's a hole in her leggings? Practicing body neutrality helps liberate the body from being the center of someone's self-image. We're shaping how our children see themselves, so if we drastically reduce commenting on how they look, it becomes less a part of the story they tell themselves.

You might be saying, "Sure, I can stop fussing," but can you refrain from telling them they're beautiful? When our daughters look adorable, it feels natural to tell them so. It's especially tempting when they're balled up in tears, feeling ugly, to insist they're beautiful because, to us, they are. But this only emphasizes pretty is important. And they don't buy it. They're well aware certain bodies are revered while others are denigrated. It might seem counterintuitive to withhold compliments when confidence in their appearance is a huge part of their self-esteem. But if we're ever going to decouple those two things, then we have to focus on other identity-shaping qualities.

Instead of their cute noses and outfits, we need to notice the things that offer depth of character and make someone interesting—those things that can be developed, not something you either have or don't (or you apply in a mirror). Girls learn simultaneously that their attractiveness is determined by other people and that it's synonymous with their value, so the takeaway is they aren't in control of the thing most important for their self-esteem. We can help undo that by praising attributes that help build resilience such as handling frustration well or being a good friend. We can observe their wit, smarts, courage, imagination, or any of the other nonaesthetic qualities previously mentioned so they expect to be heard and respected, not eyeballed and appraised. "Your creativity reminds me of the wonderful painter Frida Kahlo," or "I'm proud of the courage you showed standing up for what you believe." Or simply, "Playing in that game took serious physical strength and mental endurance." There are hundreds of ways for our daughters to feel good about themselves that have a more profound effect than being pretty ever will.

Notice with your daughter how often people comment on her appearance and teach her she's allowed to say, "I don't want to talk about how I look. Let's talk about something else." We often find others most beautiful when we're in the midst of sharing joy or intimacy. When you and your daughter are pausing to catch your breath from the belly laugh she just gave you, or after that thoughtful discussion on climate change, tell her she's beautiful and she'll know you mean *all* of her.

⮑ *Your Body Image Matters to Your Daughters. A Lot.*
None of this reframing will have lasting effects, however, unless we're mindful of our own self-objectification and commentary on the appearances of other women. Girls are watching what we eat, how we look, and how we treat others to determine what they should do.

Research repeatedly shows a mother who frets about her weight or criticizes her appearance is more likely to have a daughter who says she dislikes her own body. Negative body image is essentially contagious, even if girls just overhear it and even if it lasts only a few minutes. It's also true that even when mothers feel critical of their daughters' physiques but don't disclose those feelings, their daughters have lower body esteem. When parents, including fathers, nitpick or objectify themselves, their daughters, or other women, they're influencing their daughters' self-evaluations.

Girls also pick up on their parents' body issues even when their parents keep quiet about them. Carrie came to therapy after her thirteen-year-old daughter, Tanya, was diagnosed with anorexia. Like many parents in similar situations, she was caught completely off guard and beat herself up for missing the signs. Her daughter was a committed lacrosse player, so the exercising and focus on eating "right" seemed to go with the territory. It wasn't until Tanya passed out for the second time during a game and was given a workup by her pediatrician that it became clear. What floored Carrie was that because her own mother frequently talked about being fat, Carrie had made a conscious effort to never mention her own chronic weight concerns around her children. But kids, especially daughters, are attuned to their mothers, and silence isn't enough to blunt the messaging. Active engagement around the topic of beauty culture is necessary, and fortunately the data show mothers who use positive language about their appearance and don't accept "fat" as an insult can help their children develop healthy body image.

We can't expect to raise a child with body confidence if we're miserable about our weight or some other aspect of our appearance. If the goal is to make them feel worthy whatever their size, then we have to feel it about ourselves too, especially if our daughters are going to grow into genetically similar bodies. We can't safeguard girls from diet culture—a lifetime of pointless dieting and disordered eating—if we're avoiding whole food groups to lose weight or getting tummy tucks. The best-known environmental contributor to the development of eating disorders is the sociocultural idealization of thinness. So don't idealize it. We needn't adore our reflections, but basic respect for our bodies is a must.

➔ *Show Appreciation for How Bodies Function and Feel*

Even if you don't love your body, you can notice all the amazing things a body can do, and chances are your daughter will too. You don't have to run marathons to observe that your strong legs allow you to play chase with the family dog, and that your arms allow you to shovel snow and give comfort. When your girl sings, you can say, "Isn't it cool that the air from your lungs makes your vocal cords vibrate so you can make that sound?" When she recites forty-five cat facts, notice how wild it is her brain can absorb so much in so little time.

Teach her, too, to value her body's many sensations. Crack an invisible egg on her head, letting the pretend yolk drip down her back, and say, "Doesn't that light tickle feel nice?" Encourage her to notice the juice of an orange in her mouth and the flavor on her tongue. The message is there are many ways to feel good in your body having nothing to do with how it looks to someone else. Your body is for you; it isn't an object to be adjusted for the pleasure of others.

➔ *Don't Be the Unintentional Weight Bully*

Weight is the most common reason girls are bullied. Parents whose children are gaining weight are desperate to protect them (and maybe themselves given they're frequently blamed when their daughters are fat). They point out their kids' pudgy belly, encourage them to eat less and exercise more, drawing attention to "flaws" girls sometimes hadn't even noticed yet. One college student I saw in therapy traced her disordered eating to the day her father asked her at age nine if other kids made fun of her for being chubby. She told me she went to the mirror to see what he meant and never looked away. Parents tell me they feel stuck between a rock and a hard place as they try to prepare their daughters for how the world might interpret their appearance (which helps girls accurately calibrate their sexism detectors) without enforcing those interpretations at home (which misaligns them).

It's painful to watch your child's confidence drain away, but the wish to save them from suffering can cause more suffering. Women tell me they wish their parents had replaced diet tips with observations their bodies were unconditionally good bodies, and that's precisely what science tells us is best too. A large-scale study of more than two thousand girls found those who were labeled too fat by age fourteen had unhealthier eating thoughts and behaviors over the next five years—regardless of body mass index (BMI)—and these effects "may be most pronounced when labeling comes from a family member."

If your daughter expresses dismay about her body, ask her what's making her feel that way to try stimulating a discussion. Rather than trying to convince her she's not fat, remind her that contrary to sexist cultural messaging, fat isn't a bad thing or a measure of her worth. I once asked Geneva if her worth was measured in inches and pounds, a comment she returned to often. If your child comments on someone else being fat, don't shush them. Instead, you might shrug and say, "So what?" as a reminder that fat is a description, not a value judgment, or say, "She's lovely," to remind her no body has more value than another. This allows you to be an ally to people in bigger bodies, which is especially important for your daughter's body satisfaction no matter her objective body size.

Unless we really consider the phobia we all have toward fatness that underlies our goals of thinness, we'll continue to create a generation of girls with unhealthy relationships to their bodies. Indeed, research shows it isn't her BMI that predicts a girl's appreciation of her body but the acceptance of her body by important people in her life. By accepting their bodies, we help girls resist adopting an observer's perspective of them. If we remind her *it's not her,* it's the culture and the bullies (who might be us) who need to change, we might just avoid heightening years of insecurity. Looking for tangible changes that can help? Don't put a mirror in her room when she's young and get rid of your scale (consider a ritual smashing of it with your girl). She may come home some days in tears, but she'll be coming home to someone who sees and appreciates all of her.

⮕ *Help Her Understand the Nature of Fat. And the Effects of Fatphobia.*

You can validate her wish to be smaller given the world she's growing up in, but she should hear that her desire may be incompatible with her physiology. Researchers have identified more than a thousand genes and variants that contribute to being fat, which might explain why thinness for many people isn't sustainable. So, when we tell kids (and adults) to lose weight, we're telling them to do something that isn't necessarily natural for their bodies and setting them up for failure and hopelessness.

We've all heard that fat leads to high blood pressure, heart disease, and type 2 diabetes, yet research shows just the stigma of fatness alone, independent of BMI, is associated with increased blood pressure, cortisol, and inflammation in the body due to the fight-or-flight response it elicits. And stigma alone is also related to poor psychological functioning. When we hold girls personally responsible for their size and blame them for lacking willpower, we may harm them more than fat does.

Similarly, research repeatedly tells us that dieting inevitably results in regaining even more weight and is associated with increased morbidity, mortality, and disordered eating. It's just not true that anyone who is determined can lose weight and keep it off through diet and exercise, yet we've been conditioned to believe weight loss is the only option for improving health, preventing disease, and living a full life. A recent review of hundreds of studies concluded physical activity was far superior to weight loss when it comes to a long and healthy life.

It's not inherently unhealthy to be fat; there are "healthy" and "unhealthy" people at all points on the size spectrum. By conflating fat with poor health, we contribute to the stigma of fat, which we know has the paradoxical effect of worsening health. But the myth is if we're not torturing our bodies into skinny submission, we're doing something wrong. If we're going to help girls avoid a lifetime of self-loathing and food preoccupation, we need to shift the focus from weight and good/bad food to health-promoting behaviors that improve quality of life. Rather than saying, "I need to hit the gym to burn off this lasagna," help your kids associate exercise with being strong and energized so it becomes a get-to, not a have-to, activity. Mention how wild it is that we naturally produce "feel good" chemicals called endorphins when we exercise.

➲ *Teach Them to Trust Their Bodies and Their Hunger*
Babies trust their bodies. They know when they're hungry and full and when they're ready to roll, crawl, and stand. But our culture has made it

scary to watch a chubby kid eat. We worry they'll be bullied and unhealthy. We start asking them if they need that second helping, sowing distrust in their bodily cues and interrupting the pleasurable experience everyone deserves with food.

We can help our kids return to being the intuitive eaters they were as babies, before hectic lives, tempting ads, and well-meaning caregivers distracted them from their hunger and fullness cues. Some core elements of intuitive or mindful eating include honor your hunger, no foods are off-limits, engage all senses, honor your health, feel your fullness. As mealtime nears, you might ask your child to rate their level of hunger. Instead of chiding yourself for eating sweets, remove moral judgment and say, "This cake is delicious." When you're full, say, "I'm going to save some for later." It's time for us to turn up the volume on girls' sexism detectors around fat and drown out the drumbeat of diet culture.

It's time for us to turn up the volume on girls' sexism detectors around fat and drown out the drumbeat of diet culture.

If we can make peace with our own bodies and advocate fiercely for our daughters no matter their size, we might just be able to free a generation of girls to love their bodies and value their health more than counting calories and feeling guilty for eating something delicious. For anyone who's already sparked the fear of fat in their daughters, even adult children benefit from hearing their parents take responsibility for bringing diet culture into their homes and admitting it was destructive. This can help reorient them to overall health rather than a number on a scale and reintegrate all of their parts so when they look in the mirror, they can see the whole package.

· · ·

AS A YOUNG woman of color, Geneva had to manage conflicting messages about what constituted an appropriate body. She'd unconsciously absorbed and aspired to the thin ideal. As her body developed, she took conscious action to maintain thinness, but that goal was blurred among family and kids from her somewhat more diverse high school who appreciated a more curvaceous figure. The body politics literature explains intentionally resisting Eurocentric beauty standards is a collective effort to resist racism. While this has largely been seen by (primarily white) scientists as a buffer against negative body image, more recent research shows Black women are by no means unscathed in this arena, having to contend with being judged deviant and unhealthy in broader society. Furthermore, when thickness is idealized and essentialized in communities of color, women can feel stigmatized for having too few or excessive curves. In other words, women can't win, and that's exactly how Geneva felt.

A turning point came when Geneva was able to make meaning of why she expressed her pain through food. Food had been how Geneva felt most nurtured by her mother, whom she otherwise experienced as distant. After her parents divorced when she was seven, her mother would hand her a homemade roll as she tearfully left for visits with her father. Years later feeling pulled between two cultures was a reminder of feeling pulled between two households. Bingeing and purging were enactments of the nurturance and deprivation she felt each time she'd say goodbye. Therapy focused on finding constructive ways of managing her emotions, as well as seeing herself as somebody, not *some body*, so she could have a healthy relationship with food. Geneva began noticing how restricting led to compensation, which made her want to binge, which led to spending precious resources on thinking about food, which she began to feel was "boring and the opposite of life affirming."

She also worked with a skilled dietitian who introduced her to intuitive eating. She discovered it was perfectly fine to eat for nutritional needs *and* pleasure. "Who knew eating a cookie wasn't a crime?" she said, only half joking. As she gained an internal sense of freedom to embrace a self beyond her appearance, she could allow her weight to settle where it was most comfortable, keeping active but not obsessive. She quit her job dancing and started doing private tutoring. She saved for college rather than cosmetic surgery. Therapy terminated when she left for college, but Geneva stayed in touch. She was double majoring in women's studies and education. She last sent me a picture of herself wearing a T-shirt that said, "Self-love is a virtue . . . fitting into your high school jeans is not."

CHAPTER 5

Plugged In

Making Friends with Mass and Social Media

When my daughter was seven, we started streaming the popular cooking competition show *MasterChef Junior,* watching as a family. As season one was nearing the end, Gabi said excitedly, "I think the girl is going to win," referring to twelve-year-old Dara Yu, the only girl or minority to make it to the finale. She was heartbroken when Dara lost. The next season, she was more tempered, saying, "I hope a girl wins this time." But, alas, she'd have to wait four seasons to finally see that happen.

Until that point in their lives, I found it much easier to point out sexism around my son than my daughter. With her, I worried that talking about it would rob her of the notion she lived in a fair world and create feelings of inferiority that weren't yet there. Mostly, I stuck to pointing out positive counter-stereotypical role models, rather than overt sexism. For example, I might casually notice their friend Helen's dad takes care of Helen during the day while her mom's at work. Or when they were watching a show that demonstrated equality, like *Odd Squad,* I might say, "Olive and Otto work well together using their math skills to solve cases." I might also point out stereotypes or things I wished were different ("I wish Ariel didn't have to give up her voice for a man"). But during these seasons of *MasterChef Junior*, Gabi was voicing a clear wish. And, in that wish, I heard a plea to see herself represented out in the world, to find proof girls like her could be winners too.

As it happens, I had a parallel experience that convinced me it was time to get real with her: An article in *The Atlantic* by Caroline Framke came out during the third season, titled "On *MasterChef Junior,* Innate Biases Are Hard to Beat." She pointed out aspects of the show that had made me cringe. It wasn't only that all of the winners had been boys and that the judges were three white men, but as Framke noted, the judges seemed to identify with the white boys, making motivating remarks like "I see a lot of myself in you." Teasing about dating and marriage was reserved for the girls. "These jokes," Framke wrote, "undercut their legitimacy as young chefs." But what most irked me was the difference in the feedback the boys and girls got, with male contestants getting questions about how much they'd charge for their astonishing dish at their future restaurants, and female contestants with spectacular dishes being asked, "Is this a fluke?" and "Could you do that again, or is this luck?" As a culture, we somehow find it hard to believe girls can be successful or every bit as good as a boy. Virtually every girl and woman I see in therapy feels as if they got away with something when they experience success. They bring up the term "impostor syndrome" and say, "That's me exactly."

When we don't address the pervasive sexism baked into our kids' lives, it's akin to withholding the truth. After the third season ended with yet another boy taking home the $100,000 prize, Gabi declared sadly, "Girls never win." That's when I told her the show might make her think boys are better cooks than girls, but that's just not true. I told her there's something called sexism, which is when girls and women are treated unfairly just because they're female. I explained the judges weren't trying to be mean to girls, but since they're men and they get to make the decisions, they might give preferential treatment to people who look like them without even realizing it. I told her our country is run mostly by men, so she might see sexism in other places too. "But soon it might be run by a girl president," she noted optimistically. "It might be," I agreed, knowing the importance of balancing darkness with hope, "and the good news is women everywhere are fighting the unfairness." (Six months later, Hillary Clinton would lose the election to a man who'd bragged about sexually harassing women.)

I also explained that one of the most confusing things about sexism is not knowing for sure that it's happening, and I referenced some of the judges' behaviors that had made my sexism detector chirp but not blare. Had we been watching Spain's edition of *MasterChef Junior,* when a twelve-year-old boy offered a concrete example of sexism by saying his female teammates instinctively know how to clean because of genetics, it would've been easy to say to Gabi, "That's sexism. He's repeating a stereotype he learned," or "This little boy learned somewhere girls are born better at cleaning. He doesn't realize girls are taught to clean from a young age and boys aren't." The judge in that case addressed the sexism cleverly by making the boy do all the cleanup for his team by himself. I decided to use the less clear examples at my fingertips because I wanted Gabi to understand that we can't jump to conclusions, *and* it's important to listen to ourselves when we notice something's off.

I wished my daughter could have gone another year, another decade, without knowing about sexism. But she was already absorbing unfortunate messages about girls; giving voice to that wasn't going to suddenly reveal something she didn't know. It was, instead, going to reframe something for her, give her a vocabulary for what was happening and why. Given the dangers and drawbacks of absorbing bias without understanding it, this was the lesser of two evils and would make her path forward easier. Mass media supplies an easy avenue both for talking about sexism as a concept in the world and for helping girls become the critical consumers of media they need to be.

Discerning Mass Media's Hidden Misogyny

There's little doubt that TV influences kids' understanding of who matters and of what they can aspire to be. Studies find that girls and Black children consistently feel worse about themselves after watching TV, while white boys consistently feel better. A Common Sense Media report analyzing decades of research found that TV and movies promote the idea that being male is more valuable than being female. Another study showed that four-year-olds who watch a lot of TV repeat that message. The need to teach girls to be active interpreters of media messages— rather than passive consumers—who can challenge the realism presented, and understand the salience of sexualizing images, cannot be overstated.

However distressing it may be, the media's your partner in raising your kids. Unless you live off the grid, divorce isn't possible, so think of it as a partner with whom you have to learn to work well. Fortunately, research finds that co-viewing and actively discussing media with girls can protect them against its negative effects. But before we get into how best to intervene, it's helpful to understand three common themes in the way the media represents gender.

First, girls and women are often underrepresented in media, "which falsely implies that men are the cultural standard and women are unimportant or invisible." With recent progress after sixty years of stagnation, girls and women are still only 38 percent of the roles on channels like Cartoon Network, Disney, Nickelodeon, and PBS Kids. And as Geena Davis, founder of the Institute on Gender in Media, says, "The female characters that do exist are often underdeveloped, sidelined, uninspiring, or simply eye candy." Such low representation exists in most forms of media. One twenty-year-long study looking at 114 countries discovered girls and women constitute only 24 percent of the people we read about, see, or hear from on television, on radio, and in newspapers. Erasure in the media is erasure in girls' imaginations of what they can become. The popular hashtag #RepresentationMatters is borne out by research showing role models motivate us, give us someone to emulate, and teach us how to overcome obstacles.

In graduate school thirty years ago, a Black friend mentioned to me that as children she and her neighbors would rush to call each other on the rare occasions they saw themselves represented on TV by another Black- or brown-skinned person. I was stunned and ashamed that I'd never realized how few people of color were on-screen. As a white person who watched white actors all the time, the homogeneity didn't register. But neither did the dearth of female representation. Kids who are underrepresented or negatively portrayed unconsciously absorb that they don't fit the larger image of American success—white and male. It's what researchers call "symbolic annihilation."

Aspirational women on-screen or in public life, I realized, were rare. Change is slow. In 2022, the videos of young Black girls viewing the trailer to the remake of *The Little Mermaid*—in which Ariel is played by the Black actress Halle Bailey—were as heartbreaking as they were thrilling. Their shock and delight—"She's brown like me!" "Her skin is like mine!" "She's Black! She's Black!"—demonstrated seeing someone like themselves on-screen was still an anomaly. As far as I know, no white child has ever screamed in surprise over a character being white.

Television presents a world where seemingly everyone is rich, white, cisgender, straight, and able-bodied. The fewer of those identities a child possesses, the more likely they are to feel excluded. Only 2 percent of characters are portrayed as having lower socioeconomic status, and 1 percent have a physical disability, yet about 12 percent of people in the United States live below the poverty line and 20 percent with a disability. A girl from a working-class family watching TV may feel even more excluded than an upper-middle-class girl, and a gay, working-class girl with a disability even more so. This invisibility desensitizes kids even more to significant portions of the population. It's important for kids with more social power to see people who look different from them, and those with less to see people who look similar or share a similar background so they can identify with them. Unless, of course, they're portrayed in ways that limit a child's perceptions of what's possible, which brings us to the second theme.

It's not an overstatement to say females and males are systematically portrayed in stereotypical ways in the media. For example, females are twice as likely to solve problems using magic, while males—who make up 70 percent of characters in STEM professions—are more likely to use science, technology, engineering, and math, or their physicality. And there's reason to believe television exposure may have lasting effects on children's career aspirations. Girls who are shown TV clips featuring stereotypes of women's behavior (for example, talking about their outfits) express less interest in being a scientist or architect or joining another STEM profession than girls who are shown no content or who are shown clips featuring female scientists. One exposure to one small clip may fade, but imagine the effects of watching thousands of hours of small-waisted, submissive girls (think every Disney princess ever) or hideous, powerful ones (think wicked witches and stepmothers).

Girls in children's television and films are also two to three times more likely to be sexualized and are thinner than male characters. In a damning report by the American Psychological Association summarizing years of research, we learn systematic sexualization and commodification of girls are indeed as detrimental as many of us suspected. They affect mental health in the form of eating disorders, low self-esteem, and depression while also negatively influencing physical health, academic performance, and sexual development and contribute to reductionist beliefs about women as sexual objects.

The third consistent theme of gendering in the media is the normalization of traditional gender roles and violence against women in relationships. More often than not, men are portrayed as pursuing physical relationships, avoiding commitment, and treating women as sexual objects, and women are, confusingly, expected to set and enforce sexual limits while also being sexually passive. This is important because researchers find significant connections between young people's screen use and their gendered behaviors in real-life relationships. Teens who think reality TV lifestyles are realistic have more stereotypical views of women and believe social aggression is necessary to get ahead. Worse, screen use predicts more tolerant views of and engagement in sexual harassment, acceptance of dating violence, and blaming women for sexual assaults. Violence against women in the media is so common as to seem trivial. Girls who internalize these sexist messages are also less likely to protect themselves against pregnancy and STIs. If we're going to change these pitiful gender narratives, we need more females on-screen *and* behind the scenes. But until that happens, it's up to us to create a more balanced narrative for our children.

If we're going to change these pitiful gender narratives, we need more female characters on-screen *and* behind the scenes. But until that happens, it's up to us to create a more balanced narrative for our children.

Combating Negative Imagery

Unfortunate depictions of girls may lead to lower self-esteem, but luckily the reverse is also true. It's vital that we become effective media guides to our kids and make sure they're exposed to a diverse array of characters who counter gender stereotypes. When kids are younger, you can deliberately choose to read *The Paper Bag Princess* and watch *Doc McStuffins* and every Hayao Miyazaki film ever made. During the preteen years, it's relatively easy to find relatable and powerful female characters in media. During Gabi's tween years, we read and watched together *The Mary Tyler Moore Show*, *Anne with an E*, and more modern stories like *Harry Potter*. But as time went on, and Gabi's TV taste matured, those smart, strong, capable girls who follow their own paths, have adventures, solve mysteries, and delight in themselves (rather than needing a man to feel complete) became harder to find. They were replaced with teenage characters who were saddled with the need to perform femininity. I started insisting on shows she, almost a teenager, reflexively rejected, but she quickly changed her mind. These included *Gilmore Girls*, *The Fosters*, *Jane the Virgin*, *Buffy the Vampire Slayer*, and *Huge*. No media is perfect, though, which is where proactive parenting comes in.

◐ *Building Media Literacy*
Research shows that when adults refute the stereotypical behavior depicted in media their child is watching, kids later evaluate those shows less positively and express greater acceptance of nontraditional gender

roles. Knowing this, I pointed out the insane number of times Buffy's eye-catching outfits were changed each episode and the fatphobic comments in *Gilmore Girls*. While watching *The Fosters*, I was concerned that twelve-year-old Gabi was seeing too many examples of teenage sex, but instead of turning off a show with many lessons about acceptance, inclusion, love, and diversity, I used it as an opportunity for discussion and to share our family's values about sex. In *Jane the Virgin*, they refer to the Bechdel-Wallace test, which Gabi and I still apply to media we're engaged in together. To pass the Bechdel, a show must have (1) at least two women in it, who (2) talk to each other, about (3) something besides a man. Some add a requirement that the women both have names. The test started as an industry joke, but given how long we've failed at representation, it's become a real thing. You can also tell your kids about the "sexy lamp" test, which takes the bar even lower and asks whether a woman can be replaced by a sexy lamp without the plot changing in any way.

As we comment and discuss, we're helping build media literacy, which is the ability to decode and assess the influence of media messages and to differentiate fact from fiction in images and representations of sexuality. And we really can make a difference. After an episode of the sitcom *Friends*, researchers interviewed a national sample of twelve-to-seventeen-year-olds. The episode centered on discussion of a condom failure that had resulted in the pregnancy of a main character. About half the viewers saw condoms as less effective in preventing pregnancy (and possibly by extension not worth using) than they had in a previous survey. The kids who watched the show with an adult, though, were twice as likely to recall that the episode reported that condoms were more than 95 percent effective.

➲ *Girl, You're Being Manipulated*

Our kids see anywhere from four thousand to ten thousand ads per day, which is nearly double the number of ads the average person saw in 2007 (before the internet exploded) and more than five times as many as in the 1970s. To stand out, advertisers rely on more extreme and hypersexualized images. When they're very young, we can teach our children how advertisers are trying to convince us something's wrong with us that only their products can fix, or that we need things we really don't, because they're trying to make money.

As they get older, we can explain to them that, although it's changing, the entertainment world is controlled mostly by men, so girls are reflected through "the male gaze"—the way men might want to see them but not necessarily how girls see themselves. Knowing heterosexual male desire is prioritized can lead to a discussion about why, even in cartoons, the few female characters receive the majority of the comments about physical appearance; why movies with male nudity are more likely to get NC-17 ratings than those with female nudity; and why, on the rare occasions fat female characters are given character development, it's usually related to their weight, not their hopes and dreams. I might ask, "Is it because only thin girls are worthy of hopes and dreams?" or "Where does that princess keep her uterus given the impossibly small size of her waist?"

We can help them notice whether media they're consuming has strong, smart female characters whose speaking parts are equal to those of male characters and who are treated respectfully by those males while also being valued for what they do more than for their appearance. We can ask them why they think we see so many more stories about the sexual victimization of women than we do about sexually empowered women. We can decide in the middle of a show that we don't want to watch or listen because we don't want to participate in a girl's exploitation. We can wonder with them about the absence of LGBTQ+, non-white, and over-thirty-five women in their favorite shows. By the time they're on social media, they'll have the digital literacy skills they need to better challenge and resist insidious messages about femininity.

. . .

Social Media: Misogyny at Her Fingertips

I wasn't the pearl-clutching adult sighing that the internet was ruining childhood. I've watched my kids use it to learn to code, start Etsy and drop-shipping businesses, and become savvy and thoughtful about the world. But then they became teens, a pandemic hit, and more and more of their life shifted online. As they'll tell you, I started clutching. By the time the CDC report came out showing teenage girls were in crisis—a global phenomenon mounting since 2012—I wasn't surprised fingers pointed to social media. As the NYU professor Jonathan Haidt explains, "Instagram was founded in 2010. The iPhone 4 was released then too—the first smartphone with a front-facing camera. In 2012 Facebook bought Instagram, and that's the year its user base exploded." Enter the corrosive selfie. Data from my therapy office told the same story. My work with teens has increased exponentially in the last decade, mostly girls with high levels of anxiety, depression, and suicidal ideation often citing social media as a contributor. The most salient issues—social comparison and social dynamics, online harassment, and sexting—require us to pay attention to the quagmires girls constantly face online.

Just as our children's electronic lives are slipping from our grasp, our kids are increasingly exposed to disturbing content, interactions, and quantifiable popularity. Boys can have a hard time online too, of course, but many problems stem from social media, which is both more popular with girls and where they're ridiculed and abused more than boys. Being online brings the world's misogyny and women's ever-diminishing human rights into focus, making girls' depression and hopelessness seem quite reasonable.

To try to get ahead of all this or at least be in a position to help, I joined platforms I knew my kids would be most likely to use so I could understand what to expect. There's no doubt social media is toxic to girls. It's also pleasurable, educational, social, creative, and motivational and gives voice to the voiceless. The ways girls use social media often foster deeper connections and many LGBTQ+ teens and those with mental health issues have found community without stigma. We want girls to be aware of the perils of social media, but how can we do that without demonizing something that's part of the fabric of their lives and risk alienating them?

Social Comparison, Social Dynamics

It's not just the more obviously disturbing content such as pro-anorexia posts we have to worry about; it's also the proliferation of doctored images that make our girls feel ugly and undesirable. In a digital world that amplifies depressogenic content like debates about women's rights, a "manosphere" full of hate speech against women, and women's abuse, kidnappings, rapes, and murders, the one thing girls may feel they can have some control over is the pressure to be liked by hundreds of people on a daily basis, or at least look as good as their "friends." I've yet to meet an adolescent girl who doesn't use some of the widely posted "model tricks" for taking photos, including angling her arms away from her body, tilting her head up (or is it down? I can never remember), positioning her eyebrows just so, and "smizing" (smiling with her eyes). When we were younger and coveted the glamour of celebrities, we mostly understood it was unattainable, but our daughters are comparing themselves with their peers. Research shows it's much harder to apply critical thinking skills to images of peers, so girls forget Snapchat's "Smooth Soft Skin" filter was probably used and conclude they're just not as pretty.

Teenagers are figuring out who they are; comparing themselves with others comes with the territory. But as they scrutinize the posts of their peers, they're measuring their complex, imperfect offline selves against the idealized online selves of others—usually a two-dimensional, highly curated, and meticulously selected photo. Like many of us, kids fail to remember our online presence is, more or less, carefully crafted, often in order to tell the story of how we'd like our lives to be. This breeds feelings of inadequacy, jealousy, and resentment. Seeing social media posts of friends who look happier and more successful is linked to more social anxiety and less self-esteem. Not surprisingly, girls who are heavy users are more likely to be depressed than light users. Even beyond the greater frequency of girls' use, social comparison is harder psychologically on girls than on boys, probably because of the primacy placed on girls' looks.

Most girls know they feel more anxious and depressed when they spend too much time on social media, but that doesn't mean they want to change their behavior or feel they can. Beyond the addictive quality, girls feel pressure from friends to be constantly available. Their friendships are cultivated by supporting each other's daily struggles and successes and by bolstering friends' reputations with adoration and fire emojis. Helping friends be seen as well loved on social media is crucial, and girls notice which friend isn't up to code. They're caught between our wish for less screen time—maybe their wish too—and their friends' insistence that they interact online.

When social dynamics bring our kids crying to us, it's tempting to shake our heads and tell them to just stay off social media. This, though, is unrealistic after a certain age, and if we're willing to engage, we have a real shot at helping them navigate the complex digital lives that will be with them forever.

➲ *Help Her Tune In to Her Feelings and Encourage Her Critical Eye*

As the psychologist Jean Twenge, author of *iGen,* outlines, there is now direct evidence showing that social media—particularly Instagram—is a *cause,* not just a *correlate,* of poor mental health, especially in teen girls and especially when used more than three hours a day. Social media algorithms are tracking what our kids watch and whom they follow, and the subsequent algorithmic suggestions determine whether they have a fun, social, informative online experience or one that immerses them in whatever insecurity or vulnerability they're struggling with and convinces them their faces are warped and they're mentally ill. It's enough to make you want to stand over them every time they pick up their phones. But rather than hyper-monitoring our kids' tech use, we're likelier to see long-term success if we mentor them instead, according to Devorah Heitner, an expert in the world of youth and technology. Toward that end, share the research with your daughters that shows kids feel worse about their bodies when they spend too much time on social media. Explain how algorithms are designed to keep them hooked and can identify when they feel insecure or worthless, and are extra vulnerable to advertising. Ask to see whom they're following, and have them reflect on how they feel when they look at certain images. Can they stop following an account that induces negative feelings? If it's a friend, the social consequences might be too high. Maybe they can start following accounts with empowered messaging by searching #GirlPower or #StopSexualizingWomen. As they become more conscious of their feelings while using social media, they'll likely choose more encouraging content. Of course, if it's taking an obvious toll on their mental health (and sleep, grades, and so on), then it might be necessary to delete unhealthy accounts and re-implement some of the parental controls from when they were younger to limit which apps they can use and for how long.

When it comes to their friends' posts, encourage them to develop a critical eye by asking questions about why a certain picture might have been taken and whom it's for. Remind them that just as their own posts give only a tiny glimpse into their lives, other people's images don't tell the whole messy, human story either. Ask them whether they feel pressure to get their own pictures just right. Sympathize with the tightrope they walk knowing they're expected to look like a TikTok baddie or It Girl, always "on fleek," but if they succeed, they might be ridiculed for being too filtered or fake, yet "too natural" could get them dinged with negative comments or fewer likes. And an undefined amount of cleavage might garner likes or render them slutty. Make dinnertime conversation about the effects of social media by asking general questions like "Do you think social media makes kids your age feel more lonely or less?" Recently, I asked my kids why they thought social media was harder on girls, which led to a rich conversation about beauty standards and marketing. When the questions are abstract and not about them personally, kids are less likely to be defensive and parents can learn more about their lives. I was pleased my kids could identify the patriarchy's "master narratives" and name the social constructs being built around them. That doesn't mean the adverse effects aren't seeping in, but the more consciousness they have, the better.

❥ Teach Her to Be a Force for Good on Social Media

"Hot!" "Fire!" "Drooling!" "What a babe!" These encapsulate the comments on many girls' posts. I'd love to see girls' social media minds move beyond the facade. We can encourage them to notice other details and build their friends up in other ways, hoping it expands their view of their own posts and themselves. "Love the vintage chair and the girl in it!" "Must have felt amazing to make it to the mountaintop!" Similarly, encourage them to reflect on their own content before they post. Why am I posting this? What reaction am I hoping for? Am I hoping to stir envy in others? Am I seeking validation that I'm sexy? Will the responses

I get determine my mood? Is a social media world full of bikini shots and come-hither eyes the world I want to live in? We want our girls to eventually understand when they're turning themselves into a commodity, hoping to be (and show) they're "liked" by everyone, and how this alienates them from themselves.

The best part of social media is that it offers them a space to develop their own voice and potentially mobilize others. Encourage them to post about books they like or causes they're interested in, or to express themselves through writing, photography, and how-to demonstrations rather than just selfies. Being a creator, instead of a passive consumer, challenges traditional gender roles in and of itself and may lead them to actively challenge stereotypes.

➲ Follow Body Positivity Accounts

There are plenty of social media accounts that can help stanch social comparison by exposing kids to images that counter beauty stereotypes. Encourage your kids to follow body positivity accounts or hashtags like #BodyPositive or #NormalizeNormalBodies so their Explore or For You pages will begin suggesting more realistic, helpful posts. Since they're inevitably going to be inundated with celebrities wrapped in shiny packages, it's a nice counterbalance, especially if your child is headed down Self-Loathing Row.

Researching the body positivity movement for this book, I watched countless Instagram feeds of fat women genuinely loving on their bodies, dancing in bikinis, lifting weights, or posing in clothes that make them feel their best. It made me more aware I'd been living at the intersection of misogyny, ageism, and fatphobia, and to my surprise I found myself less critical of my body's changes and mundane imperfections. And I'm not alone. Thousands of comments from followers of these feeds tell a similar story. @Sophthickfitness, whose profile reads, "You are MORE than your body," is regularly thanked for helping people heal their relationships with their bodies. One commenter wrote, "It wasn't until I started following you that I realized how much weight I was giving my weight to define who I am." Another wrote, "I needed this reminder today. Literally no one's ever told me I deserve fulfilment [*sic*] and happiness in life without the condition I could have it if I'd just lose weight." Maybe we all need this reminder.

Online Harassment

Bullying is nothing new, but with social media reinforcing a culture of sexism, it's become much more public and no longer stops when the school bell rings. Nearly half of U.S. teens have been bullied or harassed online. Teen girls aged fifteen to seventeen are especially likely to report being cyberbullied, often related to their appearance, and they experience exclusion from group chats or games, malicious rumors, threats, stalking, nonconsensual sexting, and revenge porn.

Online abuse replicates the widespread discrimination girls and women face off-line, but it's even trickier and more prevalent, because cyberbullies can hide behind their screens or remain anonymous by creating fake accounts. It's by no means just boy-on-girl harassment. Girls bully and belittle each other too, often spurred by internalized misogyny. Competition for "likes" can mean girls portraying themselves in ever more sexualized ways, which may get a big thumbs-up from boys but be labeled slutty or skanky by other girls. Most difficult perhaps is the ambiguity of subtle aggression girls must chronically decipher: Was I cropped out of that group photo because they're embarrassed by me or because I looked bad and they're protecting me? Did they forget to tag me in the photo, or were they being mean? Plausible deniability at the ready.

Girls are also more likely to harass boys in digital spaces than they do in person. A friend's sixteen-year-old son had a gaggle of girls repeatedly ask for pictures of his "sexy chest" or "hot bod," both online and in person. He found it embarrassing and wanted it to stop, but when I asked him if he felt threatened, he laughed. "Threatened by a bunch of girls? Nah." That girls are now joining boys in this type of behavior may indicate a step toward gender equality, but it's certainly not one we should celebrate. Still, it's worth noting this young man's reaction echoes the research. Boys who are harassed by girls usually feel less threatened than the reverse. Boys' greater social power and physical strength may make it easier to shrug off harassment, whereas with girls, it's found to take a psychological toll.

Girls' posts, especially if they contain opinions, are frequently policed for "correctness," so they risk being labeled hypocritical, insincere, or insensitive, especially if their posts get traction. Alarmingly, they also risk being appearance shamed, told to go back to the kitchen, and hit with rape threats, all of which can silence or censor girls' online presence. In essence, just as they are off-line, the voices of girls, and girls of color in particular, as well as LGBTQ+ kids who suffer even more harassment, are erased from the public conversation. Such harassment is harmful to identity formation and a more diverse online environment. This is yet another way we find ourselves in the not always reconcilable position of wanting to protect our daughters *and* make sure they have equal access.

➲ *Make Their Accounts Private Until . . .*

The safest (though certainly not foolproof) way to protect kids from danger and harassment is to keep their accounts private, interacting only with people they know well in real life, for as long as possible. Girls aged eleven to thirteen are especially vulnerable to negative effects of social media because they're concrete thinkers and have trouble considering hypothetical situations, such as how a post might be perceived. A private account buys them time to develop interpersonal skills and learn to navigate social media risks. We can explain that with a public account adults can pretend they're kids and use praise and positive reinforcement to trick them into dangerous situations like sending pictures, meeting off-line, and giving their addresses. As they're honing their instincts, ask them to think of their account as their home; we keep our homes safe by not allowing strangers inside. Remind them if they ever feel even the least bit worried, or someone's telling them to keep a secret, they can always talk to a trusted adult and they won't be in trouble.

Private accounts also buy us time to impress upon girls that each person online is a *real* person who can be hurt by what they say or post, and of the benefit of making only positive comments, of seeking consent before posting images of others, and of imagining who might feel excluded by a picture of, say, a group sleepover. They should be aware they can mute or block someone posting upsetting comments or content, and if they feel threatened, remind them they don't have to be polite and should take screenshots of it and report it. No one's ever ready for harassment, especially not venomous misogyny, but when they finally allow a wider group into their social media homes, they'll be better prepared for any discrimination they encounter because you've been fine-tuning their sexism detectors for months or years.

Sexting

"We were so shocked," Daphne's father told me in our initial consultation. "I mean, Daphne herself seemed completely confused about why she did it." Daphne's dad, a lawyer from the suburbs of Chicago, was worried about his eighth grader, who was being relentlessly bullied after she sent a nude photo to a boy who shared it with other students. She couldn't stop crying and was refusing to go to school, tormented by the mushrooming posts on social media that she continuously monitored.

It's all too clear why girls share explicit images: it's an exciting way to seek approval and reassurance from boys, and even if they're hesitant, they get worn down by pestering from boys who themselves feel pressure to collect nude pics to prove their masculinity. We all did wacky or ill-advised things for approval and attention when we were adolescents. The problem is, the internet has made the dumb decisions of today's teens and tweens widely—and permanently—available.

And puberty's on a collision course with social media. Girls are now hitting puberty before adolescence, before their prefrontal cortex is prepared to manage their environment, particularly the thorny social media environment. They already understand the importance placed on their appearance, but as they cross the threshold to puberty, they learn sexual objectification is often required for recognition and power, especially with boys. A 2020 survey asked two thousand kids aged nine to seventeen about their sexting behavior. Tweens nine to twelve years old reported sending twice the number of nude selfies compared with similar findings from 2019! Of kids of all ages who shared nudes, 50 percent had shared a nude photo or video with someone they hadn't met in real life—an increase from 37 percent of youth in 2019—and 41 percent reported they'd shared a nude photo or video with someone aged eighteen or older.

Daphne was shy but emanated a sturdiness beyond her years. She was completely baffled by doing something she never thought she'd do, directly in opposition to the "Grandma Rule" her parents stressed: "Don't post anything you wouldn't want Grandma to see." In addition to her embarrassment, her confidence in what she once considered good judgment was deeply undermined.

It can be tempting to jump on a kid for doing something we explicitly forbade or that seems like an obvious don't, but it's important to remember this is the first generation of kids whose developmental impulses to explore their own identities, to connect and be liked, is bumping up against the new world of technology. Leading with empathy and curiosity is more likely to help us navigate this. In Daphne's case, it began when she created an alternate Snapchat account, one her parents didn't know about. She wanted to see what it was like to chat with people outside her friend group. The anonymity made her feel less awkward, and eventually flirtatious banter started with someone she thought was a stranger. She was having fun and hadn't planned on giving personal information, so she rationalized it was safe. She'd never dated anyone and didn't even really want to, but the attention she got from this boy, from a "safe" distance, felt fantastic.

When he finally asked for a nude photo, he promised never to show it to anyone. She'd responded, "lol, NO," but he was hurt and said it proved she didn't really like him. Afraid he'd move on and vaguely excited about breaking the rules for once, she took the selfie, impulsively sending it before she could change her mind. When he immediately took a screenshot, the shock of what was happening set in and she quickly deleted her account. But it was worse than she thought. It turned out it was a boy from her school—a "sort-of friend"—who'd "scored" her photo and went on to share it.

As Daphne's picture got around, kids snickered in the hallways and made lewd gestures, and boys fantasized loudly in the cafeteria about what sex acts they'd force on her. More than anything, they called her a slut, and though she'd never kissed anyone, she wondered if they were right. Daphne encapsulated a girl's dilemma beautifully when she said, "I guess I do want to be the girl everyone wants to fuck even if I don't actually plan to sleep with anyone." We live in a sexualized economy; being hot is what girls trade for approval, however illusory.

In an instant, Daphne's social and school life changed, her trust in herself and others was undermined, and she lost any sense of stability she'd had. But she was warned by other kids not to ruin the life of the boy who'd faked his identity and shared her photo without consent. She observed boys sexting too, but no one ever made a big deal of it the way they did with girls. Daphne was right. A study called "Damned If You Do, Damned If You Don't . . . If You're a Girl" found both boys and girls sext, but girls in the study were coerced more often and were harshly judged whether they sexted or not, whereas boys were virtually immune from criticism regardless.

Once Daphne started to see the double standards and mixed messages girls are subject to, she got mad. She decided she'd punished herself enough for slipping up and it was time for her harassers to face the consequences. Under Title IX—the federal law prohibiting discrimination based on sex in schools—unwanted distribution of nude images and the taunting that nearly always goes with it constitute sexually harassing behavior; her school was responsible for taking action. She could have gone to the police, but she was adamantly against that. The school took swifter action than most and briefly suspended the boy who'd shared her photo and two of his friends. There were only three months left of middle school, but they were miserable for Daphne and included rifts in friendships and continued circulation of rumors. Although she had a lot of support from family and friends and discovered courage she didn't know she had, she'll likely struggle for a long time with the shame of having become the sexual entertainment for her peers and with self-image issues stemming from the cruel comments about her body. Her trust in justice had also been shattered. When the ostracism you face is less important to peers and their parents than your tormentor's fate, you learn all you need to know—but never wanted to—about misogyny.

● *What Girls Need to Hear*
Here are the facts:

If you're under eighteen, it's illegal to sext.

"Self-generated child sexual abuse material" can lead to charges for child pornography possession and in some cases distribution. Laws don't differentiate between predators and teens in love.

If there's a big enough age gap between the two sharers (usually about three years, but it depends on the state), the older party can be tried as an adult.

While all kids need to hear these facts, it might just feel like a scare tactic, so make sure to address the following five points as soon as they're old enough for a cellphone:

1) These are usually no-win situations. If they refuse to send a photo, they're often called a prude or a tease or threatened with rumors. If they do, they're a slut. Remind them no one gets to decide their sexuality for them even though they'll try to. And if they don't send a photo, at least there's no damage legally or reputationally.

2) Tell them to always assume the photo will be shared, if not right away, maybe next month or next year. Maybe their peers will see it; maybe a college admissions counselor will. The internet is forever.

3) Girls often think it's okay to send nudes if they're in a relationship, so ask them to consider whether they'd want this person to have their nude photos if they break up. Explain revenge porn: power dynamics in relationships can change when someone has something that can be used against you during fights or if you want to end the relationship.

4) Tell them it's a big red bullying flag if someone, even a boyfriend, is trying to wear them down. Like any other sexual endeavor, sexting should never involve pressure or guilt—evidence their boundaries aren't being respected. Because digital pressure is so common in some circles, a girl who's not comfortable sending photos might feel immature. Girls really do benefit from hearing you say, "It's absolutely inappropriate for a guy to ask for a nude, let alone ask you repeatedly once you've said no."

5) Acknowledge that being asked for nudes and feeling comfortable enough with her body to send them can feel empowering. But it's also critical to help her consider it from the boy's perspective. He may not be thinking "Wow, what a confident girl" as much as he's high-fiving his friends or feeling pressured to fit in. As kids age, you can expect to hear a version of "I know, I'm not dumb!" but that doesn't mean your words don't matter. You can always respond, "I know. I just like to check in occasionally to make sure we're on the same page."

Because Daphne was so upset, she couldn't hide what happened from her parents. But it's often parents who come across a child's explicit text as they're exercising their right to check her phone. If you do find a nude, remember that shaming them only makes it harder for them to seek our help if they get into a dangerous or nonconsensual situation. Instead, say as neutrally as possible, "Hey, you know how I sometimes spot-check your phone? Today I noticed there were some naked pictures on there." Remind them you're there to protect them, and then remind them it's not okay: "It's exciting to share your body with someone else, but it's illegal and it can be weaponized against you."

Now that I've recommended putting the kibosh on sexting, it's important for us adults to remember that consensual sexting between teenagers isn't actually developmentally inappropriate and is fairly common. And kids who aren't coerced don't seem to experience sexting as harmful, according to research. There is such a thing as safe (or safer) sexting especially when it's between older teens who may want to demonstrate interest or take their relationship to the next level. Kids are increasingly savvy about hiding their faces and other identifiable features like birthmarks, jewelry, and backgrounds. Some are even deleting metadata or superimposing watermarks on the images with the name of the boy to decrease the risk of his leaking them. Consider saying, "The safest route is never sending one, but if you really feel the need to with someone you trust, I'd hope you'd take these precautions." Ask them too to consider sending a Google image in lieu of *their* body (and to then screenshot the search results as proof it's not theirs just in case it gets shared), or taking pictures that are suggestive rather than explicit. And always add, "If someone threatens you with exposure, come to me and I'll help you."

THE TWEENS AND teens in my world have taught me that helping them means listening to what empowers them, even though that might look different from what we imagined for them. Before we assume they're being damaged by social media, we have to tune in to their particular strengths and vulnerabilities and ask them how a particular app like TikTok or Snapchat is making things like self-regulation, interpersonal issues, and body image better or worse for them. Some girls are naive to social media's effects, and some are more critical users and generators of it. If we assume all tech is bad, we shut down conversations instead of opening them.

Our cultural understanding of how to navigate social media with our kids is in its infancy. The good news is, most kids do want to figure out how to have a healthy relationship with technology. And hopefully soon we'll see improved infrastructure around them, with better algorithms and big platforms held accountable for their content. Then parents will feel less alone in their fight to keep children safe online.

Potential, Lost and Found

From Unentitled to Healthy Entitlement

Finding Her Voice

Robyn, a bright and curious college student, told me she could add value to most conversations, "but only when I'm relaxed." When it was time to speak up at work or in certain classes, her doubts kept her quiet. If she was given an explicit opening to talk, she got anxious and her thoughts often became muddled. Even in therapy, feeling in the spotlight, she sometimes let her sentences trail off like someone turning down the volume. In her job as a research assistant, her co-workers were almost all male. When she tried to intervene in meetings, she found she was interrupted a lot by both male and female co-workers. One of the male supervisors asked her out on a date. A co-worker mentioned her "smokin' bod." She had boisterous conversations about books, movies, and the latest party with close friends, but was quiet and somewhat withdrawn with her family. Robyn liked to say her parents always had ears for her two brothers and eyes for her. By this, she meant they'd listened to and shown interest in her brothers, but mainly focused on her safety or appearance, complimenting or nitpicking. She withdrew because she said she was "done begging for space."

Adolescence is, as the Bill & Melinda Gates Foundation found in their global examination of inequality, when girls' and boys' futures really start to diverge. It's the critical moment—made up of an abundance of smaller moments of being interrupted, dismissed, ignored, scolded for being angry, and mocked for having a strong feeling or any opinions—when girls realize, consciously or not, that women aren't seen as serious creatures. If we want our girls to grow into women who feel deserving of their share of public space, to help make the world better with their ideas and talents, to negotiate more effectively for a job and equal pay, and to become our future leaders, we need to teach them to feel, deep down in their gut, that they're entitled to it.

Being called entitled is usually pejorative, used when we believe someone expects too much. But over and over, I see girls in my practice who aren't entitled enough, who lack a healthy sense of entitlement. To put it into concrete terms, as early as third grade girls begin to ask for less than boys. In a study of four-to-nine-year-olds, when children were given the opportunity to negotiate for their favorite stickers, the older girls asked for two fewer than the boys, but only when negotiating with a male, reflecting the same gender gap in negotiation we see in adults. What lessons are we imparting to girls, subliminally or directly, that lead them to believe that they deserve less? Without even realizing it, girls begin to feel they aren't entitled to the things boys grow up knowing they're entitled to: speaking up, respect, and money. This chapter will focus on the ways we can interrupt the subtle (and not-so-subtle) influences of sexism before our daughters become less likely to share their ideas, to speak up if they're harassed or assaulted, and to believe they're equipped for an independent, powerful future.

Girl Interrupted, Boy Interrupting

It's not all in Robyn's head (or in yours or your daughter's). It's a fact: women speak less in mixed company and are interrupted more and taken less seriously when they do speak. A study at George Washington

University found men interrupted their female conversational partners 33 percent more often than they interrupted other men. Decades of research find similar results: girls and women are disproportionately interrupted by both men and other women, but women rarely interrupt men. You might think it's because women talk more, but that's a false cultural perception. Men are actually the more talkative gender in classroom discussions, professional contexts, and even romantic relationships. And interruptions can't be explained by men generally holding more status; male doctors are more likely than female doctors to interrupt patients, which is especially true when their patients are female. While patients rarely interrupt male doctors, they do interrupt female doctors. Even female Supreme Court justices are three times more likely to suffer interruptions than their male colleagues.

Given the difference in respect afforded to girls' and boys' speech, those adult patterns should come as no surprise. In schools, boys are encouraged to take up more airtime. They're eight times more likely to call out answers than girls, and when they do, they're more likely to be listened to by teachers. When girls call out answers, teachers interrupt them and tell them to raise their hands before speaking. We reward boys for being assertive but call the same behavior from girls impolite or aggressive—and do the same with adult men and women, respectively. Nearly 50 percent of girls believe speaking their mind will make them unlikable. Boys come to trust their voices and girls to doubt theirs.

Talking over people and penalizing them for speaking out are ways of asserting social dominance. When you add race and class to the equation, the incidence of this marginalization is even higher. We live in a society that both accepts male dominion and teaches men their knowledge and opinions are worth more, sometimes even more than those of women much more qualified than them. The term for that is "mansplaining" and is defined in *Merriam-Webster* as "what occurs when a man talks condescendingly to someone (especially a woman) about something he has incomplete knowledge of, with the mistaken assumption he knows more about it than the person he's talking to does."

Not all men mansplain, but all women know what it is to be bullied out of their own perceptions and interpretations; to not be considered credible; to be treated as less knowledgeable than they are. If you're female, it's tempting to assume men are just cretins with overinflated egos. More likely, however, it's a function of unconscious bias and learned behavior. Your interrupter has been exposed to gendered linguistic patterns since birth. And he doesn't live with the cultural mandate of feminine politeness either.

Interrupting can seem like one small behavior—a minor indignity—especially compared with something like sexual assault (which itself is often considered no big deal). But its frequency has huge, long-term consequences. Chronically talked over, girls unconsciously absorb their insignificance over time. This diminished sense of self creates a vicious cycle: by being denied a sense of their own credibility, girls and women are more likely to speak softly and with more hesitation, making it easier for them to be interrupted. And, like Robyn, they're less likely to share their ideas. That's a loss not just for women but for the world, deprived of so many ideas and potential future leaders.

ROBYN'S PROBLEM AT work was immediate, but it's also a long-term one for two reasons. First, decades of research emphasize that a person's ability to speak up and effectively assert herself in group settings is critical for how much influence she'll attain. Second, experiencing sexual harassment early in a career can have long-term negative consequences, including altered career paths, lower overall earnings, and greater susceptibility to further harassment and violence in the workplace. Robyn didn't consider her work environment hostile, but she did feel her gender was an impediment. She said being viewed as dating material "sucks, but it's the kind of thing you just have to expect." She was bothered by being dismissed when she spoke but also wondered if it was her imagination. When girls accept disrespect at work as the norm, they've effectively muted the sexism detector that might help them contest it later.

In therapy, we explored Robyn's dislike of being treated differently but also her tendency to downplay or deny it was happening. She considered the effect of having been treated differently growing up female, of having her appearance valued and emphasized over everything else about her, and of experiences that made her feel her body was not really her own. Robyn's stories, accompanied by feelings of anger and hopelessness, illustrate a lifetime of being held in a gaze not reflective of her.

Shame also surfaced as she recognized that she, too, had focused excessively on her appearance, especially her weight, at the expense of other hobbies or talents. She came to understand the unconscious benefits of doing to herself what had been done to her. Being noticed and getting approval were beneficial, but seeking that as much as she did was also an ingenious way to hide, even from herself, her anger toward her parents and others who seemed not to notice or care about her internal world. Focusing on her appearance also allowed her to convince herself she didn't have much to offer beyond her looks, giving her good reason to avoid taking interpersonal risks that would reveal more of her.

As Robyn came to better understand her feelings, she gained more control over her behavior and self-doubt. By reconnecting with a sense of herself as smart and capable, she became increasingly proud of speaking up, insisting she be allowed to finish what she was saying when interrupted, and offering her ideas at home, work, and school. But a frustrating, if predictable, thing happened. Robyn found herself smack in the middle of a gender double bind: when asserting herself more, she was sometimes accused of being too demanding or overconfident. Knowing Robyn, I found it hard to imagine either of those. Instead, it fits with research on women in the workplace showing that they're punished and criticized when they speak in ways considered masculine (for example, being direct is interpreted as abrasive). It's an unfortunate trade-off girls and women sometimes have to make. Despite the discomfort it provoked, rather than internalizing this sexist interpretation of her and shrinking as she had in the past, Robyn felt better able to stand her ground. As therapists witness time and again, once people have the experience of being deeply listened to and valued, they know they're entitled to more, and the intimidation loses its power. Parents can do that for their daughters.

⤳ *Making It Safe to Speak*

When our daughters get the experience of psychological safety at home that Robyn craved, they have an easier time participating in work and personal conversations and standing up for themselves and their beliefs.

Parents are crucial in creating this self-assurance through communicating that their daughters' thoughts and ideas are important, even if they're quieter than their brothers, even if they speak hesitantly or say "I think" a lot. If you really listen to them and appreciate their unique way of seeing the world, their quick-wittedness, their interesting perspectives or amazing memory, they'll be more naturally willing to fight to be heard in those spaces where there's a risk of being called ignorant, intrusive, or incompetent. Make a conscious effort to invite your daughters to participate in family discussions and to debate with you. If they believe in their mind and have the experience of being listened to by you, they'll expect it from others.

> Make a conscious effort to invite your daughters to participate in family discussions and to debate with you. If they believe in their mind and have the experience of being listened to by you, they'll expect it from others.

➲ To Curb or Not to Curb Feminine Speak?

Some experts suggest encouraging girls to curb the uptalk, apologizing, and hedging so they'll sound more authoritative and therefore be interrupted less. Does your daughter ask for permission to speak ("Can I ask a question?"), apologize first for no reason ("Sorry, I just want to say . . ."), or qualify what she's about to say ("I'm not sure but . . .")? These are called softeners—a linguistic tool to soften the tone or to show politeness. This can be a useful way to connect, but when it's an unconscious habit rather than a choice, it's problematic, leaving more space for interruptions and projecting less confidence.

Bringing it to your daughter's attention might look something like this: "Hey, I noticed you say 'I think' a lot when you actually know something. You might get people to listen better if you give yourself permission to be sure of yourself and say 'I know.'" You could also include that girls are socialized to hide confidence so as to avoid being seen as bossy.

Others, however, argue it's unfair to hold girls responsible for the culture's sexist response to them by encouraging them to emulate masculinized expression—to code switch—in order to deserve participation in the conversation. Moreover, these tactics don't always work. Equivocating—considered more feminine and likable in a woman—sometimes wields more influence, especially when asking something of a man. Plus, they're behavioral fixes and won't undo years of believing your thoughts are unimportant. And in the end, as the linguist Deborah Cameron points out, judgment about female speech patterns is really judgment about the speaker and is just another way to blame women for their own oppression. Teaching young women to accommodate the linguistic patterns of men is, she says, doing patriarchy's work for it.

It's unclear, though, whether we're asking girls to go against organic speech patterns arising from their tendency for more one-on-one collaborative play, or if we're trying to override socialization that preaches female modesty and cooperation and asks girls to be nonthreatening. Probably a bit of both. We're in that knotty position of prodding our daughters to take up space they're entitled to without telling them it's better to be like boys, and warning them that when they do take up space, they may meet with angry reactions resulting from believing men are losing something they deserve, rather than a recognition that they had more of it than they should have had. There's no privilege without underprivilege.

➜ *Creating Space for Strong Voices*

I tried to teach my reserved girl to be assertive, direct, unapologetic—to take up space in a loud world where listening is undervalued. I once said to soft-spoken Gabi, when she was complaining about being interrupted at the dinner table, "You're right. We're not being good listeners and we need to do better. I also want to tell you it's okay to be more assertive, because it absolutely is and it's important to practice it. But I know it can be hard because when girls are more assertive, sometimes they're seen as hostile. It's an unfair dance we have to do."

It's important for girls to test out the power of their voice outside the home, so I harnessed small moments where Gabi could practice: ordering her own food at a restaurant or asking questions of the bookstore owner, the pediatrician, or the vet. Self-assertion is integral both to a girl's safety and to her future in the work world, so rather than step in, teach your daughter to advocate for herself. We want girls to feel entitled to speak up when they know the answer in class, or to voice their concerns when they're mistreated by a friend or significant other, or repeatedly interrupted or overlooked. It's impossible to say what, if any, influence I've had, but over the past couple years I've watched Gabi become entitled to own some verbal real estate in all these arenas.

No matter how strong their voice, we want to prepare girls for that first time they're spoken over—or down to—when the stakes matter. We can set expectations from a young age by modeling appropriate behavior. For example, "I'm going to explain the rules of this game, and then I'll take questions, but please don't interrupt," or by intervening if brother tends to speak over sister or Dad mansplains to Mom. A simple "Your sister was talking. Let's allow her to finish and then you can talk" or a good-natured (if your kids are listening) "Ahem, honey, remember that word for explaining something someone already knows?"

We can encourage our daughters to make it known when they have something to say but aren't being listened to (firmly but in a neutral tone, "Let me finish"), to hold up a finger when they're interrupted (indicating "I will cede the floor to you when I'm done") while continuing to speak without allowing the other person to chime in, or to pull a Kamala Harris and firmly repeat, "I'm speaking."

Soraya Chemaly, an author and activist who writes about gender norms, says there are ten words every girl should practice: "Stop interrupting me." "I just said that." "No explanation needed." Boom! Imagine your daughter growing up and setting a similar tone in a meeting or presentation at work. Let's tell our daughters that the longer female justices serve on the Supreme Court, the more they learn to just jump in—as their male colleagues do—rather than waiting for exactly the right time to speak. Finally, we can—no, we must—teach our sons to make space for girls by being mindful of listening to them and making sure they aren't dominating conversations.

. . .

The Invisible Work of Girlhood: Performative Femininity

When we talk about invisible work, we usually think of the mental load and emotional labor of adult women. But women's struggles with unfair expectations start when they get the message as girls that they're responsible for managing others' feelings. Taking on the cognitive and emotional tasks that make lives and relationships run smoothly is costly work that draws from our emotional, mental, or energetic tank. And even for young girls, the social consequences for refusing to do that work, or doing it badly, are often enormous. As a result, girls are chronically and anxiously evaluating the effects of small everyday actions.

Remember Rebecca from chapter 1 who was tired of her mother being too nice? Rebecca could be "bitchy" to her mother, but when it came to her friends, she was always trying to get it right so she could avoid being labeled a bitch/drama queen/loser, or, heaven forbid, entitled. *Will Julie think I'm bitchy if I want alone time after school? Will Olivia believe me when I tell her why I can't go to her party? If I tell my teacher I don't have time to tutor that kid, he'll think I'm rude.*

It was exhausting just listening to her unceasing list of concerns, so I could imagine how tired she felt. "Well, aren't you entitled to alone time if you're needing it?" I asked. "You don't understand," she said, pulling rapidly on a crease of her jeans. "Julie and I said we'd go over our lines for the play every day this week. It's kind of rude to change the plan on her."

I did understand, though. My own teen years were full of tiny missteps and long hours puzzling over the most artful way of declining requests or delicately sharing an accomplishment. From a young age, girls are expected to accommodate others and ensure they don't hurt anyone's feelings. And while empathy and cooperation are important for all children to learn, girls are pushed into unproductive ruminations that are distracting and anxiety provoking and that sap them of valuable mental and emotional energy.

Rebecca had asked her parents for a therapist because she found herself feeling "not like myself." She described being someone who was normally laid-back but more recently found herself "being snarky" with everyone and working overtime to cover it up because, she explained, "that's just not cool."

Over the next few sessions I came to understand why she was irritable. She was in all AP classes and repeatedly took on the bulk of group projects at school, rarely asking for equal help for fear she'd make someone mad. She rarely said no to volunteer or social requests even if she had a ton of homework, and kept quiet when friends left her out. She played volleyball, sang in the choir, and had been talked into the school play by a friend she didn't want to disappoint. Even her sense of humor was starting to feel like a burden. "Being funny is like the one place I can kind of be snarky without getting in trouble because it makes people laugh. But now that I'm not in a joking mood, people ask me what's wrong, and I feel like I've fallen down on the job."

I asked, "It's your job to make everyone happy?" "Absolutely!" she said without hesitation. Then, quietly, she said, "But there's a selfish element to it because I guess if I'm honest with myself, I do it because I'm scared people won't like me if they really knew me." I reflected back the fantasy that she could control other people's feelings about her and she said, "Ugh. All of this is making me sound like my mother. Bleh!"

As teenagers are trying to forge their own identities, they don't relish seeing their similarities to their parents. Rebecca could see her mother's unhealthy need to be perfect but hadn't been able to see it in herself. Rebecca had, in part, learned to stop listening to what she needed and wanted by watching her mother.

Mothers are bound by the same norms that restrict their daughters. No matter your age, where you grow up, your race or ethnicity, if you're female, the caregiver archetype—with the expectation that you be unerringly good and self-sacrificing—is projected on you. We've all heard the argument that women are more nurturing, but even if that were true, gender differences are never an excuse for inequality. And being the Nice Girl is inherently limiting. Science, however, is finding that women aren't more natural caregivers than men. Instead, our brains and hormones change based on time spent giving care. So it's time and behavior, not gender, that make a difference.

Whatever girls' unique sensibilities are or aren't, they do need the tools to say no, to ask for what they need and deserve, to say what they think and behave with confidence. But when we ask them to always "be nice," we erode their ability to do those things and to experience a full range of emotions. Selflessness requires them to prioritize others over themselves, repressing their own needs and desires, and modesty deprives them of permission to own what they're good at, for fear of seeming conceited. Perfection is unattainable, so, like Rebecca, girls are constantly docking themselves for every centimeter they fall short. Yet, because their sense of self rests precariously on being good, even a shred of negative feedback from someone else can be devastating.

Rebecca's mother embodied the caregiver archetype, according to Rebecca's descriptions, which just made her feel guilty and confused about being mad at her mother. Being a Good Mother isn't the same as being a connected mother, and no matter how hard Rebecca tried, she felt she couldn't reach her mom. The pressure to be a Good Mother can hinder a woman's ability to model positive behavior for her daughter. When she tried to be real with her mom, suggesting her mom might be repressing feelings, thoughts, and needs, it was always met with denial. "But I'm not dumb. I can feel it," Rebecca said. When she tried to get a rise out of her mother, her mother would become tearful or grow stony. Rebecca came to understand her longing for her mother to admit she wasn't necessarily happy was not only to validate her intuition but to give her permission to have her own "bad" feelings.

Words like "bad," "rude," "negative," and "selfish" permeated Rebecca's sessions. She saw everything she did as a choice because, consciously, it was. When I'd ask her why other people's needs were more important than her own, she'd list what she was getting out of it: "I can't stand conflict, so I'd rather just show up," or "Volunteering looks good on my résumé." What was more difficult for Rebecca to see was she'd never really been given another choice. The alternative meant drawing outside the lines of traditional femininity, and Rebecca told me, even as a toddler, she'd go ballistic if she colored outside the lines of her coloring book. Free expression, or as she called it, "failure," had never been an option. As she focused on external symbols of success, she became increasingly alienated from her inner life. She was so busy managing her image, she didn't have time to figure out what made her tick or have the bandwidth for even small mistakes. Her irritability turned into a deep sense of emptiness.

Some girls more consciously reject the good girl stereotype but get pushback for being "unfeminine," which can lead to an unstable sense of gender identity. Donna, a woman I'd worked with when she was pregnant, returned thirteen years later to talk about her challenging relationship with her daughter, Frankie. According to Donna, Frankie had changed from a well-behaved, fairy-loving girl to a foulmouthed kid who didn't brush her hair. "I have my fill of messy burpers and farters," she said, referring to her two sons. "I just want my girl back." As a young fairy, Frankie had flown around the house singing at the top of her lungs a line from *Cinderella,* "My heart has wings and I can fly. I'll touch every star in the sky," while chronically getting food or paint on her wings. Donna missed that happy, spunky little girl, but as I listened to her, it seemed that the older girl she described had much in common with her younger self. Sure, she was more sullen, pissed off especially about what she described as the expectation to be "perky and perfect" and having to let go of being a free spirit. She was anxious, and didn't have the language to articulate that, or understand why she felt oppressed. Donna huffed, "I would never have sworn in front of my mother or walked out of the house looking like that." Recalling she'd described being a free spirit herself as a young child, I asked, "Could it be that Frankie's free spirit is trying not to sequester itself in Neverland with yours?" Rather than fully swallow the good girl stereotype, Frankie seemed to be trying to hold on to the "bad girl" who sings loudly and reaches for the stars; who takes up space with her voice and body; who resists convention—things now inexplicably and confusingly considered masculine.

Donna herself felt frequently on the verge of "imploding." She felt guilty for desiring to have a life outside of her children and was angry at her husband for not shouldering more of the mental and emotional work of family life. It was easier, though, to focus on her daughter's rage. And Donna was hurt because it seemed to her Frankie was making a statement that she didn't want to be like her. "You mean she'd rather be a 'big, angry, graceless galumph'?" I asked, conjuring up Donna's own description of herself, "masculine" qualities she'd worked to conceal with elegance and good manners. Donna sighed a big sigh: "Maybe what bothers me is that she *is* like me, not that she isn't." Donna had internalized the culture's limited definition of femininity and perceived herself as missing the mark. Splitting off those pieces of herself that felt masculine, she projected them onto Frankie, who, I suspected, internalized them and then felt unfeminine herself.

The unconscious projection of a parent's unresolved emotions, fears, and insecurities that get internalized by their child profoundly distorts the child's reality because their experiences are systematically invalidated. To kids, this can feel like lifelong gaslighting. Donna was a Good Girl who became a Good Mother whose daughter was a painful reminder to her of what she'd sacrificed. As Donna came to identify her own anger and mourn the spunkier pieces of herself she'd long ago rejected for being unladylike, she began to see Frankie's anger as justified and as healthy resistance. And to see Frankie's "rough around the edges" personality as lovably Frankie. Frankie, in turn, was relieved because she'd secretly begun wondering if she were a boy, despite not feeling like one. The false dichotomies of "Good" and "Bad," "Selfless" and "Selfish," cheat girls by telling them who and how to be. As Donna became more integrated herself, she was in a better position to get close to Frankie and undo some of the confusion she'd wrought. But it would be up to Frankie to grapple with how that conflict—the wish to conform and be liked and the wish to be herself—lived inside her.

The narrow range of acceptable "girl voices" straightjackets girls and undermines how they're regarded. I outline below five important voices—integrity, resistance, ambition, authority, and economic self-sufficiency—that adults can and should help girls cultivate.

➔ *Developing Her Voice of Integrity: Trading Being Liked for Being Respected*

The need to be liked is hardwired into all of us. But the message we've accidentally given girls is that it's more important than being respected. To be likable, they learn, they have to make themselves more palatable by downplaying their strengths and accomplishments and watering down their feelings, as if the goal were a charming, somewhat vacant robot instead of a sincere, evolving human.

Girls often remember when they went from being cherished by their families to being outcasts, seen as rivals, or the subject of gossip (how she carries herself, whom she's dating). They trace it to becoming independent and strong-willed, whether at three or thirteen. When you learn being loved means pleasing others, you chronically look to them for approval, giving up an enormous amount of agency. You want everyone to like you. Everyone! And you'll put in the cognitive and emotional labor to get as close to that goal as possible.

If we teach our daughters that social harmony always trumps self-advocacy, they won't learn that their opinions, abilities, or achievements help them garner respect, which might make them more likable too. But liking someone doesn't always mean respecting them, especially if they've hidden away the things unique to them. Rebecca felt liked, mostly, but it didn't feel meaningful because it was superficial. Like those of many teenage girls, her relationships were full of intensity—big *I love yous* and *BFF forevers*, all heartfelt. But realizing that neither she nor her friends really knew her, she started to loosen her grip on the need to be liked, becoming curious about who she was without her mask and testing out being real with friends.

One afternoon she came bursting into my office a few minutes late. "You'll never guess what I just did," she said. "I told Julie directly I'm realizing I'm not an actor and don't want to do another play." She expected Julie to be mad, but instead Julie surprised her and said she might not want to either. "It's weird, though, because it felt like she was just saying that to please *me*. I hope I won't wake up to the silent treatment tomorrow, but liking different things is a stupid reason to freeze someone out."

Related to this is teaching kids the difference between being nice (pleasing others, a socialized response) and being kind (acting with benevolence, a choice), and that it's okay—essential even—to put themselves first. This doesn't mean never doing something they don't want to do; it means learning to give weight to their own needs and desires.

This is a conversation I have often with girls and women. It came up with my daughter when she was twelve. She and her friend Bella were hanging out on our front porch after school, chatting and playing with the dog. Or at least Bella was; Gabi was sprawled out half-asleep on the floor, listening with her eyes closed, exhausted after having been up most of the night with terrible growing pains. When it was time to part ways, Bella asked if Gabi could walk her home. "Do you feel up to it, Gabs? You're looking pretty out of it," I said to intervene. "You don't have to!" Bella said. But Gabi quickly agreed and roused herself for the stroll.

When she stumbled home an hour later, I asked about her decision process. Compared with the prospect of having to turn Bella down, Gabi felt denying her exhaustion was no big deal.

"I'd rather be mad at myself for saying yes than have her be mad at me for saying no or thinking I'm mean," she told me. "That's a tough one," I said, an expression I use a lot with kids as I'm trying to help them through dilemmas. "On one hand, it's nice to want to make someone happy, and it can be scary to risk having someone be mad at you. But on the other hand, it seems like that extra walk today was pretty hard on you. What happens if she expects you to walk her home next time and you can't, or now expects it every time? Are you ever allowed to say no?" As we talked through her options—make up an excuse to get out of walking Bella home, continue to acquiesce whenever Bella asked despite mixed feelings, let her friend know when she doesn't want to—I reflected back to Gabi what the pros and cons of each approach might be. We brainstormed how she might handle Bella's possible negative reactions and discussed how much weight to give her friend's potential feelings versus her own real ones. (And then, probably much to her relief, I suggested she go lie down.)

The difficulty in this scenario, and in many situations, is that there isn't one right answer. And fortunately, a little extra walking or slightly delayed rest isn't enormously consequential. But these tiny moments of discounting personal needs can add up. As Brené Brown writes, "Because true belonging only happens when we present our authentic, imperfect selves to the world, our sense of belonging can never be greater than our level of self-acceptance." My goal in talking to Gabi wasn't to tell her she'd made the wrong call; it was to help her replace anxiety ("Bella might think I'm a bitch") or catastrophic thinking ("Bella might tell everyone I'm snobby, and then no one will hang out with me ever again") around failing to please with a realistic sense of how to prioritize and balance her and others' needs. In other words, to replace the need to be liked with the desire to be respected.

⮕ *Accepting Her Voice of Resistance*

Conflict is inevitable, so allowing it in our homes rather than quashing it has many benefits, unpleasant as it may be. Girls are notorious for dealing poorly with each other when "bad" feelings like anger, hurt, or betrayal arise. They simultaneously worry it means they're unkind, the relationship will end, and they're overreacting. When you've never learned to manage difficult feelings or have had limited access to a full emotional lexicon, your feelings will come out sideways, either passive-aggressively or just aggressively. Girls need to practice their voice of resistance, which is really a voice of honesty and integrity, so they can be both real and respectful when they disagree. If our girls feel entitled to resist, they'll be less likely to compromise their values or principles for the sake of preserving relationships or avoiding conflict.

Suppressing feelings, coupled with the need to be viewed as Good and in the right, can ultimately lead to confrontation that lacks nuance and curiosity about the other's perspective. As a fifth grader, I came to school one Monday morning after getting stitches in my lip. Embarrassed by the string hanging off my face, I held my books up to shield my lips and stayed to myself. Not knowing what had happened and feeling slighted, my best friend began giving me the dreaded silent treatment and marshaled other friends to do the same. I'd planned to show her my mouth privately, but before I could, she'd assumed, I later discovered, I either had candy in my mouth I didn't want to share or was mad at her. For my part, I wondered what I'd done, not recognizing my misstep. It took several painful days for us to untangle the misunderstanding. Guessing is a staple in Girl World. I can't count the number of times I've asked a girl, "Could you just ask why she's angry with you?" Or "What's the fantasy of what would happen if you just explained why you're mad?" Relationships are the lifeblood of teenage girls, and they fear that anger will harm the connection. And because the anger they're not supposed to feel has been mismanaged, sometimes it does.

Girls need to practice their voice of resistance, which is really a voice of honesty and integrity, so they can be both real and respectful when they disagree. If our girls feel entitled to resist, they'll be less likely to compromise their values or principles for the sake of preserving relationships or avoiding conflict.

Expressing anger is also crucial for a girl's relationship to her body. Mounting scientific evidence (and the testimonies of every therapist I know) suggest there's a real connection between bodily pain and suppressed anger. Perhaps not surprisingly, then, women make up 70 percent of chronic pain sufferers. Over the years, I've seen chronic rashes, migraines, and back, neck, knee, and eye pain recede with therapy after scads of other treatments, including surgery, have failed. Patients report that having their pain taken seriously and being permitted to express rage is what helped. Their pain often has a medical basis, such as a herniated disk or an autoimmune disorder, but is exacerbated by unexpressed or unconscious anger—especially when related to perceived injustice. One patient with an autoimmune disorder who was prone to inflammation spent a lot of energy defanging her anger. But as she became more aware of it, she started to notice that when she suppressed it, particularly with men who crossed boundaries, she'd get a flare-up of pain in her hands. When she expressed herself, the pain would ease. She said, "I'm done sacrificing myself to be nice." It was as if her hands had been manifesting all the punches it wasn't safe for them to throw.

We've been telling girls it's okay to speak their mind but haven't helped them learn to do it effectively. The girl guru Rachel Simmons in *The Curse of the Good Girl* writes, "Relationships are a girl's primary classroom, and what they learn about responsibility in relationship forms the foundation of lifelong habits. Honesty is as much a skill as it is a value. Admitting a wrong is a high-stakes, nerve-racking experience;

the longer girls go without these formative moments, the more terrifying they will seem."

Their other primary classroom is their home, where, fortunately, we can help them tolerate and express their feelings and learn to repair conflict. That starts with being able to tolerate conflict in our homes, which can be difficult, especially if we've gone from Good Girl to Good Mother. Ask yourself whether you're effective at allowing your daughter to dislike you when you set a rule or, you know, chew wrong. It's hard to remember in the moment just because she says you're mean (or disgusting) doesn't mean you are. Teens are infamous for making us feel how they feel, rather than *telling* us how they feel. By externalizing their feelings, they feel better, but we get stuck feeling crappy. Lisa Damour calls it collecting their "emotional trash"—a loving service we provide.

It helps to remember that disrespect in kids is really a sign of emotional dysregulation. Some useful ways to approach this include "You can be angry, but how you express it matters. I can't hear what's bothering you if you're eviscerating my character" or "I don't let people speak to me that way. I hope you don't either. Let's try again." If a girl sees her negativity doesn't melt her mother, she learns to tolerate those feelings in herself and channel them more appropriately. And if she witnesses Mom speaking up kindly but firmly when disgruntled with someone else, she'll learn girls can still be liked or respected even when voicing their true feelings. A warning, though, Moms: You'll be violating the Nice Girl rule, so your daughter may be mortified. But do it anyway (while tolerating her feelings). The point is, conflict isn't an emergency, and negative emotions don't need to be extinguished; they need to breathe.

This may be especially important for a father who has the opportunity as a man to show his daughter she can question his authority, disagree with his opinion, and even leave the room if she's feeling too mad. The message is, you don't have to keep talking to a guy just to be polite. One study found more than half of girls, compared with a third of boys, feel they can't talk to their father about important issues. Again, that doesn't mean allowing her to be rude (though it's important to tell her that sometimes it's advisable to drop the politeness and be a jerk; girls have spent too much time trying to be nice to people who do them harm). Teach her to say, "I'm too mad to talk. I'll come find you later when I'm calmer."

Whether you're a mom or a dad, when you behave during an argument in a way you regret, repair it by apologizing and letting her know how you wish you'd handled it. You can explain how you calmed yourself down ("I just took a walk," "I paid attention to my breathing") and that you'd like to try again. In our household, we call it a "do-over," and our kids now use that expression occasionally when they regret their responses. You can make a repair while still imposing limits; after apologizing, say, for example, "The rule is still no cellphones at the table." Developing a strong, respectful voice of resistance will ensure your daughter can speak up and demand better if those sexist alarm bells ring.

➔ Nurturing Her Voice of Ambition: Tolerating Competition and Envy

When my daughter was eight, she was in a production of *Annie*. She was dying to be cast as Sandy, Annie's dog, the Airedale terrier mix who had no lines. But as casting got closer, Gabi started to hedge, saying maybe she didn't want to be in the play after all. With a little prodding, I found out her close friend Zoe also wanted to be Sandy. This troubled Gabi. "I feel bad wanting it when she does too," she told me. "It's good to want," I told her, adding, "even if you won't always get what you want." But to help her further reflect, I asked her what bothered her about the situation, and after a pause she said, "Well, I don't want to make her feel bad if I get it and I'll be really jealous if she gets it so maybe it's better to not do it at all." I realized this was about the age girls' emotional labor kicks into gear. I asked if she might have any other feelings, both if she did and if she didn't get the part. She named being really happy if she got it and sad if she didn't, but added, "I'd also be happy for Zoe, not just jealous." "Right," I said. "Lots of feelings can live together. And having feelings is never a problem. It's what we do with those feelings that matters. If you decide to drop out of the play because you're worried about hurting her feelings or being hurt, that's acting out your feelings rather than learning to experience them."

Just like with speaking their minds, we've been telling girls it's okay to be ambitious without helping them reconcile their competitive feelings with the mandate to be nice. The competitive edge girls have over boys in school doesn't last into adulthood, because intelligence and diligence alone aren't sufficient for success. Girls need to be given permission to "go for it"—to promote themselves and ask for what they deserve. These are increasingly important skills in a twenty-first-century world. When women don't negotiate their first salary, and research shows they often don't if their boss is male, they lose approximately half a million dollars during their careers. Raises, bonuses, and the starting wage for their next jobs are frequently based on that lower starting salary.

Negotiation opportunities abound in everyday life. She wants a sleepover? Let her make a good argument for it. Then address issues she doesn't cover, such as being tired for her piano lesson the next day. She wants a puppy? Let her PowerPoint presentation begin. Later curfew? Two-paragraph essay should suffice. Even if you know your answer in advance, she's learning what's important to her and developing effective communication skills. She's becoming an authority on what she wants and why.

It turned out Zoe got the part of Sandy, and Gabi was crushed. "It's not fair. She didn't want it as much as me," she said, sobbing. Then, looking a little guilty, she asked, "What if I'm not happy for her?" "Oh, honey," I said. "You get to be sad and angry and jealous because that's just how you feel. That's completely normal. You need some time to process your feelings, and you'll probably realize they don't cancel out your good feelings for her." The next day when Zoe's mom reached out for a playdate, Gabi asked me if it was okay to say no because "I'm still processing." Gabi needed some space from Zoe, and she asked for it.

Envy is a difficult emotion that girls often feel ashamed of feeling, which can lead to burying it in themselves and finding instead a negative quality in someone else ("She's a bitch," "She thinks she's so great"). Tween conflict patterns emerge among grown women who haven't learned to tolerate their own feelings of competition and envy and end up bad-mouthing, backstabbing, or power grabbing. If Gabi had been older, or in a situation where she had to see Zoe that day, I would've encouraged her to be honest rather than avoiding Zoe or pretending to be nice so she'd know she's entitled to honesty and her friend is entitled to an explanation. It might sound something like this: "I'm having a hard time with the play stuff right now. It's not your fault; I just need a little space to understand my feelings." As it turned out, the next day was rehearsal and Gabi happily embraced her part as an orphan and Zoe as Sandy.

➲ *Maintaining Her Voice of Authority*

We can help girls feel better about competing by underscoring the difference between being a competitive contender and being an aggressive rival. A tailor-made example might lie in the difference between how you play a game with her (trying to win while also celebrating her smart tactics and victories) and how her sibling plays with her (finding great joy in defeating her and rubbing it in her face). We're teaching them to stay with their desires and maintain their determination, but to be a good sport when they lose.

What about when they win, though? Largesse is valued in boys, but being a Good Girl means minimizing skill and authority. When incoming college students were asked to predict their first-semester grades—with half making public predictions and half private—women who'd made public predictions predicted lower grades for themselves than men, whereas private predictions were similar to those of men and aligned with their actual grades. The tendency for men to minimize their doubts and women to downplay their certainty has been called the male hubris, female humility problem.

When girls don't own their abilities, it has ramifications not just for self-esteem but for respect, influence, and payout in the real world. Admitting you got a good grade or believe you deserved to win the student election and being gracious aren't mutually exclusive. Girls must learn to hold onto their sense of authority because they're growing up in a world that frequently omits the titles and credentials women spend years achieving. The effects of "untitling" or "uncredentialing" aren't trivial. They shrink the already diminished authority and expertise associated with women and contribute to the "gender respect gap." It's hard to imagine a man being condemned for insisting on his title, as the First Lady and college educator, Dr. Jill Biden, publicly experienced in *The Wall Street Journal*. As girls come to feel entitled to compete, learn to tolerate the envy and pride that come with ambition, and demand recognition for their achievements, society will be quicker to acknowledge their expertise.

⮑ *Money Talks: Cultivating a Voice of Economic Self-Sufficiency*
The annual T. Rowe Price survey of parents with children aged eight to fourteen repeatedly shows parents talk more about money with boys than girls. They also pay boys shockingly more allowance for chores. A chore app called BusyKid looked at ten thousand families using its app and found boys earned more than twice what girls earned. To boot, boys were awarded larger bonuses. And *that* is how we implicitly tell girls money is a man's domain.

The World Economic Forum tells us it'll take women two and a half more centuries to catch up to men if economic progress continues at its current pace. We have the opportunity to help shorten that timeline just by teaching our daughters about money (and paying them equally!). Building girls' awareness is the first step to financial literacy and to setting them on the path to independence. By talking to them about money, helping them open and manage their own bank accounts, and having expectations for how and when they'll use their money, we can give them the skills to make their own wise purchasing, saving, and investing decisions.

If girls aren't encouraged to become financially independent, they certainly aren't being empowered to build wealth. Financial literacy allows us not just to understand and earn money but to make optimal use of that money. It's difficult to take risks with your money if you lack financial confidence. Being more cautious financially has its benefits, but for women that means keeping excess money in savings rather than in mutual funds or stocks, despite healthier long-term return rates of typical index funds. Even so, a 2021 Fidelity study showed when women *do* invest, they actually outperform men because they possess characteristics that make for good investors. They're more likely to make informed investment choices, stick to their investments, and seek advice. But only 9 percent of women think they make better investors than men; only 33 percent feel confident making an investment decision; and only 42 percent feel confident in their ability to save for future milestones like retirement. Numerous studies have documented women feel undervalued and talked down to by financial institutions, which likely contributes to the confidence gap. Is your sexism detector blaring right now?

You don't need a lot of money to teach them about investing. Let them create their own investment club with their friends. A parent can scaffold their research, but the kids get to decide the companies or funds in which to invest small amounts of money. Pro tip: investing in women-owned businesses isn't solely altruistic; a recent article in *Forbes* shows they're more profitable too.

There's also a growing list of resources for teaching kids about money. Jumpstartclearinghouse.org is a good place to start. It's an online library of financial education resources such as Money Mountain, a board game for early elementary kids, and *Bite Club*, an online video game for teens about a vampire nightclub that teaches about retirement planning, APR, interest, and paying off debt. For a more typical learning experience with a dedicated teacher, the Council for Economic Education has a three-course series called Invest in Girls. Building a girl's financial foundation will provide a lifetime of dividends, and not just for girls. A large and growing body of evidence tells us the key to a healthy economy is financial equality.

GIRLS ARE ENTITLED to be heard. Listening to them might just lead to a healthier (and more prosperous) world.

CHAPTER 7

Discovering All Geniuses Born Girls

Parenting Girls to Reach Their Potential

The nineteenth-century novelist Stendhal once wrote, "All geniuses born women are lost to the public good." Though we now know unequivocally there's no smarter sex, it wasn't until the development of objective measures of intelligence that the myth of men being the smarter sex was disproven. Still, stereotypes are tenacious, and girls' abilities are being squandered, not just intellectually, but physically too. The focus on girls' bodies at the expense of their minds and voices leads to a loss of confidence in their intellectual strength and ambition. The focus on their sexuality and femininity comes at the expense of their physical prowess. By the age of fourteen, girls are dropping out of sports at twice the rate of boys. As you'll see in this chapter, the additional biases girls encounter in the classroom and on the field eat away at their self-confidence. Girls try and fail over and over again to be Goldilocks—to find the sweet spot between being too hard and too soft, too smart and not smart enough, too strong or competitive and too weak or unambitious. "Just right" is usually out of reach, though, because it doesn't exist. They can be competent or liked, but not both.

How Girls Lose Intellectual Confidence and Ambition

"To my SENIOR BOYS who are becoming YOUNG MEN this year, you are now ready for my best life lesson. It's one of the biggest reasons why I'm pushing you to start your college and career journey right by PLAN-NING, EXECUTING, MONITORING, then ADJUSTING your plan if desired results aren't being achieved. Why do all this? To build up your financial resources in the future. WHY?"

Before we get to the answer, I'll tell you these were the words in a Google chat sent to the entire multi-gendered high school class by my nephew's well-meaning economics teacher. The answer to why building financial resources is important was in a YouTube video he included, titled "8 Reasons Women Want Men with Money and Why They Should."

In the same message, the teacher addressed the girls, "And to the girls in the class who are becoming YOUNG LADIES soon, just know WE KNOW your secret [that they want men with money]. As you get older, you will be able to admit that to yourself out loud. And it's OK, Mr. Williams understands, and the young men you encounter will come to realize this as well," followed by a winking emoji.

When you're writing a book about sexism, new material falls into your lap every day, but on that particular day I knew the writing gods were here to help. The video Mr. Williams shared was by Jeff at the Style O.G. and rested on the premise that it's a man's job to provide for and protect a woman. Jeff tells the audience it's natural for the average woman to care about a man's money because it springs from her natural desires to feel safe and protected. "I'm not talking about the gold diggers or the saints who don't care about money. I'm talking about the average woman," he clarifies. He goes on to say that just as it's natural for him to be attracted to a woman who's beautiful and nurturing, it's natural for a woman to want a man with resources. Yes, he uses the word "natural" countless times. He also says things like "We're men, so we understand logic," and "Trust me, women want to get married."

Jeff's message, the one I think the teacher wanted the class to hear, is that a man with money represents a man with a good work ethic, discipline, and resilience, someone a woman can count on. Mr. Williams wanted to inspire the boys to make a solid plan as they were considering their futures during the very important first semester of senior year, but his message got lost in the chauvinism. The boys jumped in with comments such as "That video assumes a woman's primary purpose is to rely on a man financially" and "MODERN women can make their own money now." Let's hear it for the boys! Sadly, not a single girl commented. But the message that a boy's future career is more important than a girl's was loud and clear and echoes the messages girls get, albeit more subtly, throughout their academic careers—messages that diminish their aspirations and erode their intellectual self-confidence.

PARENTS ARE TWO and a half times more likely to ask Google "Is my son gifted?" than "Is my daughter gifted?" and twice as likely to search "Is my daughter overweight?" Though it may not be conscious, the belief that boys should be smart and girls should be pretty runs deep. *The New York Times* explains, "It's not that parents don't want their daughters to be bright or their sons to be in shape, but they are much more focused on the braininess of their sons and the waistlines of their daughters." Still, across the globe, parents estimate their sons have significantly higher IQs than their daughters, despite there being no actual difference. "It's weird," said Robyn, the college student who'd had trouble speaking up. "I always thought my brothers were smarter even though I got the higher grades." One in three girls with a grade point average above 4.0 do not think they are smart enough for their dream career!

Piles of research suggest parents' stereotypical beliefs influence children's beliefs about their own abilities more so than their past achievements do, and are also predictive of later academic achievement. This has long-term implications for girls' aspirations and career choices. At five years old, children don't hold gender biases about who can be "really, really smart." That changes by age six, when girls start to categorize more boys that way and shy away from games meant for the really smart kids. As kids grow up, beliefs about the importance of innate talent or brilliance for success in fields such as physics, philosophy, and economics shape academic and career paths, and, unsurprisingly, women are underrepresented in those fields.

Girls simply don't have exposure to representations of female genius, whereas Albert Einstein, Sherlock Holmes, and Elon Musk roll off the tongue. A Google search for the top ten smartest TV characters didn't include any women on it. When I expanded it to twenty-five, three showed up, two of whom are animated characters—Lisa Simpson, and Velma Dinkley from *Scooby-Doo*. The same is true when searching for flesh-and-blood geniuses; the only woman included is Marie Curie, coming in at number nineteen. Glaring omissions include Jane Goodall, Ada Lovelace, and Simone de Beauvoir. It's true, many female geniuses like Maria Anna Mozart (Wolfgang Amadeus Mozart's sister) had their careers cut short because they had to settle down. Other women's legacies have been lost to history or were given due recognition only recently, such as Rosalind Franklin's discoveries about the structure of DNA or the brilliant African American women of NASA, Dr. Katherine Johnson, Dorothy Vaughan, and Mary Jackson, whose work on the space program in the 1960s (and beyond) was finally acknowledged through the book and later film *Hidden Figures*. Simply put, the idea of female geniuses just hasn't had the time to saturate public consciousness, and we contribute to that as a culture by failing to commemorate female brilliance the way we do male.

What happens between ages five and six when girls go from believing they're every bit as smart as boys to not believing that? Kindergarten happens. Whatever our girls are picking up in the world about the importance of their appearance, their intellectual modesty, and the primacy of boys gets exacerbated when they begin school, even as they outperform boys. Part of the problem seems to lie in the intense gendering of schools, from "Good morning, boys and girls" to sex-segregated sports, clubs, and classroom activities, highly gendered social groups, and gender-differentiated policies and treatment (for example, dress codes and acceptable play). Such gendering can trigger *stereotype threat*, which means the mere act of being reminded you're a girl can activate internalized stereotypes, putting girls at a disadvantage.

Rebecca Bigler, a developmental psychologist, has spent years studying the effects of labeling on children's development of stereotypes. In one experiment, she divided elementary school teachers and students into two groups: half were instructed to organize the classroom based on gender using both physical and verbal cues. This included sex-segregated seating and desks marked with either pink or blue name tags, separate male and female bulletin boards for displaying artwork, referring to the groups by gender, and having them line up boy-girl-boy-girl. Teachers were required to *treat* boys and girls equally, however, demanding similar tasks of each group, and couldn't express any gender-based stereotypes (for example, asking boys to be "big and strong" or asking girls to sweep the floors). The teachers solely used gender to sort and label, creating a typical classroom environment.

In the other group—the control classroom—the teachers referred to students using individual names and treated the classroom as a unit. No attention was called to gender. The day might start with "Good morning, *children*," and instead of "You're such a helpful girl," they'd say, "You're so helpful, Lucy." After just four weeks, students in the gendered classroom developed stronger gender stereotypes than those in the control classroom. They were more likely to say only men could be doctors, construction workers, or president and only women could be nurses, house cleaners, or babysitters. They also said "only women" can be kind and gentle and take care of children. Also disturbing, the children in the gendered rooms were more likely to see girls and boys as separate and homogeneous groups, disregarding individual variability. They perceived all boys to be one way and all girls to be another, an environment that makes it more likely a child who doesn't fit the norm will become an outcast.

A girl's school experience is frequently marked by implicit and sometimes explicit sexism and racism that can affect her learning and diminish her intellectual self-image. As mentioned, teachers unconsciously call on boys more often and also ask them harder questions than girls, restricting girls' influence and voices. They also show major bias about girls' math abilities. Equity in STEM disciplines is particularly important because achievement in these subjects is considered crucial for economic success in today's increasingly technological world. In certain STEM fields like molecular biology, women have achieved parity, but in the more math-intensive fields like computer science they're still largely underrepresented. Math achievement for boys and girls is "virtually the same in fourth and eighth grades in the United States, and eighth-grade girls actually outperform boys by five points in technology and engineering." But over time the gaps grow as girls are tracked away from STEM subjects, and attitudes toward math ability bend strikingly in favor of boys. One study, for example, showed girls outscored boys in two math exams when they were graded anonymously, but boys outscored girls when graded by teachers who knew their names. This bias wasn't found in other school subjects. Another similar study found when assessing the math ability of fictitious students, those with Black, Hispanic, or female names were judged lower than boys and white boys. The lowest-rated group was always girls of color.

Parents too hold biased views about math. They believe their daughters must try harder than their sons, and they prioritize advanced math for their sons because it enables them to enhance "natural" talent. Girls themselves express less confidence in their math abilities, even when they have the same grades as boys. Low self-efficacy explains a considerable amount of the gender gap in STEM. And bias is contagious; a mother may see her daughter struggling and comfort her by saying, "I wasn't good at math either," allowing her story about math to become her daughter's story. Teachers, too, with math anxiety can pass it on to students. Almost from the get-go, little girls are getting the message math isn't for them.

The focus on girls' bodies at school is another way our girls get the message their minds count less than their bodies. Take dress coding. Why do schools care so much what kids wear? Purportedly, it's to establish an appropriate learning environment. But in recent years, many school dress codes seem less focused on education and more on controlling girls with arbitrary and sexist rules, such as "three fingers width of coverage on the shoulders."

There are three main reasons schools employ dress codes. The most common reason cited is to minimize distraction. While this is technically a gender-neutral rule, it's almost exclusively applied to girls, which, by the way, is discriminatory and against the law. When a girl is told she can't wear leggings, shorts above the knee, or a tank top because it's distracting to boys and male teachers, this is just another form of objectification and victim blaming (not to mention heteronormativity).

Twelve-year-old Ari Waters wore a sweet knee-length yellow dress to her school's dance but was told to cover up because it was sleeveless. Her mother, perplexed, asked why that violated the school's dress code. Hearing the answer left Ari feeling dirty and embarrassed. They were told Ari's bare arms were "sexual objects." Dress codes don't teach modesty; they teach girls to be ashamed of their bodies. Claiming bare shoulders are "distracting" to boys makes it the girl's "fault." And what does it say about our faith in boys if we imply they can't learn or control themselves if there's a bare shoulder in the room? How many shoulders do we need to bring down patriarchy?

We want to ensure boys can learn without distraction, but where is the concern for girls' education? Their learning process is disrupted when they're pulled out of class until their parents can bring another set of clothes; given an in-school suspension; humiliated when they're forced by the dean to "stand up and move around" to judge whether their breasts look appropriate, or to change into a shame suit: bright red sweatpants and a neon-yellow shirt that reads, "Dress Code Violator," which I'm sure isn't distracting to anyone. You can't make this stuff up.

Another reason schools put dress codes in place is for the "safety" of their students, particularly their female students, even though there's no proven relationship between clothing and assault. Girls and women and even toddlers get catcalled, harassed, groped, or raped in everything from bikinis to burqas. The onus shouldn't be on girls to control male behavior. And if schools are so concerned about protecting girls, why do so many of them not only fail to properly report but also make it difficult for students to come forward when incidents of sexual harassment and violence occur? By the end of high school 90 percent of girls have experienced sexual harassment at least once. Surely not all of them were violating dress codes, and if they were, does it mean it's their fault?

A sometimes more hidden reason for dress codes is to enforce gender. Trevor Wilkinson, a gay boy in Texas, was suspended for wearing nail polish, something perfectly acceptable for any of the girls in his school to wear. Demanding girls and boys present differently is an example of adults placing their need for categorization onto kids. Gender expression doesn't seem to affect learning, so there's no educational value in enforcing a dress code that upholds a gender binary.

By calling girls out, we're focusing on their bodies instead of their minds. We're teaching them their naturally developing bodies are shameful and require covering up. This is particularly true for curvier girls and girls of color, who receive dress code violations far more often. Black girls in particular are unfairly targeted for their bodies, attire, and hair. We're teaching girls even at school that they can't escape having their bodies sexualized. Children want to be seen for their developing intellects, not their developing bodies. Maybe schools worry that if they risk letting girls feel smart, they'll speak out against absurd policies.

Though most parents and teachers don't consciously endorse gender stereotypes about intelligence, implicit beliefs about gender and intellect are widespread. Girls' intellectual self-image erodes slowly across the years with dire consequences. It becomes a self-fulfilling prophecy: if you think you can't, you won't. Men routinely overestimate their IQ, and women underestimate theirs. Both girls and the adults in their lives take girls' futures less seriously. To wit, a nationwide survey of a thousand families showed parents of boys save more for and are willing to pay and borrow more for college than parents of girls. Not having equal financial backing from their parents sends a strong message and may stop daughters from both believing in and optimizing their academic potential. Let's make sure we're sending our daughters more hopeful messages.

➲ *Encourage Courage, Make Room for Failure*

When I think of the girls in my practice who questioned their intelligence, I think of Robyn, who didn't feel safe speaking up outside her friend group, and Lulu, who felt she had to be "some dumb girl" with boys. Dozens of others come to mind, too, like Trinity, who refused to speak in class despite losing participation marks, because, she insisted, the boys laughed at the girls; Laila, a straight-A student who was too worried about looking stupid to ask for her teacher's help "until the assignment is perfect"; and Clara, who stayed quiet about a major mistake in a group project at school because she didn't want to seem like a know-it-all. It's essential for girls to take risks, trust their instinct to express a thought, and ask questions. But to feel safe doing that, they need to know they can survive failure or "looking dumb" and that making mistakes leads to growth.

Some studies suggest the most significant factor in determining someone's level of influence is the sheer amount of their verbal participation. It's concerning, then, that female college students are two and a half times less likely to ask or answer questions than their male counterparts. Being able to self-advocate is a vital life skill. And as discussed, sometimes it's a matter not of confidence or competence but of modesty, so we have to help her transform inner confidence into action by speaking up.

To help her harness her voice, explicitly invite your daughter to make a contribution. Let her know she can think aloud because a thought is the first step in a discussion people build together. That may go against the grain of our individualistic approach to success, but it's also the wave of the future. Being a collaborative problem solver who adapts well in teams is where our technology-driven world is headed. It also speaks to what girls already do well, especially when we nurture these abilities from a young age. If she's hesitant or says she doesn't know, say, "Every time you share even a half-baked idea, or ask a question, we're discovering the way your beautiful mind works." Help her appreciate the value of her voice especially at school by asking how she contributed in class. Instead of the generic "How was your day?" ask her what questions she asked her teacher or whether she shared that thing that happened over the weekend that reminded her of the book they're reading in class. The objective is to help move her away from obedience and perfectionism toward grit and resilience so the narrative changes from "I'm not smart/I might not be right" to "I can develop confidence/knowledge by stepping outside my comfort zone."

> To help her harness her voice, explicitly invite your daughter to make a contribution. Let her know she can think aloud because a thought is the first step in a discussion people build together.

❥ *Instill a Growth Mindset*

We've known for two decades that a child's belief about whether human attributes are fixed or malleable can have important consequences for their motivation, cognition, and behavior. Carol Dweck, who coined the term "growth mindset," and her colleagues have shown that when someone believes abilities can grow, they attribute success to hard work and are motivated to pursue challenges and generate strategies for improvement. In other words, they believe that with effort and deliberate practice they can reach their goals. When they believe their abilities are fixed, however, they're less likely to show persistence and motivation when they hit a roadblock. They become more cautious, avoiding challenges that might expose poor ability and withdrawing effort that seems pointless. If someone with a fixed mindset is having difficulty drawing a face, they might decide: *I can't draw a face. I'm a bad drawer. There's no point in continuing.* Someone with a growth mindset, though, would believe they just have to practice to improve.

How, then, do people develop these mindsets? It turns out how we praise our kids has a lot to do with it. Praise is an important way to convey our beliefs and values. When we praise a child for their good grades by saying, "You must've tried hard" or "Your strategies worked," we're using process praise and letting them know we believe they'll succeed with effort. Asking after a setback what they'd do differently next time gives them a sense of control. When instead we use person praise like "You're so smart," which emphasizes a fixed quality, they may come to believe the sources of their accomplishments are predetermined, unchangeable traits. Either they have it or they don't.

Although girls and boys are shown to receive similar amounts of praise overall, process praise accounts for 24.4 percent of the praise boys receive and only 10.3 percent of what girls hear. And here's the important part: being given more process praise between the ages of one and three predicted the development of a growth mindset five years later and in turn predicted better academic achievement seven years later. It's hard to say why boys get more process praise if we think boys are the geniuses, but maybe it's because we believe they're more capable of mastery so we more naturally reward their learning and hard work. This gender difference in praise puts boys at an advantage by promoting their ability—their right—to learn.

Not surprisingly, perhaps, girls more than boys tend to attribute failures to lack of ability and thus show less willingness to try after a setback. This gender difference in children's attribution styles is especially pronounced in the areas of math and science. Taking stock of the amount of unintentional influence, both good and bad, we have on our kids can feel overwhelming. We certainly can't catch it all, but a little mindfulness goes a long way.

➲ *Explain Affirmative Action*

"It sucks to be a guy right now," said my friend's son, complaining that 50 percent of college engineering spots were going to girls. "Why should gender matter?" he wanted to know. He argued the spots should go to those most qualified. As my friend explained, "Boys don't understand they're not losing something they deserve. They've had extra privilege all along they shouldn't have had."

Affirmative action was put in place to help members of groups that have been kept down by historic discrimination. The narrative, though, when affirmative action affects our kids directly rather than merely conceptually, is that we're doing girls and people from minority groups a favor, rather than righting a wrong (or many wrongs). This leaves boys feeling victimized and girls questioning whether they really deserve what they got. Yes, including a characteristic other than demonstrated scientific ability adds incrementally to an applicant's score, but that doesn't negate the applicant's scientific ability. Because women and people of color aren't part of the public consciousness of intelligence, affirmative action can be seen as unfair without adequate explanation. I wonder what my friend's son would think if he knew elite colleges disclosed giving boys a leg up in recent years to even the gender split.

➲ *Vet Your Daughter's School*

Girls may outperform boys academically, but if we measure success by levels of confidence, pay, and political ambition as they emerge from college, boys come out ahead. Girls grow up hearing "girl power," but in school they learn mostly about male power. When women are ritually erased from history lessons, their books don't include strong female protagonists, and boys command more of teachers' time and energy and overwhelmingly dominate the class proceedings, girls learn "girl power" isn't actual power.

Given the effects of school settings and curricula on your daughter's self-esteem, you want to choose a school that's aware of the need to actively seek girls' participation and is conspicuously appreciative of their contributions and tenacity. Girls need this so they'll continue to claim space in the verbal marketplace, and boys need to see girls being valued for these qualities. Suss out whether the school and teachers are committed to a gender-balanced curriculum. Find out if textbooks were chosen with gender parity in mind and whether 50 percent of the literature they're exposed to portrays strong female characters. Thumb through her homework assignments and textbooks. Of course, we often don't get to choose a school, but we can request they do better and compensate at home for what's missing. When we pay attention to the education our daughter's getting and how it's shaping her sense of herself as a girl, we're making sure her potential—her unique genius—isn't being lost to the public good.

. . .

How Girls Lose Physical Confidence

We know as girls reach the tween years, they start to place greater emphasis on their body's appearance than on its competence. Everything they've learned about being feminine calls for subdued body language, quiet voices, and gentle handshakes. Starting in infancy, we handle girls gingerly while tossing those "tough" boy babies in the air. When girls explore their environments, we caution them more and use the word "no" more often than with boys, whom we encourage to investigate their surroundings. In one famous experiment, mothers were asked to guess the steepness of a slope their eleven-month-old child would be able to crawl down. The results showed boys and girls were able to crawl the same degree of incline and showed identical levels of motor performance. But mothers of girls consistently underestimated and mothers of boys consistently overestimated their performance. Because of these stereotypes, boys are given more opportunities and encouragement to be physical than are girls, and, voilà, they become more physical.

In graduate school, I lived with my cousin Elaine, who graciously lent me her car on a weekend she was away. And then it snowed. And snowed. I heeded warnings to stay off the road and didn't use the car. But as the snow slowed and Sunday arrived, digging it out felt like the right thing to do. Borrowing a neighbor's shovel, I grudgingly got to work on the giant white mound that hid a blue Honda Civic within it. Passersby pointed and laughed at this young woman tackling something thirty times her size, and one yelled from across the street, "Never gonna happen!" Nevertheless, she persisted. My back hurt, my fingers were numb, but I did it, realizing I'd never before felt such a sense of physical accomplishment in my life. I was twenty-five! I grew up in Montreal, for goodness' sake, but I was never the one who shoveled out the cars. Had I held a shovel since my sandbox days? I thought about how regularly boys get to experience how their bodies feel, move, and function, and how often we deprive girls of that sense of mastery.

Physical and emotional confidence are deeply entwined, especially for girls who must constantly concern themselves with safety. Feeling strong, agile, and capable makes it easier to project that you're not someone to mess with. Physical confidence allows you to do things even when you don't want to—to get in the water, try out for the sport, carry the suitcases, claim space on public transit. It gives girls permission to walk through the world in a way they don't often feel they're supposed to. Every kid has different levels of physical confidence, but regardless, if your daughter is able-bodied, the best thing you can do is get out of her way. Land your helicopter and allow her to climb that tree, scale that fence, jump off that river rock. Let her struggle to get the giant bag of garbage out of the can and walk it to the dumpster or to bring in the groceries.

Bias and Sexism in Sports

My daughter showed little interest in anything athletic and was less flexible and coordinated than her big brother. It would've been so easy to forget about the importance of physical expression, because she didn't seek it out, and instead believe she was limited from the outset by the two X chromosomes she (presumably) inherited. But with the passion her brother and some of her friends had for sports, I was reminded to keep offering her opportunities to engage in physical activities alongside her more artistic activities. Softball didn't take (too hot!), soccer was just okay, circus was cool but not compelling enough to continue, and then, finally, we hit on karate. After a year in karate, Gabi found a strength and grace she hadn't known before, and when the opportunity arose, she announced to my great surprise she was joining the school basketball team. This was the sport she stuck with until middle school. She's still more of an artsy kid, but I'm grateful I continued to encourage her because I know girls who are challenged physically gain so much.

Playing sports is a powerful source of physical confidence and is repeatedly shown to help girls resist traditional gender roles that push them to be sexy, compliant, and powerless. The American Psychological Association explains, "Because athletic activities inherently require a focus on body competence, agency, and action, they provide girls with the opportunity to develop a self-concept founded on what they can do rather than on how they look." To boot, gender differences in visuo-spatial abilities more or less vanish in girls involved in sports.

There are numerous other benefits for girls who play—better grades, body image, psychological well-being, social skills, and less likelihood of an unintended pregnancy or eventual breast cancer, to name a few—and sports are also shown to benefit families, fostering communication and trust between parents and children. They also have significant effects on girls' futures because they teach important life skills such as teamwork, leadership, and perseverance that position kids for success.

Yet by age fourteen, girls drop out of sports at twice the rate of boys, often listing obstacles such as negative body image, perceived lack of skill, and feeling unwelcome. Indeed, girls are considered less valuable athletes by coaches from the get-go, sometimes being ignored or humiliated. They list teasing and taunting from boys as a major barrier to being more physically active. Three-fourths of adolescent girls report hearing disparaging statements about girls in sports, sometimes from their parents. A third of parents say boys are better at sports than girls.

Specific sports are coded as feminine or masculine, so children exclude themselves or get excluded from sports that don't align with their pre-scribed gender role. Getting—and keeping—girls in the game involves more than just permitting them to play.

As a culture, we just don't invest in sports for girls the way we do for boys. We don't involve our daughters at the same rates and ages as our sons. Instead, we bypass sports altogether or start them at a later age. And even though half a century has passed since the enactment of Title IX, a landmark civil rights law prohibiting sex-based discrimination at feder-ally funded schools including their athletic programs, noncompliance is still common. Schools frequently offer better training, facilities, uni-forms, and locker rooms to male sports programs. While girls notice these discrepancies, three-quarters of teenagers and nearly 60 percent of parents don't know about Title IX and the protections it offers.

Sydney Prenatt and Danielle Ellis were high school seniors at a San Diego–area high school, playing varsity softball, when they lobbied their school board for a new field. Interviewed on the *PBS NewsHour,* they described having to carry their thirty-pound sports bags throughout the day for lack of locker rooms, often changing in parking lots and bath-rooms before games and practices on their run-down, patchy field. Meanwhile, the boys' baseball team had it all. When asked what they'd thought about the discrepancies at the time, Ellis responded, "We'd never seen an example where girls were kind of treated more equita-bly. . . . It just kind of seemed like that was just the way things are, and, as girls, we just had to kind of tough it out." No "kind of" about it. Like so many forms of sexism, girls notice something is amiss but tell them-selves it's normal.

That's where parents or, in this case, teachers come in. The day in social studies class when Sydney and Danielle learned about Title IX, they looked at each other and knew without a doubt their school was in violation. Taking their fight to the board even though they were gradu-ating and wouldn't benefit themselves, they said, "We're asking you to all stand with us, so that future girls don't have to grow up thinking equality has to be earned. They grow up believing that equality is expected." A few weeks later, the board approved, quite literally, to level the playing field.

Sometimes the examples of differential treatment are on a smaller scale but still pack a big punch. One high school sophomore, Penelope, told me she'd just quit basketball. For the second year in a row, the boys had gotten all the good practice times. Cate, a senior, talked about her team's disappointment the year before when they realized how much more pomp was involved in the boys' Senior Night than the girls'. Senior Night is a celebration that marks the last time seniors will play in their own gym. The girls had homemade decorations and posters and felt good about the results—that is, until they attended the boys' Senior Night a week later, walking through a giant balloon arch into a gym decorated with professionally printed posters and a live announcer. On top of that, Cate told me, the Poms and Cheer squads share their Senior Night with the boys, making it that much more exciting. They also cheer at all of the boys' games and only some of the girls'.

This year, Cate and her team worked hard to "balance things out" by asking the Poms to attend their Senior Night and raising money for a balloon arch and other decor. Cate told me there's far more student turnout for boys' games than girls' despite the girls' team having a better record and being in a higher bracket. Surely, some of that has to do with all the spirit attached to the boys' but not the girls' games.

In addition to the poorer quality of experience in girls' sports, the Women's Sports Foundation lists five other reasons girls stop participating: lack of access—even for girls who are committed to playing, there are 1.3 million fewer opportunities for girls to play high school sports than boys; cost—fewer opportunities within schools mean families must pay to play in private programs; transportation and safety issues getting to these facilities; lack of positive female role models—coaches, referees, reporters, and commentators; and social stigma—being tagged as gay or unfeminine. In her best-selling book *Queen Bees and Wannabes*, Rosalind Wiseman interviewed high school girls who told her girls can be both athletic and popular but only if they have thin, "feminine" bodies, and that a large, "masculine" build was unacceptable. Girls of color and those from urban areas face even more barriers and participate in lower numbers than white girls.

Jenna—straight, white, and slender from Wisconsin—seemingly faced none of these barriers. She played sports from a young age, both in school and in private leagues, and her parents drove her to practices and cheered her on at games. In her senior year at a large and diverse public high school, she made the unusual decision to try out for the position of kicker on the boys' football team. There was no girls' team, and girls' varsity soccer and basketball—her main sports—were over for the season. Competing against four kickers—all boys—Jenna became the first girl in the history of her school to play varsity football. Jenna told me she likes to prove people wrong. "If someone says I can't do it, especially if it's because I'm female, I'll do it." These days, she's an avid snowboarder and rides a motorcycle. She also plays club soccer, dodgeball, Ultimate Frisbee, and flag football. It certainly helps that Jenna is both athletic and highly determined, but that year she also had the support of the other players, which she said made it far less intimidating. After years of playing coed soccer and basketball with them in elementary school, she said "they were like brothers to me." The coach's son practiced with her before tryouts, and the quarterback, who held the ball for her to kick, was "super supportive" throughout the season.

When I asked Jenna whether she'd experienced any bias or sexism, she initially said no. The biggest difference she noticed between girls' and boys' sports was the number of spectators, which echoed Cate's and other girls' complaints that they'd get only a handful of students coming to watch, whereas boys' games were packed. The hardest part, she told me, was being unprepared for "the celebrity aspect of it." Walking down the halls, people would stare and point, or ask her if she was "that girl on the football team." There was a lot to live up to.

"But," I pushed, "no one took issue with you being a girl?" That's when she remembered that during the first game the kick got tipped due to no fault of hers, and some frustrated parents in the stands shouted to put one of the boys in. Thankfully, Jenna hadn't heard it, but her parents had. The backlash toward Jenna in that first game—not uncommon when girls play male sports—was unlikely due to her athletic abilities. The play had been out of her control. In addition, children of various skill levels are happily accepted onto the football field—when they're boys. Instead, it's often precisely because someone's female that parents, coaches, and other children feel a need to exclude her. The fans' knee-jerk reactions seemed to settle down once Jenna showed she could perform, but not every girl is so lucky.

After that, more stories poured out. Jenna's coach had been skeptical, not of her abilities but of the dynamics that having a girl on the team might create. He was concerned the boys would get protective of her and get into fights. Indeed, during one game against a superior team, Jenna's kicks all got blocked. The defense got through and landed on her leg, taking her out. Her teammates quickly surrounded her, angry at the other team and coddling her—something that didn't happen when boys got hit. She told me she "calmed the boys down"—perhaps the way a girl might her jealous or overprotective boyfriend—explaining she was fine. And she was, except when she got to the sidelines, she started crying and couldn't stop. "I think all the pressure of being the only girl on the team finally got to me and I was emotionally releasing. But I played up getting hurt because I didn't want to say it was emotional and be labeled a girl." Jenna regrets not being honest because accentuating the physical aspect confirmed what skeptics believed; she'd heard some boys were saying, "She gets hit one time and she cries." I noted that showing vulnerability for whatever reason might be proof she didn't belong. "Meanwhile," Jenna said, laughing, "when we lost the final game, the boys were all bawling like babies."

That last game, as she charged through the boys' locker room, eyes averted and announcing herself like usual as she headed to the athletic training room to change—the only private space provided—her teammates were waiting for her, pants down, mooning her. One slapped her on the butt, saying he'd wanted to do that all season. "It's the only sport I've played where people slap each other's butts. They mostly treated me like one of the guys but drew the line at slapping me." I asked her how she felt about how it ended, and she shrugged and said, "I just laughed it off. I thought it was immature but I just laughed."

When I asked more pointed questions, I found out Jenna did experience some of the things that keep other girls away from sports. She got tagged as a tomboy and called gay despite having boyfriends throughout high school. "I knew who I was and didn't think being gay was a big deal so it didn't bother me much." Most of her coaches were male, but she said, "I didn't think much of it. I had female role models outside high school like Alex Morgan and Abby Wambach," naming well-known professional soccer players. "And I looked up to some of my teammates."

When I asked whether she or her parents ever worried about assault either in the locker room or when traveling with the team, she said it never crossed their minds, explaining, "I think partly because one of our neighbors was a coach and his son was on the team." Then she added, "My freshman year of college I had an uncomfortable experience with that coach and he's no longer in our lives." It turns out this coach, whom she'd known since she was five "and had complete trust in," had been sexually inappropriate with Jenna in her college dorm room. Allegations had been made against him by a high school student at one point, and Jenna said, "I remember everyone, including me, thinking he could never do something like that. He was cleared and went back to working at schools." She sighed and said, "It's ironic how the ones we trust most sometimes are the ones that are the least deserving of that trust."

This last bit was especially disheartening. When we first met, I knew only that Jenna had had a good experience playing football on a boys' team. She did have a good experience overall, though she was relieved when it ended. She's especially proud of paving the way for other girls who've followed in her footsteps. As with every girl I talked to, though, sexism, whether blatant or "ordinary," was inescapable. I got the sense that part of what made Jenna so successful as a girl in sports, especially as the only girl playing football, was getting good at ignoring the pressure, attention, and chauvinism that came with being a girl. Having her farthest record be forty-five yards from the goalpost (typically fifty-two in the NFL) probably didn't hurt either.

Girls need us to support them in building their physical confidence. And with all the pressure they face to drop out of sports and the deficiencies they run up against, girls need strong encouragement to offset the temptation to quit. What can parents do to help?

➔ *Let's Get Physical*

Fathers spend about three times as long each day engaged in rough-and-tumble play with their sons and use more "achievement-related" language, including words such as "proud," "win," and "best." With girls, they sing and whistle five times more and are more vocal about emotions, all of which is lovely. But as we discussed earlier, the assumption that sons and daughters have different needs, even though they're actually quite similar at young ages, is creating or magnifying gender differences. We've got to normalize girls being physical. It turns out not only do girls enjoy rough play, but it's found to protect children from developing anxiety disorders. So, dads (and moms!), feel free to throw your toddler girls in the air, wrestle with your school-age daughters, and challenge them to a race as you do your sons. Go one-on-one in basketball with your older girls. Celebrate being capable and strong, and notice when you're treating them as more fragile than their brothers. When the Women's Sports Foundation asked girls what they like about playing sports, current players said "being strong" (that is, celebrating the capabilities of their bodies), while girls who'd dropped out named more appearance-based benefits, such as losing weight or looking better.

➔ *Make Sports Appealing: Closing the Gender "Play" Gap*

There are a number of ways parents can help link girls to sports, such as valuing athleticism ideologically and supporting sports financially; offering lots of encouragement; providing opportunities at home; and participating themselves—especially mothers. The more positive you can be about its benefits, connecting it to positive body image and mood, the better. That might sound like "Wow, win or lose, I always feel so powerful after a game of tennis." Going on family hikes, throwing a football or Frisbee around, or doing any other exercise-related activities with your daughters helps movement and sports become a logical choice for having fun, which girls report is an essential ingredient for participation. When we practice their chosen sport with them, we show them we take their participation and improvement seriously.

Finding her sport might be a process. Some girls love competition and get excited about being a top scorer. For girls who are more motivated by social reasons, like having fun or being someone the team can rely on, a highly competitive environment might turn them off. Listen to what your daughter says she wants and don't be afraid to ask about the organization's or individual coach's style as you're searching for options.

The demands of academics are one of the top reasons cited for not playing or dropping out of sports. This becomes especially true as kids get older and academics more rigorous. While it might be tempting to cut down on extracurriculars if your daughter is struggling, keep in mind that sports have consistently been shown to support all aspects of academic achievement, including positive academic self-concepts, a positive attitude toward schoolwork, better performance, and higher educational aspirations and attainment. From all the research I've seen on sports, it makes more sense to build in academic supports rather than stop playing to bolster academic benefits.

➲ *Ungender Sports, at Least Until High School*

Research finds there's no statistical difference in the capabilities of girls and boys until age twelve, so whenever possible, go coed. The more kids play sports in mixed-gender groups, the more they'll see each other as friends and allies, rather than as dissimilar. This was something Jenna wholeheartedly endorsed. She attributes the determination she has today and the ease with which she socializes with all genders to playing coed sports during elementary school. In high school, she was "forced to do all-girls," which initially upset her because, she explained, it was more satisfying to steal a ball from the boys, who were more selfish with it and got more upset than the girls. She summed up her experience like this: "Learning that your physicality is just as beneficial as boys' was really beneficial to me growing up."

We also need to chip away at the idea that sports are default male. It's true, organized sports were originally designed for boys in the nineteenth century for fear they were becoming "feminized" when fathers moved outside the home for work and feminism was on the rise. But if our modern world were genuinely equal, the distinction between sports and women's sports would be nonexistent. Lately, I've had fun calling the FIFA competitions the World Cup (referring to the women) and the Men's World Cup. Mothers who practice with boys are showing them girls play sports too. My friend Leah made a point of regularly bringing both her son and her daughter to see women's sports—which she just called sports—at their local university. She said, "When a six-year-old boy who just started playing soccer watches a college woman do a somersault when doing a throw-in, it makes quite an impression."

➔ *Name Sexism and Know Your Title IX*

After the champion golfer Tiger Woods handed his playing partner a
tampon in February 2023 to indicate he was playing like a girl, CNN
reported, "Some on social media said the incident had sexist overtones."
That bothered me more than the joke itself because it's the kind of language that makes girls feel crazy, deceptively suggesting it could possibly
be something other than sexism. Calling something sexist isn't political;
it's calling it what it is. As for the joke, Tiger is a leader and role model,
not to mention a father of a fifteen-year-old girl. It's astounding that
even if he thought it was highly amusing, he didn't have the wherewithal
to restrain himself and do better. The joke is even less funny when you
consider that periods are a real issue for girls in sports due to cultural
bias coupled with the striking lack of innovation around period products (which would never be the case if most men menstruated).

"Jokes" like these are a great way to explain the nuances of this kind
of sexism and show girls you've got their back. Coming from a father,
the message would be even more effective. When you hear a "plays like
a girl" joke, consider saying something like "The reason I don't think it's
funny is that girls and women have been kept out of sports for eons
because they're the so-called weaker sex and have their periods used
against them. Jokes like these are designed to make them feel as if they
don't belong, which is a real shame because sports do everyone so much
good."

Thanks to Title IX, 3.4 million girls now play high school sports and
can experience the joy, confidence, strength, and sense of belonging that
boys have always enjoyed. And yet. That number is still lower than boys'
pre–Title IX participation, which was 3.6 million in 1972 and is now
4.5 million. If we can impress upon girls the benefits of sports and their
legal right to equal opportunity, they may just be more willing to find
ways to stick with it.

CHAPTER 8

The Slippery Slope from Gender Bias and Sexism to Sexual Harassment and Assault

"When they watch you lean over the water fountain to drink, it's the worst," said Amanda of boys in her class. "Or when they push into you from behind," Ronny added, laughing and rolling her eyes. Then Harley chimed in: "Once this guy said in front of everyone in biology, 'Maybe your boobs are getting in the way of oxygen flowing to your brain,'" because I disagreed with him. Already self-conscious about her body, she'd frozen and teared up. "I'm still angry for being such a girl for crying. But he made me think I was stupid for a long time."

I was interviewing a group of eighth graders about sexual harassment in their middle schools. All of them gave multiple examples of being harassed. Boys had pestered them and then called them gender-based slurs if they fought back. Girls sometimes used those slurs too as a means of bullying.

Ava, a quiet girl with long brown hair she twirled nervously around her fingers, waited to speak. "I stayed home for two days after the biggest jerk in our class called me a slut and said I was begging for attention because I'd worn a miniskirt, kneesocks, and Uggs. I felt like I totally bombed girl power—my parents' favorite motto. I started analyzing all my clothes and finding things he could use to say I was slutty until I couldn't get dressed in the morning. I realized no matter what I wore—no matter what anyone wears—boys can always find a way to make you feel stupid. And now I don't know what to think. I mean I guess I do dress cute because I want to look good for others, but does that make me slutty?"

That's when Elena jumped in: "What's the point of getting upset? It's always going to happen and you have to get on with your life." As you'll hear, Elena hadn't yet registered just how disturbing her own story was.

WHEN PARENTS CALL me to discuss helping their daughters process sexual harassment or assault, they almost always say the same thing: "I can't believe this happened—she's still so young." But becoming the target of unwanted sexual attention and violence starts increasing significantly between the tender ages of ten and eleven—about the time many students start their middle school years. (This is yet another way attention is pulled away from girls' minds and placed on their bodies.) The stats are grim: by the end of high school, 90 percent of teenage girls will be harassed, and 33 percent—one in three—will experience dating violence (physical, emotional, or verbal); 27 percent (compared with 5 percent of boys) can expect to be sexually abused or assaulted before they turn eighteen; and 14 percent of high school girls report they've been physically forced to have sex. Sadly, the actual numbers are probably higher given underreporting and inconsistent tracking of sexual assault by schools.

As an adviser for the organization Stop Sexual Assault in Schools, I've learned that in order to inoculate themselves against legal action and bad press, schools regularly deny claims of harassment and assault, shaming and isolating the victim and violating their Title IX civil rights, further traumatizing the student. Schools are legally responsible for notifying students in writing of their harassment policy and complaint procedure so that students understand their right to attend school without fear of being harassed. But because many schools don't, the education and messaging need to be reinforced by parents. Unfortunately, in a large 2018 poll (taken *after* #MeToo) only one in three girls (and even fewer boys) said a parent had talked to them about how to stop sexual harassment.

Though sexual harassment and "minor" assault (like being grabbed or having clothing yanked) are often justified as part of growing up, they're associated with a host of upsetting outcomes. In fact, Title IX was created, in part, because studies show that it can be traumatic when demeaning words and actions of a sexual nature are imposed against another person's will. The emotional toll it takes manifests itself in trouble sleeping, absenteeism, and difficulty concentrating. Longitudinal studies show those who've been sexually harassed by ninth grade have more mental health issues by twelfth grade, including self-harm, suicidal thoughts, maladaptive dieting, substance use, depression, and low self-esteem. Moreover, sexual harassment at the beginning of high school is a strong predictor of future victimization by peers and dating partners. Certainly, the narratives I hear from girls in my psychology practice confirm these findings.

While most people readily agree sexual assault is wrong, there's still much debate over its definition. Even people who understand that rape by a stranger is a violent criminal act will still sometimes make excuses for rape in other contexts: She went to his house and was willingly kissing him, what did she expect to happen next? Others dismiss the idea that less violent assault or harassment is worth taking seriously. I repeatedly hear—even from girls themselves—that these less obviously harmful experiences should be brushed off: having your bra strap snapped; being called ho; having your feelings attributed to PMS; being shut down by boys when you try to speak; having your butt grabbed. "It's fine," they tell me, or "It's not the worst thing; I can handle it," or "Getting upset just fuels the fire." Girls are so desensitized to it, they accept it as a fact of life.

Maybe if these casual infringements happened rarely over a lifetime, we could accept them (though I think it would likelier be even more obvious such behavior isn't normal). But that's exactly the point: the problem is in their sheer persistence. While one instance of low-level sexism may seem trivial in isolation, these microaggressions belittle girls and make them feel inadequate and unsafe over time, the way even the hardest marble stairs can be ground down by years of trampling. If girls do complain, they're told to lighten up.

The repeated minimization and denial, often by trusted adults, lead girls to question, trivialize, and negate their lived experiences. Girls learn they have little power to do anything about these violations so they suck it up or laugh, erasing themselves to survive. We can view this through the framework of learned helplessness, a powerful source of depression, anxiety, and post-traumatic stress disorder. Learned help-lessness was first studied by delivering electric shocks to dogs. The dogs who learned they couldn't escape the shock stopped trying in subse-quent experiments, even when they were given a path to freedom. In the same way, girls have so often had no path out of the daily indignities that they're conditioned not to look for one.

Fourteen-year-old Elena embodied that sense of powerlessness, but she masked it with bravado. She listened skeptically to the other eighth graders as the discussion morphed from talking about the lewd boys at school to the double standards at home to the unwanted touches on the subway and everywhere else. One girl complained she'd go to the gro-cery store every Saturday with her mother while her twin brother got to play outside. Another girl, shuddering as she spoke, told us about her uncle who frequently brushes past her so closely she can feel his breath on her neck. And yet another told us her sister had failed her driver's test because the instructor kept putting his hand on her thigh. That remark seemed to jog Elena's memory, and she said cheerfully, "Oh, I have a story like that."

Elena had been walking home from school one afternoon when a man rolled up beside her in a car. He asked her—a young teenager—for directions to a liquor store that was around the corner. As Elena pointed, he grabbed her wrist, pulled her arm to his face, and sniffed it. She jerked it back, yelling, "Hey!" He didn't let go. Instead, he caressed her arm and said, "Sorry, honey, you look so good I knew you'd smell good too. No need to get bent out of shape." Then he twisted her wrist until it hurt, let it go, and drove off.

At that point in her story Elena looked up at us from her fidgeting hands and pretended to put her finger down her throat to simulate vomiting. She was surprised the other girls gaped at her. Her story was distressing, made more so by the fact it didn't register for Elena just how disturbing and dangerous it was. I told Elena I thought she'd been through a frightening situation and wondered whom she'd told. Elena shrugged.

"I texted my boyfriend like a couple hours later. He said he wanted to kill the guy, which I appreciated." Then, after a pause, she added, "But he also said I should save my perfume for him. I think he was trying to help, but for some reason it made me mad. But he's probably right."

She didn't tell her parents, because she worried they'd be mad at her or would take away her already minimal freedom. Elena never talked about the incident again and told the group she never thinks about it except when she hears someone say "Don't get bent out of shape," which leads to what she calls "a disgusted feeling in my stomach." I asked her if she thinks it affected her in other ways.

She shrugged and sat silently thinking for a moment. "I don't wear some of the clothes I like best . . . and I mean, I'm not stupid. I make sure I'm ready when a car drives past me now in case it's another creep."

As the group listened and asked Elena questions, it became clear this one supposedly fleeting event had myriad lasting effects on her. She no longer felt safe walking alone (few women do), and she believed it was her responsibility to be prepared for any passing driver to lunge at her. The fact that she might have been wearing perfume, an ultimately irrelevant detail, distracted her from noticing she felt blamed and also blamed herself for the assault. Without support and validation that what had happened to her was terrifying and the fault of the adult man who grabbed a child from his car window, she had nowhere to point her feelings of fear and distrust but back at herself.

Fixating on her perfume and avoiding certain outfits illustrated Elena was doing what many girls do in response to harassment and assault: change to accommodate a hostile environment. Most important, because she wasn't badly physically harmed, she told herself it was no big deal. A few months later she'd end up in my therapy office.

Whose Body Is It Anyway?

In our culture, the bodies of girls and women are treated as public domain—open for discussion, critique, scorn, and desire. Unwanted touch starts in childhood, with a squeeze of the cheeks or waist, being pulled onto laps and into uninvited hugs; it moves to shoulder rubs, a hand "innocently" resting on the thigh, a brush of the butt or a hand on the back as a stranger passes behind them. After much practice ignoring unwelcome touch and dissociating from their bodies, girls and women are understandably confused about whom their bodies belong to, about what's okay and when to speak up.

This discouragement from listening to our own sexism detectors—even the blaring Klaxon we should be able to hear when we may be in danger—can lead to assumptions that unwanted encounters are our fault. Months after telling her story to the group, Elena oscillated, in therapy, between dismissing the significance of the car incident and berating herself for being confused when the man grabbed her, for not telling him off or noting his license plate number. Girls and women frequently freeze or avoid making a scene in situations where their sexism detectors should be helping them fight back, escape, or call for help—and then blame themselves for the consequences of a lifetime of confusion. (It doesn't help that others almost always blame them too.)

Indeed, many women find they're taken more seriously when something happens to their houses, cars, or dogs than when it happens to their bodies. We'd find it absurd if the police asked us, "Why did you wash and wax your car if you didn't want it vandalized? Why did you renovate your house if you didn't want it burglarized? Why did you groom your dog if you didn't want her stolen?" Yet these are precisely the kinds of questions a woman is asked when she's brave enough to report assault or harassment. As Elena's classmate Ava said, addressing the double binds that inundate girls, "It's like you're expected to look good and then you're punished for it."

Somehow, we can imagine ownership of a lot of things, but a girl's body being truly her own isn't one of them. Commodifying and sexualizing women's bodies is standard practice, and now girls are bracing for a new era of repressive legislation that, in many states, denies them access to reproductive health care, forcing them to give birth against their will, including to children conceived against their will. And they're regularly shown it's no big deal if their bodies are grabbed and groped. If you steal someone's bike, you're a thief, but not if you steal a kiss or "grab 'em by the pussy," to quote the forty-fifth U.S. president. The concepts of rape culture and victim blaming are based on a woman's body being treated as an object to be used as the culture sees fit.

Rape Culture, Really?

I used to think the idea of rape culture was extreme. So many women keep rape and assault to themselves it was hard to wrap my mind around the sheer prevalence. And there's a psychological incentive to assume rape is mostly something that happens to women who aren't careful or put themselves in dangerous situations. Once we accept it happens to other women simply because they're women, and that most perpetrators are never held accountable, we have to live knowing it could happen to us, and that if it did, we'd likely never get justice. Who wants to believe they live in *that* world?

Unfortunately, the proof is in the numbers. In the United States, a sexual assault occurs every sixty-eight seconds. Every nine minutes, that victim is a child. One in seven girls and one in twenty-five boys will be sexually assaulted by their eighteenth birthday, and one in two transgender people will be sexually assaulted at some point in their lives. Survivors of sexual assault are more likely than combat veterans—people shot at with machine guns—to develop PTSD.

Rape remains exceptionally hard to prosecute. Only 2 to 10 percent of sexual assault accusations against men are false, similar to rates of false reports for other felonies, yet 56 percent of Americans believe they're "very common"—the specter of the manipulative woman ever-present. Male aggression and sexual boundary pushing are considered normal. Girls and women struggle to find just the right words with just the right tone to make unwanted attention and harassment stop, hoping that protesting "correctly" will help them avoid escalation and violence, being blamed and called names, and losing out on valuable things like work promotions or social connections.

Importantly, though, rape culture isn't just about rape. As Rebecca

Solnit describes in her memoir, *Recollections of My Nonexistence,* "The threat of violence takes up residence in your mind. The fear and tension inhabit your body. . . . Even if none of these terrible things happen to you, the possibility they might and the constant reminders have an impact." Rape culture is the burden of knowing you could be "fair game" at any moment; it's those things you must do to make sure you're no one's "game." Most of the time, we barely notice these precautionary measures that form the white noise of womanhood. It's looking over our shoulders with keys pressed between fingers just in case. It's peering through our car windows to make sure no one is hiding and quickly locking the doors when we get in. It's making sure we don't take our eyes off our drinks at the party. It's limiting where and when we exercise or even which jobs we consider, paying extra for a cab home if we work late, budgeting time and money for self-defense classes, home security systems, or other defense measures. It's choosing an outfit based not on weather, comfort, or occasion but rather on what might avoid making us look as if we were "asking for it." (It's worth noting that girls who aren't straight experience high rates of harassment, so unsavory behavior by boys has nothing to do with how girls dress or the "vibe they're giving off.") It's knowing that if we're assaulted after drinking alcohol, we'll be told it was our fault. It's sacrificing a host of freedoms and opportunities for achievement and progress that could put us in jeopardy, like my adult patient who decided not to attend a coveted out-of-town work conference with her manager because he was a known harasser.

After a terrorist attack, leaders often urge law-abiding citizens not to let the attackers win by changing their behavior or living in fear, but women are routinely advised to cope with the chronic threat of gender-based violence with a litany of behavioral changes. Imagine if the response to reports of sexual assault were to tell women to stand firm, assuring them authorities were using every resource to track down those responsible! Instead, we spend more time telling girls not to get raped than teaching boys to recognize, value, and wait for enthusiastic consent.

Rape is a problem not of individual crimes of passion but of a culture that admires male sexual aggression and devalues women as plunder. From pornography to pop culture, our daughters grow up with erotic and thrilling depictions of the torment and death of beautiful women.

Yet each dot in the pattern of objectifying women and excusing or fetishizing violence against them is labeled an isolated experience, and addressing the picture in aggregate is considered overreacting. But just as terrorism functions to instill fear across a large population even though many people never experience the direct violence of an attack, rape functions as a powerful tool to keep the whole female population in a position of subordination even though most men don't rape and some women are never assaulted.

I'm heartbroken my teenage daughter is entering such a daunting world without the inalienable right to safety, a world where being a young woman means regularly facing attacks on her dignity and physical integrity. Her TikTok feed is full of other teens telling their horror stories of being groped, stalked, or sexually abused and warning her to check under her future car from ten feet away, lest her Achilles tendons get sliced by an attacker lurking beneath it. Her own mother warns her to stay attuned to the world around her; though I don't use the term "rape culture" with Gabi, I do remind her to keep her wits about her and notice who's around, who sits down next to her or walks behind her. Eventually, I'll talk to her about parties and parking lots.

I'm aware I'm requesting she swap her daydreams and musings— where ideas and creativity are so often born—for vigilance. I'm also aware I'm contradicting myself. Asking her to watch her back is the opposite message I've given her her whole life—live large, be whoever you want to be, think whatever you want to think, don't worry about others. I wish there were another way I could let her be a child for a while longer, but the cost of naïveté is too high. So we talk about the contradictions, because acknowledging them reduces confusion, gives her more of a sense of control, and, I hope, makes her feel less alone. I tell her the goal is still for her to live large, even though she must take all sorts of precautions she shouldn't have to take; that these precautions can be useful but are also misleading because they obscure the fact that most sexual assault is perpetrated by someone known to the victim, in the privacy of their own homes; that all this depleting safety work we tell girls to do to avoid stranger rape is a form of social control that reinforces that girls are vulnerable; that she should be careful but also know that if she's targeted, it's not because she did something wrong or was sniffed out as a weak gazelle in the herd. It's a slippery slope from prevention to victim blaming. I tell her to hold on to all of herself even though she'll often have to tamp it down; I'm asking her to join me in keeping herself whole, spiritually and emotionally, while keeping herself safe, knowing it's not fair when those two things don't mesh.

Isn't It Just Harmless Flirting?

I remember—I can't seem to forget—that as a young kid after each doctor's appointment I had to hand over my urine to a tall, lanky lab manager in his late thirties. As if that weren't embarrassing and degrading enough, he would stare at me intently and command me to call him when I turned eighteen. Was this recognition that I was underage supposed to make hitting on a child acceptable? At other times, he'd "flatter" my mother by telling her what a beautiful daughter she had. Every single time, I left feeling dirty, mad, and envious he never said anything like that to my brothers. Though I dreaded these visits, I never spoke up. I was a kid; this "harmless flirting" was just what girls had to deal with. It's taken years for me and our culture to realize it's not normal or acceptable, and it's certainly not flirting.

The #MeToo movement has made sexual harassment part of the public conversation. The idea behind the hashtag is to destigmatize survivors of sexual assault and harassment by highlighting the widespread prevalence and effects on countless women. Instead of depicting women as unreliable and at fault, the movement offered a fresh narrative, granting women credibility and demanding we listen to them. Hearing that beautiful, successful, privileged women like Angelina Jolie and Gwyneth Paltrow had been manipulated, demeaned, threatened, or raped underscored for many people that sexual harassment and assault can happen to anyone, and while power and fame aren't enough to protect victims, they've all too often protected perpetrators.

As #MeToo opened the floodgates to news coverage of successful men across high-profile industries taking advantage of positions of power, our young daughter heard graphic stories from the media, her older sibling, and her friends. My husband and I asked her what she knew so we could gauge her understanding. We answered all of her questions. She had trouble grasping why grown women couldn't just say no. She'd gotten pretty good at telling others when they were "in her bubble," as she'd heard my husband and I say so often to teach about personal space. It required us to describe power dynamics and the fear of retaliation. She wanted to know why they didn't "just tell on him," so we talked about fears of not being believed and their own confusion about what had happened to them. She was only nine at the time, and while I wished we didn't have to talk to her at that age about women being hurt, it gave us the opportunity to reinforce the lessons we'd been instilling all along about boundaries, consent, and prioritizing bodily safety above hurting other people's feelings. And to celebrate the exhilarating rectification that was happening for women everywhere.

In the style of a still feisty and straightforward nine-year-old karate enthusiast she declared, "I'm not going to let anyone do things to me even if I have to lose my job. I'll kick him in the balls." And I remember praying she would.

➔ *Differentiating Flirting from Harassment*
The comedian and writer Kate Willett brilliantly describes the difference between sexual harassment and flirting in a post on her Facebook page:

> *Good flirting is fundamentally empathetic. It's about building desire and it's often pretty subtle. It's paying such deep attention to another person's emotions and body language that you create more intimacy with them. It's a two-way, playful, fun exchange that makes everyone feel good. Sexual harassment is the opposite. It's devoid of empathy and it's about forcing your will upon another person without having any regard for their desire. You're comparing a paint brush to a wrecking ball.*

When talking to kids, I usually keep my references to the differences between flirting and harassment fairly simple. I tell them flirting is welcome attention. It goes both ways, and both people enjoy it. It's perfectly normal to want our desirability affirmed—especially as teenage girls who've come to know it as their most valued quality—and flirting can do that. Sexual harassment, on the other hand, makes you feel icky, embarrassed, angry, helpless, or hopeless.

I also tell them the unconscious brain is often good at detecting hostility and, once it does, it'll activate the amygdala—an area of the brain that processes fear—or other regions of the brain associated with the fight-or-flight response. Therefore, feeling anxious or uncomfortable is a crucial signal. If they've asked the person to stop, or aren't in a position to do so, because they worry about the consequences (for example, a bad grade, being alienated by kids at school, getting fired), and it continues, then it's harassment. And it's illegal.

Street Harassment
"Smile, baby!" "You're hot!" "Marry me, beautiful!" While these words, usually from strangers, may sound like compliments, they rarely feel that way. Girls who hear these commands from men as they walk down the street often find they freeze momentarily and try to pretend they didn't hear. Being commanded to do something is a power play, and the object is to dominate. If you're a woman, this story of freezing, flinching, and fear is written on your body. You know the pounding heart and leaden feet, the hairs that prick up on the back of your neck, the pretending you don't hear or care, and the praying you're not followed, wondering all the while if a given man enjoys belittling girls only verbally or uses that as a prelude to something more violent.

As I walked alone to my favorite café one afternoon to work on this book—you know, the one about sexism—a stranger started hissing at me: "Baby, hey, baby, baby, where you going, baby?" Doing my best to ignore him and appear unrattled, because we all know appearing rattled can intensify the onslaught, I walked on. Then I heard him say in a loud, friendly voice to a man passing in the opposite direction, "What's up, boss?" Fascinating, isn't it? I was the recipient of a creepy, aggressive voice and infantilization, and the dude got a nonthreatening voice and was referred to as, literally, someone in charge.

➲ *Teaching Our Daughters What to Do When Compliments Aren't Compliments*
I chose to ignore this catcaller, but there's more than one right way to respond to this kind of harassment. As parents, we must strike a balance between validating our daughters' feelings of indignation and their right

to speak up while still encouraging them to use caution. It's unfair that girls and women have to make quick, calculated decisions about this, but they do, so learning to trust their gut is essential. I tell my daughter the best thing to do if she's being harassed is whatever makes her feel safest. I suggest she engage as little as possible and try to appear unrattled. If ignoring a harasser makes him mad, she might acknowledge him with a nod. If he follows her, she can call 911 and tell him firmly she's not interested. If he's shouting from a window three stories up and her ride is pulling up, she might give him a piece of her mind, but only if it feels empowering. We've listened to *Bossypants* in the car about three hundred times, and Gabi loves that Tina Fey screamed "Suck my dick" the first time she was catcalled as a teenager. But will my sometimes softspoken daughter be more likely to show fear than assertiveness in the moment? The point of harassment is to make the harasser feel powerful, and he might feed on that fear. On the other hand, being assertive can also lead to escalation: harassment is about exerting power and intimidation, and the fear of it leading to violence is reasonable.

Most girls and women say nothing and then later wish they'd had the wherewithal to handle it differently. We can generate some responses with our girls so they have a few up their sleeve if safety allows. They might choose to be direct and say, "Don't talk to me like that," "Leave me alone," or "That's harassment." They might attempt to get the harasser to reflect on his behavior by asking a question, "Why are you trying to embarrass me?" or "Do you always compliment someone by trying to scare or humiliate them?" or "What would your mother (or wife) think of you now?" If the harassment continues or they're being followed, they can use their phones and film it, though I'd recommend that strategy only if they're out of reach or there are other people around. If they're genuinely worried for their safety, they should approach someone else and ask for help.

Despite the major advances in laws against sexual harassment, women reporting harassment are frequently told they're too sensitive, lack a sense of humor, or are acting like the "PC police." Girls who complain about being harassed are made to think their feelings and concerns are petty, not legitimate, all in their heads, or their fault. It can feel crazy-making when an experience feels wrong, when something feels off, yet the people around you dismiss your concerns.

There's a name for the kind of denial that manipulates or makes someone question their own sense of reality: gaslighting. And if we don't want our girls growing up second-guessing their feelings—because undoing that distrust of self takes years—we have to help them recognize gaslighting in action and avoid perpetrating it ourselves.

ELENA MADE IT clear to me she didn't want to give the man who'd violated her sense of safety any more energy than she already had and she just wanted it to disappear. At the same time, she knew her strategy for putting the incident behind her wasn't really working. Elena found herself angry all the time. She'd broken up with her boyfriend but didn't know why. (Later in therapy she realized his possessive nature, and the perfume comment implying she was complicit in her attack, became intolerable.) She snapped constantly at her parents and siblings. She began having nightmares several times a week and had become extremely anxious at bedtime; her parents often found her pacing tearfully in her room. Until she could get angry with the man who'd threatened her from his car, she'd continue to take out her anger on those who cared about her. But she'd need to come to that in her own time. Facing our demons and the defenses that conceal them takes courage and trust.

Often when we make room for feelings we've previously suppressed, things can feel worse for a while, and although she'd specifically asked to see me, Elena was guarded and partially blamed me for "opening a can of ugly worms." For months, she greeted me with raised eyebrows saying, "I'm here, sadly."

Elena's ambivalence was understandable. She wasn't sure she could trust me or that talking wouldn't make things uglier. When she got to something painful in a session, she'd flee the feeling by saying, "Booooring. I could be with Angelica right now, or drawing." Angelica was her best friend and drawing her favorite thing to do when she was sad. Sticking to more surface issues and current-day concerns like her not-so-ex-boyfriend, Elena tested me out. She wondered aloud if one day I'd decide not to show up because of her "all-star rudeness." Some days she refused to talk, hoping I'd get so bored I'd kick her out of treatment. If she was getting along better with her parents, she'd accuse me of disclosing her complaints and suggest they were being nicer so I wouldn't think they were bad parents. Listening to her and reflecting back her fear that I couldn't handle what she had to tell me helped Elena see I wasn't going to retaliate by getting angry, cutting her off, or betraying her, and she began to relax.

Avoidance, suspicion, and distancing are common tactics in therapy as patients are building trust, and parents often encounter similar behaviors after an assault. Sexual assault leaves a child feeling powerless over their surroundings and can lessen their faith that adults will protect them. They often feel ashamed, angry, sad, lonely, anxious, different, betrayed, depressed, or as if they'll never trust anyone again. Teens already believe nobody understands them, and a sexual assault intensifies that feeling. Someone who's been a victim of assault wants to know you don't think they're as rotten as they feel they are, but just telling your teen that won't convince them. Like Elena, they need to experience steady support and understanding—not just about the assault, but about how they're handling it, even if that means tolerating a roller coaster of moods and insolence.

Over time, Elena's tough exterior and accusations dissipated, at least in our sessions. One day, the topic of the assault came up unexpectedly, and this time Elena leaned in. She'd been talking about a conversation she'd overheard her older brother and his friend having about "the chick with the big tits" who'd attended Elena's fifteenth birthday party. "He's such a jerk," she sputtered. "He doesn't even know her name even though we've been friends for two years and, like, she's got a hard life. Her mother's sick and she cooks and everything for the family. But all he sees are her tits?" Then she added, "And it's not like I could even say anything because then he'd be all like, 'Elena, you're just jealous' or 'Calm your tits, Elena.'" She'd been tearful before in therapy, but this was the first time she really sobbed.

While Elena was genuinely hurt by her brother's comment and her powerlessness to confront it—the aspect of sexism that makes it all the more maddening—it was clear the dam she'd built to hold back her feelings had broken. After some time passed in silence, I asked her where her mind had gone. "To that asshole who grabbed my arm," she whispered, looking me straight in the eye. And then louder she said, "Sometimes I get flashes of punching him in the face and blood spurting everywhere," her right fist hooking the air.

As Elena slowly began to direct her rage at the man who'd assaulted her, the nightmares abated and she became less angry in other places in her life. It wasn't a perfect fix—she was a teenager after all—but she was relieved that everyone else seemed less annoying. She also began to show more compassion for herself. She'd been frustrated with herself for not fighting back, wondering why she hadn't yelled louder or punched him. I held that as a question for her, just as parents might do, so she could explain to herself her shock reaction—how she automatically froze in response to the fear—and acknowledge she was a child taught to respect (and not ignore or yell at) adults. When she referred to herself as an idiot or a weakling, I wondered how blaming herself might be helpful, and eventually it became clear that if it were her fault, then she'd have had at least some control. Otherwise, she had to face her vulnerability. Hearing someone else say it's not your fault is important, but it's very powerful to learn from yourself you did the best you could.

WITH THE CRISIS behind her, Elena began to explore her chronic self-doubt. She did well in school but didn't feel smart. She had friends but wasn't in the popular group, which she figured was because she was petite but had a "big butt and chest" or because she had brown skin (Elena's parents were Mexican). Though she was a bilingual, artistic, and resilient young woman, people often underestimated her intelligence and abilities. She was the child of immigrants during a rise in xenophobic and racist government policies, a girl in a patriarchal culture, and a working-class kid in a capitalist society. Surrounded by misogyny and racism, she'd internalized them. Elena's overlapping identities were alternating sources of confusion, shame, and pride. She knew she'd been assaulted because she was female, but she wondered if she'd been targeted also because of her skin color.

Elena's well-meaning parents had spoken to her about personal safety—stay aware of your surroundings, avoid dangerous situations, and so on. But those messages were delivered with sexist double standards. It seemed to her that her brothers could just be themselves while her every move was scrutinized: smile more, question less, dress like a lady, and happily help out at home. Her older brother had gotten his driver's license when he was sixteen, but she'd have to wait until she turned eighteen—a safety issue, her parents told her. Similar double standards existed for curfews and dating, all positioned as restrictions designed for her own benefit. Elena came to believe it was her job to keep herself from being a target, so when she *was* targeted, she assumed it was a failure on her part that would disappoint her parents.

Not all of Elena's issues could be singularly tied to being female, of course, but Elena frequently circled back to what it meant to her to be a girl in her family and in this world. As she made the connections between being treated differently because of her gender at home and feeling devalued based on her race and gender outside the home, she came to feel a greater sense of self-assurance. The assault had heightened her awareness of being more physically vulnerable than boys, but she began to speak up when she had something to say. Rather than scowling, she talked to her parents in earnest about the effects of their double standards. She told her grandfather his misogynistic jokes made her feel bad about being a girl, and she helped a friend report an assault at school. She continued to struggle with accepting her body but actively worked to challenge her beliefs about how her body was "supposed" to be. She came in one day with a book about body image she'd taken out of her school's library and said, "I'm deprogramming myself and my friends from thinking we have to look one particular way to be worthwhile." She also said, "I wish my mom would read it. She's beautiful but nitpicks her body."

When it was time for us to say goodbye, Elena shed bittersweet tears as she described having more of a say in forming her own identity and setting the terms for how she expected to be treated. This made me think of the learned helplessness experiment: dogs who were given some control over the duration of the electric shock were more resilient and didn't become depressed despite the pain. Elena would always have to deal with sexual harassment, sexist and racist double standards, and being underestimated, but she had better tools to control how she addressed those attacks. She understood this as a systemic problem and not her own. Seeing it this way made her less self-critical and freer to be herself. I watched Elena head off to college a curious, determined, and, though she probably would've bristled at this assessment, tenderhearted young woman.

➲ Addressing Harassment and Assault Before They Happen

A large-scale Harvard study found significant majorities of young adults report never having had a conversation with their parents about what sexual harassment is, what they should do if they experience it, and how to avoid sexually harassing others. That may explain why so many young people believe gender-based degradation isn't a problem in our society even as it's happening to them. When we address sexism (and prejudice, in general), we lay the groundwork for girls to discuss their demeaning experiences and explore traits they've come to believe make them inferior before they grow up with damaging perceptions of themselves.

We must acknowledge that girls receive unwanted attention and at least lightly prepare them for what to expect. We can explain that sometimes other kids cross boundaries that make girls feel uncomfortable, or someone on the street might choose to comment on her appearance or say something rude. In a scenario given to respondents in the Harvard study in which a man whistles at a woman, 69 percent of females reported that the woman in this situation would be offended, angered, and/or frightened, yet one in three males reported she'd find it "flattering" or "sexy." Girls and boys alike need to hear directly these behaviors are harassment. The low bar we seem to communicate is simply that rape is bad. That's woefully inadequate for avoiding not just sexist mistreatment but rape too, given most people think it's rape only if there's fighting, screaming, and someone yelling no.

Teens and adults alike tell me they never discussed the nuances of consent and what constitutes coercion with their parents. One fourteen-year-old girl I saw in therapy—who'd managed to escape being raped by kneeing her new boyfriend in the balls—told me when she'd previously approached her father with questions about sex, he'd said, "When you're old enough to know, you won't have to ask." This dovetails with the Harvard survey that found 60 percent of respondents reported their parents hadn't discussed, for example, the importance of "being sure your partner wants to have sex and is comfortable doing so before having sex," "not continuing to ask someone to have sex after they have said no," or "not having sex with someone who is too intoxicated or impaired to make a decision about sex." Only slightly better, about half of respondents said that their parents had talked to them about ensuring their "own comfort before engaging in sex." Encouragingly, those who did have these conversations with their parents said they'd been influential. We can better understand what our kids want and need to know by seeking out and sharing age-appropriate resources such as SashClub.org and LoveIsRespect.org.

Our kids want to hear from us, even though in the moment they'll shoot us daggers with their eyes, fire cannonballs of sarcasm, or run for cover. We're soldiers in a war against ignorance and misinformation; our bravery must prevail if we're to fill these troubling gaps in knowledge. Conversations around consent and unwanted touch or attention can happen at any age, but middle school isn't too soon to ask your daughter what the boys at school are like with the girls and whether they make comments about girls' bodies or call them names, or to ask if they've been catcalled. If she opens up, listen and let her know she can always come to you either just to talk or to help her resolve problems with how a boy is treating her. Regardless of the situation, I often suggest parents listen, empathize, validate, and ask if their advice is wanted. One parent told me she'd created an acronym to remember that advice in the heat of the moment: LEVA. I might add a *B* to that—B'LEVA—in cases where they're telling you something scary or upsetting and need to be believed it wasn't their fault.

Teachable moments from their everyday life are all too easy to come upon once they enter high school. My friend Allie called me one afternoon after overhearing her son and his new high school friends using words like "ho" and "thot" (an acronym for "that ho over there" or "thirsty hos over there" originating from rap music and Twitter). She'd wanted to say something in the moment, but she'd been afraid of single-handedly ruining those budding friendships. "So I swallowed my bile and I guess it's too late now," she groaned. I disagreed. I understood why she'd let it go then, but suggested she revisit it with her son by simply stating, "That language is sexist and we don't demean any genders in our house." When she approached him again, he countered, "It's no big deal. Even the girls laugh." Allie replied, "They might. But there's no reason girls' sexuality should be demeaned while guys get high fives for theirs." High five, Allie! We can wonder aloud why boys bond over girls' sexuality and remind them "jokes" influence how we think and behave toward girls and that others may assume we approve of degrading or harassing them.

> Our kids want to hear from us, even though in the moment they'll shoot us daggers with their eyes, fire cannonballs of sarcasm, or run for cover. We're soldiers in a war against ignorance and misinformation; our bravery must prevail if we're to fill these troubling gaps in knowledge.

The more we can help a girl assess her level of discomfort with various incidents, the more she'll learn to listen to her gut in deciding whether she wants to call out future incidents, ask a grown-up to step in, or ignore them. She should hear that ignoring persistent harassment is unlikely to make it stop and that harassment and assault are difficult to process alone, even for adults, and can have long-term effects if not addressed. It's important for adults to remember that what kids can tolerate and what they internalize will vary from child to child. Sometimes all a kid needs is to be heard and reminded it's not her fault; that harassment tells us a whole lot about the harasser but nothing about the victim.

It's essential to make it clear we believe they're not responsible for harassment and that we'll never make them regret coming to us, because girls need that inviting space even more when they run into situations that feel ambiguous to them (and sometimes to us). Here's a parenting tip I snagged from NFL executive Anne Doepner on Twitter: "My dad once wrote a note to us and put it in a drawer. The note said 'if you're scared to tell me something, just bring me this note as a reminder that I'm here to support you. I won't get mad; I will work with you on a solution.'" That seems like a great way to keep our kids talking to us.

➲ *Addressing Harassment and Assault After They Happen*

When Elena finally told her parents about the assault, they asked so many questions that Elena felt unsupported and suspect. Even well-meaning questions can sound like disbelief, and many girls already blame and doubt themselves. It's incredibly helpful to listen without interrupting, letting her talk and attending to her feelings first. Immediate validation goes a long way: hug her, tell her you're sorry this happened and that you'd like to help in any way you can. Stay calm and steady, even if internally you're feeling shock, anger, worry, blame, and guilt.

When Elena screamed at her parents that she knew she shouldn't have told them, they realized she was feeling attacked by their questions and quickly changed course. Their empathy and support allowed her to take stock of her feelings and eventually ask for therapy.

It's not uncommon to feel angry with a child for being in that situation in the first place. Maybe she was drinking, maybe she snuck out of the house to meet a boy she liked, or maybe she just walked to the back of the school to make out with someone. In our concern for and wish to protect our daughters, we might inadvertently chasten them. By asking about their choices, such as the street they took, the outfit they wore, the boy they hung out with, and whether they were flirting, we send the message they had a role in being unfairly treated or hurt. Most parents don't believe their child *deserved* to be hurt but still struggle to think past the rule they broke or the choice they made that allowed for the harm to take place. In part, this is a defense mechanism; it allows the parents to feel as if they and their child had control over a situation and simply failed to exert it properly. But the truisms we hear about teenagers are real: they push limits, they're impulsive, and they have intense sexual feelings. It's practically their job to test their own and their parents' boundaries as they're figuring out where their parents end and they begin. More than once I've said to a parent, "She could've shown up naked and he still would've had no right to do what he did." If we invite them to tell us what happened and what they're feeling, their fear that they contributed to their own harassment will surface, and you'll be able to talk about their choices without suggesting they "asked for it."

After a sexual assault, many parents want their child to take action, but it's vital to give your child as much control as possible. If the assault is very serious, this can be tricky, because they may require emergency contraception and to be checked for STIs. Many states have a time limit for filing a report, though most extend the deadline for minors. But an investigation is more effective when begun earlier. There's also more evidence from a medical exam within the first seventy-two hours of the assault. You can help by finding out about the processes and services available in your area and gently letting your child know her options. She might be comforted to hear that if you go to the police, there may be officers available who are trained specifically to help people who've been sexually assaulted.

If we invite them to tell us what happened and what they're feeling, their fear that they contributed to their own harassment will surface, and you'll be able to talk about their choices without suggesting they "asked for it."

As parents, we walk a wobbly line of ensuring safety without blaming, slut shaming, sexualizing, and alarming our kids, or making them feel there's something wrong with their bodies. Your daughter may wonder if her initial flirting caused the subsequent boob grab. (No, it didn't.) Or like Ava, who "bombed girl power" by being slut shamed for beginning to express her healthy sexuality, she may wonder if her wish to be noticed brought about the name-calling. (No, it didn't.) Beyond basic safety measures, we can't task our kids with avoiding or preventing their own harassment or assault, but we can help them change how they see themselves in response to it. We can also teach them about bystander intervention. Standing up when others are targeted can help reduce self-blame when it happens to them. If they grasp that their efforts can potentially prevent sexism from spreading through society, they might be more motivated to speak out.

Part IV

Guiding Her Through Sex and Sexuality

CHAPTER 9

Deconstructing the World of Girls' Sexuality

"I'm a total slut. I don't know what I was thinking. I wasn't thinking. I wish I were dead," Aimee moaned in an emergency psychotherapy session scheduled the day after a sexual experience that left her feeling vulnerable, alone, and confused about who she was, as if her whole identity rested on a single sexual choice. Aimee, a sophomore in high school who often sported two braids and pajama pants, had been hooking up with a senior named Andy for two months. Occasionally they'd hang out after school, but mostly he'd call her late at night after a party. They'd get high and make out, and it would end after she'd given him a blow job.

Aimee's story could be seen as the story of a half-finished sexual revolution. A revolution designed to unyoke women's sexuality from shame and empower them to pursue their own authentic desires. But dissociation from desire is part of being a woman. As girls learn to suppress physical hunger, they learn to deny other cravings—for naps, for novelty, for affection, and yes, for the pleasure of sex. Couple that with persistent conditioning to please men, and instead hookup culture, with its revealing clothing, shaved pubes, and porn-driven casual sex, has become a commodified performance that caters to men, according to Peggy Orenstein, Ariel Levy, and others who write about modern sexuality. The sexually active girls I see in therapy often focus on boys' desires, and describe feeling pressured to be up for anything—to be the "perfect slut"—yet avoid being labeled slutty.

At first, Aimee did feel empowered, or at least didn't mind the dynamics of her relationship. She found Andy "cool and interesting," and it didn't hurt that his attention bought her social status when other girls began seeing her in a more sophisticated light. Fellatio, rather than intercourse, is often a "get out of slut-jail free" card. But not always. Aimee soon discovered a group of girls had given her the nickname ABC, short for "Andy's Booty Call." She hated feeling as though others got to judge her choices but was determined not to let it bother her, saying, "It's not like I get with ten guys. I'm only with Andy and it's no one's business what I do with my body." While Aimee would've liked a relationship that was more than purely physical, she also didn't feel ready for a committed relationship. Andy felt like a good way to dip her toes in the thrilling yet choppy waters of romance.

Then Andy had starting pushing Aimee to have sex. She'd never had penetrative sex before and always imagined her first time would be with someone she loved, or at least "would be really romantic with candles or whatever." She was discussing it in therapy, trying to distill what she wanted amid Andy's wishes and all the noise surrounding girls' sexuality. We'd come up with a plan: she'd ask him to stop badgering her so she could tune in to what was right for her. But the night before, she got the sense Andy was getting tired of her. He'd left her snap "on read" (meaning he'd read it but hadn't responded) all day, so when he finally responded and halfheartedly invited her over, she was relieved and felt she had to decide.

A grown woman can spend her whole life fighting sexism and still partially believe her worth is dictated by her desirability to men. For teenage girls, the choices they suddenly face with their newly developing bodies and burgeoning sexuality are overwhelming. I've had a front row seat to the poor, unsafe, or regrettable choices girls sometimes make in frantic attempts to maintain a romance, choices that take them far from home, have them walking in unknown neighborhoods late at night, put them alone with someone they don't know well enough to trust, or have them being sexual in uncomfortable ways, hoping it will bring them love.

It's difficult to set boundaries with someone you're dependent on for validation, and Aimee's connection to Andy had grown into her main source of self-esteem and newfound popularity. That night, he'd said all the right things, except in the context of persuasion the right things cannot be said. He told her she should have sex only if she wanted to, and it wouldn't change his opinion of her; that he had a condom and would go slowly and take care of her. He told her he thought she was cool and beautiful and liked that she didn't care what anyone else thought, least of all a bunch of jealous girls.

Aimee liked this version of herself—a cool girl with her own mind who was both different and envied by other girls. "I wanted that to be me and figured, 'What the hell. He seems to care how I feel, and it would be fun for my first to be with someone this hot,' so I did it." The actual experience wasn't great given their youthful ineptitude. Only he'd climaxed, and it hurt her physically, though Andy did tread carefully. But it was how it ended—with him quickly pulling on his shorts and saying he better get to sleep, no different from the blow jobs—that bothered her. Then, the next day at school, she felt as if people were looking at her. Andy admitted he'd told a few friends, trying to make it okay by appealing to the "cooler than thou" status he'd granted her. But Aimee was humiliated, mostly because she saw it as a sign he didn't respect her. That's when she called me, in the midst of a full-blown panic attack.

Mostly, I just listened to what she was going through and asked some clarifying questions. If she were my daughter, I might have been tempted to soothe her, insisting she did nothing wrong, but that risked shutting down her feelings and her ability to think critically about her decision. Or I might've gotten upset with her impulsivity, not sticking to her stated plan to make an informed decision, but then I probably would've gotten shut out. Here again, listening and empathizing are the best options, even if they mean silently talking ourselves off the ledge. Toward the end of the session, I contrasted her previously stated belief about getting to choose what she does with her body with today's self-loathing and slut shaming.

"That's the thing. It somehow doesn't feel like a choice. I mean it's not like he made me or anything, but he's so good at getting what he wants, and I think I did it for the wrong reasons. I just gave in."

Aimee was realizing she'd given empty consent, a common story among girls. She hadn't really wanted to sleep with Andy; she wanted to be wanted. Like so much else we've discussed in this book, Aimee *was* choosing on one level, *and* her choices were steeped in the messages she'd internalized in childhood and adolescence about romance and sex. These experiences teach girls that feeling confused and violated are just part of growing up and being a woman.

This chapter will explore the mixed messages, the false narratives, and the role of pornography as contributors to girls' sexual experiences. My goal is to help you evaluate how you want to address sex so your daughters can identify what they're hoping for relationally and sexually, how to pursue it when ready, and how to be clear about what they don't want.

Mixed Messages

The confusing messages girls get about sex can paralyze them in deciding whether and when to have sex. Be sexy but don't have sex, save yourself but don't be a tease, sex is proof you're desirable but boys are only using you, being involved with a boy makes you cool but can also mean you're desperate, dependent, or foolish. Their personal desire and decision-making are clouded by the meaning others will make of it, and sometimes obscured by the memories of creepy experiences or childhood abuse they're trying to fend off.

I've seen many women and teenage girls like Aimee—straight, gay, and queer—bemoan that their early experiences of intercourse with a male didn't entirely feel like their choice. In the moment, they felt pulled between wanting the experience of sex and protecting their reputations, including how they might judge themselves. One girl told me floating through her mind during a tryst were those phrases that compare girls to objects and animals: *no one will buy the cow if they can get the milk for free, no man wants to buy a used car, a slice missing from the cake ruins the celebration,* and other such pearls of wisdom suggesting waiting is virtuous, yet sex is all girls have to offer. Girls who wanted to protect their reputations or simply didn't want to have sex worried about being labeled prudes. Some girls were craving emotionally what they thought they could get only by offering sex. Others felt avoiding the awkwardness of rejecting someone was worth more than their dignity. Still others were longing for the romantic story that paints sex as silent and intuitive, not really a decision at all but a deep knowing when it's right.

Given the circus surrounding girls' sexuality, they often experience a sense of powerlessness over it that can lead to detaching from their sexual desires and ultimately from their bodies. Their conflicted position can (sometimes conveniently) be interpreted as yes. "I was lying there unable to speak or move, unsure what I wanted to do. Suddenly he's having sex with me, and I'm left feeling used, empty, and not knowing if I was just taken advantage of." By losing touch with her sexuality, a girl stops being her body's gatekeeper, neglecting to actively discern what feels pleasurable or uncomfortable, not really deciding who touches her and in what way. Her sense of self-protection is muddled; sex feels as if it "just happened." She might have consented, strictly speaking, but it was empty consent. Not only do boys have to be taught to wait to hear "Yes!" but girls need to know that if they can't freely say it (and talk about sex with their partner), they're probably confused and not ready to have sex yet.

> By losing touch with her sexuality, a girl stops being her body's gatekeeper, neglecting to actively discern what feels pleasurable or uncomfortable, not really deciding who touches her and in what way.

Girls also tell me about times they didn't want to have sex but found it difficult to give a clear, verbal "No!" because they were scared they'd be forced. Maybe they did what the comedian Aziz Ansari's accuser did, and what research shows most of us (especially women) do when trying to reject someone without being rude: saying things like "Next time" and "I don't want to feel forced." Others talk about having said no but not fighting the boy off because then it would "for sure be rape," or they negotiated a lesser act to avoid something worse. In other words, girls are terrified of being raped or stripped of their sense of power and dignity, so, instead, they try to find a way to make coerced sex or routine male sexual entitlement feel less awful. Of course, too many women do say no very clearly—or fight—and still get raped. The point here is girls so often don't get to set the terms for their own bodies. They're constantly trying to find creative ways to keep themselves safe in a culture that confuses them with mixed messages and doesn't listen to them.

False Narratives

Aimee found herself in a sexual relationship few of us would want for our daughters. Double standards aside, even if we're okay with her hooking up in a casual relationship, we'd want to know that it was reciprocal and pleasurable and that she felt equally able to dictate the terms of it. Before Aimee had sex, she'd said to me, "It's kind of one-sided. Like, I don't even know if I'd want him to go down on me, but he's never tried and I'd *never* ask. I don't want to be that ho, ya know?" In Aimee's logic, going down on him was for his pleasure, but receiving oral sex "is for the girl" and justification for being labeled a ho. Wanting pleasure is slutty. When I reflected that back to her, Aimee could see the double standard she and society set for girls.

One of the false narratives we push is girls aren't supposed to like sex, especially not teenage girls, whereas boys, especially teenage boys, want it all the time. Our reluctance to see girls as sexual beings creates a troubling dynamic that says, in heterosexual interactions, boys are expected to play offense and girls must play defense. The data tell us most people, regardless of gender, want connection *and* sexual intimacy. But the narrative is that boys want sex and girls tolerate it. If owning her sexual desires and being in charge of her sexuality are shameful, a girl will expect the boy to take the lead. This, in addition to the masculine dictate to prove his dominance, can prompt him to think he has permission to go further with her than he actually does. Such misconceptions strip girls of their agency, put them at risk physically, and disregard the joy they too can get from intimacy and mutual seduction. When we put the burden of consent on girls, rather than emphasize it's a process two people undertake, it puts pressure on girls to know exactly what they want. That's unrealistic for anyone but especially for girls who are taught to not trust their voices and desires from a young age.

The narrative is harmful for boys, too, because it reinforces the idea that a "real man" must get sex, and a girl's refusal is merely a sign that more charm and convincing are needed. This, of course, puts even "good" guys in danger of either pressuring their partners into sexual acts or assaulting them. It also sends the message girls don't need to seek boys' consent and makes it harder for boys to admit when they don't want to be sexual. If we want to change the narrative, we have to address with our kids the underlying dynamics of slut shaming and homophobia that underpin bad sex and assault. We'll talk more explicitly about sex ed and consent in later chapters, but this is precisely why we have to talk to our sons and daughters in the same way about sex and jettison gender-specific sex education: aggressive advances, regardless of gender, aren't okay, and all genders have a right to sexual agency and pleasure.

OUR GIRLS ARE coming of age in a time of sexist-inspired, one-sided, sometimes exploitative sex. It's stunning to me that the assertive and politically astute young women I meet in therapy still don't believe they can assert their desire for pleasure. As with Aimee, more often than not their motivation to engage in oral sex is because they hope to attract a boy's interest, secure it, or placate him. Often, girls end up feeling used, especially because they're rarely on the receiving end of sexual favors. How is it that our daughters—that women in general—remain unconvinced that sexual agency and equality are available to them?

Fear of female sexuality is buried deep in our history (think witches, chastity belts, and now sluts), and its consequences wreak havoc in the psyches of women. In some inchoate way, girls understand that the potential for violence is tied up with male desire. In a very clear way, girls of a certain age understand that a boy's sexuality is a celebration of his maturity and virility, while her sexuality is simultaneously imbued with witchy power and shrouded in shame.

Slut shaming is one of patriarchy's most brilliant tactics, used to separate women from their own desires and from other women and to distract them from confronting male supremacy. A boy who gets around is rather favorably called a player. Even newer terms like "manwhore"—a guy with multiple sexual partners—and "fuckboy"—a guy who pretends to like a girl until he gets what he wants—aren't nearly as derogatory or shaming as "slut." Sex toys, often designed to enhance women's pleasure, are outlawed in many places in the world, including, as of this writing, Alabama and Georgia—places where guns are available with no background check and can be carried, fully loaded, into churches and nightclubs. The collective unconscious of our daughters' world holds the story that feminine pleasure is scarier than masculine violence.

The Sexual Landscape

Amid these mixed messages and false narratives, Aimee and Andy followed the rules, as they understood them. He got her to say yes. She tolerated the sex and pretended to like it more than she did. Though she consented, their sexual activity falls in the gray area between pain and pleasure commonly described by teenage girls.

Bad Sex

A surprising number of girls believe discomfort during sex is normal and talk about sex more as a performance than an experience. Young men are taught sex will boost their social status. They're not taught to think of the women they're having sex with as equal partners or how to make the experience pleasurable, or even pleasant, for them. They learn to conquer women, not relate to them.

While boys learn they're entitled to sexual pleasure, girls learn about sex in the context of disease, pregnancy, or social rejection, and are told it's virtuous to deprive themselves of it. Simply put, boys' everyday sexual entitlement coupled with girls' lack of entitlement to pleasure and reciprocity makes for bad sex.

Women might be less interested in sex than men but the differences aren't biological, according to sex researchers at the University of Michigan. Instead, lower libido can be attributed to experiencing lower-quality sex. They liken it to measuring the desirability of a plate of fresh ravioli handcrafted by one of Italy's top chefs versus a can of Chef Boyardee. Consider that, at every age, three-quarters of men report regularly climaxing during partnered sex, while only about 29 percent of women do. They argue, "If men orgasmed as rarely as women do in partnered sexual encounters, they might have an interest in sex equivalent to that of women."

Creating a paradigm of pleasure for our daughters is integral to building a sexism detector. Put it under the category of healthy entitlement. We've gotten so caught up in women's right to safety, we've forgotten to fight for their right to orgasm. The truth is, when we teach girls they deserve pleasure, we're teaching them about "intimate justice"—a term coined by Sara McClelland, a psychologist who studies power dynamics, bodily integrity, and other critical issues of intimate relationships. I was introduced to the concept in Peggy Orenstein's book *Girls and Sex*. Young women, Orenstein tells us, measure their sexual satisfaction by their partner's satisfaction (which is why lesbians are more likely to have orgasms).

> Creating a paradigm of pleasure for our daughters is integral to building a sexism detector. . . . When we teach girls they deserve pleasure, we're teaching them about "intimate justice."

After Aimee described sex with Andy as awkward, not great, and painful, she said, "Ultimately, though, I think it was pretty good because he totally orgasmed." If "good sex" means your guy "finishes," that might explain why girls are four times more willing than boys to engage in sexual activity they don't like or want, particularly oral and anal sex. For girls, the absence of pain is more important than pleasure, which, Orenstein notes, is a pretty low bar. When girls talk about bad sex, they mention pain, humiliation, and degradation. In sharp contrast, bad sex for boys usually means they didn't come or weren't attracted to their partner. What a game changer it would be for girls to feel as entitled to enjoyment as boys and to expect parity in their sexual lives.

In a world with far too much coercion, rape, and obligatory/dutiful sex, discovering a partner who prioritizes and respects their consent can be transformative for girls. But consent should be the jumping-off point, not the be-all and end-all. Our daughters deserve to know good sex is more than the absence of emotional and physical discomfort or not having a crime committed against them; it's more than emotional intimacy too. It's also about desire and feeling able to fully express that desire. That, however, is an affront to femininity. To be "feminine" is to be an ingenue. Girls might be expected to project sexual desirability and sexual availability—even as they see that very sex appeal used to justify their harassment or rape—but they're not actually supposed to be sexual.

Still, "virgin" is a slur today, and girls on average have intercourse by age seventeen, often worried if they don't lose their virginity before college, they'll be considered embarrassingly inexperienced or "unfuckable." Most of the girls I've worked with have had no intention of waiting until marriage, but that doesn't mean purity culture and femininity aren't holding their psyches hostage. Couple that with porn culture, and you have girls searching for that elusive balance between virgin and vixen.

Porn

In a piece for *The Cut,* Rebecca Traister writes, "Male attention and approval remain the validating metric of female worth, and women are still (perhaps increasingly) expected to look and fuck like porn stars—plucked, smooth, their pleasure performed persuasively." A study by Common Sense Media surveyed teenagers from across the country and found the average age of first exposure to pornography, either by stumbling on it or by seeking it, is twelve years old. By age seventeen, three-quarters of teenagers have viewed online pornography. Given the abominable sex education in this country, porn is where kids are getting most of their information, and the free porn they're accessing follows a relatively homogeneous script. Consider the takeaway: Sexual encounters begin without negotiation, sometimes suddenly. The man's in charge, is often rough, and the woman plays along, usually gratefully, even if it began by force, because women enjoy domination and degradation. Sex ends when he has an orgasm. So, while we're trying to teach them about how desire, pleasure, and safety factor into making healthy and embodied choices about sex and consent, the porn they—or certainly their male partners—are seeing tells a powerfully different story.

Because porn's now so widespread, many teens believe that's what normal dating and sexual behavior look like. Indeed, studies show teens, especially boys, who've viewed a lot of porn fantasize about and incorporate the behaviors they see into their sexual scripts with girls. The more porn boys and men see, the more likely they are to use dominant or sexually aggressive behaviors in sex, such as spanking, calling their partners "slut," "whore," or "bitch," pressuring them into doing things they don't want to do, such as penile gagging and ejaculating on their faces (often believing this means doing sex well). Twenty-two percent admitted to slipping their penis in a partner's anus without first asking. And erotic asphyxiation, referred to as "choking," has gone from fetish to mainstream, with one in five women reporting having been choked during sex, most of whom were not asked first. Though choking can cause harm or death especially while drinking, the issue isn't kink per se. It's that, increasingly, even when boys have girls' consent to mess around or to have sex, they see rough sex as a natural extension of it and don't ask their partners for further consent.

Research that followed adolescents over time found when both boys and girls were exposed to sexually explicit media between ages twelve and fourteen, they engaged earlier in oral sex and sexual intercourse. Moreover, the boys perpetrated more sexual harassment, and the girls endorsed less progressive gender role attitudes. What's most concerning is that the initial porn-watching data for this study were collected in 2001, long before access to pornography was as widespread as it is now. Subsequent studies confirm pornography reinforces gender and sexual stereotypes and appears to lead to less egalitarian attitudes and increased hostile sexism, acceptance of rape myths, and being sexually deceptive and aggressive. So our job is twofold: to delay our kids' exposure to it as long as possible, and to help them think critically about what they're seeing or are going to see. Most parents I know, myself included, are dying to dodge porn discussions. But if we know in our heart of hearts they'll see porn—and they will, given the sheer quantity and accessibility of it—then we can't avoid it.

❍ *Talking to Kids About Porn*

Viewing pornography has been a rite of passage in the lives of adolescents for generations. It helps them learn about sex and tune in to their own sexual preferences, which may be particularly useful for LGBTQ+ teens who don't have a lot of other avenues for this. But seeing the odd *Playboy* is different from the videos most kids are seeing today, and at this point there's no evidence that the good outweighs the bad—anxiety, depression, reduced well-being, sexual dysfunction, and the previously mentioned dangerous or aggressive sexual behaviors are all linked with using today's pornography.

If the average age of first exposure is twelve, that means some kids are stumbling on it at even younger ages, so introducing the concept to our kids should start around age eight. As with all sexual health, sex educators suggest multiple brief conversations over time, not just a single talk. Kids often resort to porn or search engines where they know they won't be shamed for their questions and concerns. If we can be open and truthful about sex and porn with them, and receptive to their inquiries, they'll turn to us instead.

Our overarching job is to help place porn and the erotic on opposite ends of a spectrum for our kids and to equip young people with the skills to decide what they want. Porn teaches them real intimacy is unerotic. We want kids to know that what is sexy is consent, respect, and intimacy, not the sexist hostility depicted in porn. Ideally, we want to teach them about sex and about porn before porn defines their understanding of sex or traumatizes them.

With younger kids, begin by asking if they've ever heard the word "porn" and, if they have, ask them what they know about it. That will give you a sense of how much defining you need to do. We want them to know the basics: porn is people performing sexual acts for a camera; it's made for adults and isn't appropriate for children. Tell them if they have questions or concerns, they can always come to you. If they come to you with a porn sighting before you've had the chance to discuss porn (as they might if they're younger and, say, click on an ad that pops up while playing a game), you can approach it similarly. But because what they saw might have been scary or confusing, it's a good idea to ask them first how they feel about what they saw and then help them make sense of it. Depending on what they already know, that might include explaining sex to them.

Once they're a little bit older, be clear without being judgmental about wanting them to avoid porn and explain why. Shame and guilt don't keep kids away from it; they just make kids feel badly for viewing it. You might say something like "I'll be brief, but I want you to hear why it's not appropriate for you to watch porn: It's unrealistic and I don't want you to ever think that's what sex is like. It's often violent, particularly against women, and shows them and people of color in stereotypical and demeaning ways. Lots of studies show it can warp a young person's understanding of sex, and I want you to be able to write your own story of intimacy with other people, not have your desires and what makes you feel connected to another person prodded by online algorithms." If part of their interest is learning about sex, let them know you're open to any questions and can send them some alternatives for learning about it. Amaze.org and Scarleteen.com are excellent resources for all things sex ed.

You can also let teens know there are more ethical and realistic kinds of porn, which are usually behind a paywall, so they don't feel shamed if they saw and liked porn. For older girls specifically, you might add something like "You probably know better than me that porn is shaping the landscape of sex, so I want you to be aware some boys are going to have unrealistic or even dangerous expectations of sex. You get to have your own expectations for what sex looks like." The caveat is that girls can also enjoy porn (and kink), so if we frame it as something only boys benefit from, we risk shaming them for feelings and experiences that diverge from that narrative. Ultimately, our message is good sex happens in the space where their desires and their partners' overlap. Draw a Venn diagram to give them a visual. Let them know you'll be checking back with them on occasion, given how ubiquitous porn is.

At some point, all kids should hear it's potentially harmful to rely on porn for masturbation because it can make it more difficult to experience intimacy with a partner. And it can limit access to their own sexual fantasies, which inform what will be pleasurable to them in sex. Conversations about porn enable kids to feel a sense of ownership over their safety that feeling monitored or controlled won't provide.

If you discover they're looking at porn, let them know you found it, emphasize they're not in trouble, and let them know you need to discuss it. They may deny it was them or turn the focus to their privacy, but don't get sidetracked by that. Stick to the educational piece. A great opportunity has presented itself. Just explain you've been meaning to talk about it anyway because it's your job to keep them safe and healthy.

Schools should be a part of helping kids navigate sexually explicit material. Such curricula can teach them to respond more critically and minimize pernicious ideas about sex, as shown in a Dutch longitudinal study where the more a child had learned from their school's porn literacy education, the less likely they were to see women as sex objects. School is a perfect opportunity to ensure all kids hear that most easily accessible porn is made for and by men and doesn't take women's actual desires into consideration. Consider lobbying your school to make that part of your child's health class.

Good Sex

Given women's historical lack of ownership over their bodies and ongoing sexual violence, it's tricky, even in a book like this, to talk about sex and consent without falling into the trap that makes it sound as if those were things that boys want or take and that girls give or have taken from them. Becoming a sexual being is a fundamental part of healthy development every bit as much for girls as it is for boys. There are, of course, girls who have more solid sexual identities and feel entitled to pleasure, but navigating that as a girl is complicated, especially if it includes less mainstream sex that doesn't fit a Good Girl script.

Astrid was a young woman I saw briefly in therapy who came in specifically to discuss one issue that we eventually referred to as "performing a vanilla self." At eighteen, she was more self-possessed than many adults. She was an accomplished cellist, spoke her mind, and was whip-smart. Living and traveling the world on a boat until she was eight, she was accustomed to being different.

On the day we first met, Astrid explained, "I haven't taken shit from anyone for years, but with this new guy, Sam, who I really, really like, I'm acting all good girl and sweet, as if he won't like me if I don't fit some mold."

"What mold is that?" I asked, trying to help her better define for herself what she meant.

"I don't know. Someone who's maybe unsure of themselves and assumes boys are smarter . . . or just, like, know more than them?"

"Hmm," I said while thinking. "Earlier in the session you mentioned you love that Sam appreciates your smarts."

"Okay, so yeah." She jumped in, "Being smart academically isn't a problem. I think what it is, is being experienced both in life and"—she hesitated, assessing whether I could tolerate her being herself—"in bed."

Astrid had been in a serious relationship for most of high school with a guy she loved and trusted. They were each other's firsts and discovered their sexuality together, which she described as becoming "totally hot and unencumbered." They'd had a mature breakup when he left for college, and a few months later she found herself feeling "breathless and dizzy" around Sam, in a way she'd never experienced before. They'd been together for six weeks at this point, but it felt like a year because everything was moving slowly and it'd been so long since she could "think straight."

"I just want to jump his bones, let myself go, but then I literally get paralyzed thinking he's going to think I'm too . . . too something. Too much I guess." I sat quietly and she said, "But, I mean, I don't think I'm too much and I shouldn't be with someone who does."

I responded, "Part of you believes you're not too much, but we're not sure about the other part." In many cases, this allows someone to look more deeply at their contradictory feelings, but in Astrid's case she said, "I'm willing to consider that, but I can tell you that until now I've felt pretty sure of myself." Then her words came gushing out: "I guess more than an internal fight, or even a problem with Sam, I'm just now realizing that I feel like I'm trying to fight off American culture."

Astrid's parents were Danish, and she was well versed in cultural differences. "I guess why I'm here is because I'm so mad at the world for thinking there's something wrong with women expressing themselves freely, especially when it comes to sex, and I'm especially mad that I have to worry about it. I'm not a vanilla girl and I never want to go back to having polite sex, so I guess it's not totally about Sam, but being rejected by him would be confirmation the world is shitty to women."

After that first session, Astrid marched into Sam's apartment and boldly asked if he'd mind if she jumped his bones. Sam was receptive, and for the remaining six months that I saw her, their relationship grew. Good sex often and inconveniently defies social mores, political values, and certainly femininity, starting with feeling equally entitled to desire.

Astrid realized she'd been performing gender and sexuality for fear of threatening Sam's masculinity and his potentially traditional ideas of femininity. Because of the attitudes toward women and sex she'd been exposed to through her unusual upbringing and her liberal parents, it didn't take much to help her see the dissonance in herself. In fact, my statement insinuating maybe part of her felt like "too much" didn't reso-nate for her. This serves as a great example that adults don't always have to get it right. They just have to encourage exploration and be open to hearing their kids' perspective.

In subsequent sessions, Astrid realized losing the safety of her first relationship and once again being at the mercy of male expectations did actually poke at underlying insecurities about whether she was normal *for a girl*. With her first boyfriend, she'd experienced the joy of disman-tling everything she knew about how to be Normal and discovered what so many wise older women learn: that everything they knew about desire and intimacy had only been a can of Chef Boyardee. Her insecuri-ties, however, were awakened by an uncle who'd suggested she hold on to her college-bound boyfriend because she'd probably scare off all the other boys. Comments like that are effective at getting girls to doubt themselves.

In the twenty-five years I've been a practicing psychologist, I've seen an unprecedented level of uncertainty in the past few years around sex-ual behavior. The #MeToo movement has finally provided a platform for women to voice their concerns about sexual misconduct and everyday male sexual entitlement that leads to joyless, exploitative sex. As a culture, we're feeling our way around in the dark to change the sexual relationship dynamics between men and women. As we attempt to break down the structures of sexual discrimination created by patriarchal and sex-negative cultural norms, girls are bracing for trauma and boys are bracing for accusation. I suspect this is one reason teenage sex, for better and worse, has hit record lows since the early 1990s, with kids having less sex and fewer partners and delaying sex longer.

While there's much to teach girls, listening to them is essential, especially at this moment in time when teens are often savvier than we are, sometimes with sexism barometers on overload. They want agency, and we want them to come to us so we can help them hear their own desires and decide how best to respond to confusing situations. By engaging in positive and proactive discussions about sexuality and sexual behavior, and bringing bodily autonomy and communication into the conversation, we can rebuild a fairer, more pleasurable sexual landscape for everyone that needn't lack spontaneity. As Hayley Phelan aptly puts it in her *New York Times* article about sex in the age of #MeToo, "We don't need different rules; we need two empowered individuals liberated and secure enough to explore each other's impulses, to listen to each other, and ask for what they want—even if that includes permission to *not* ask for what comes next."

CHAPTER 10

Giving the Gift of Bodily Autonomy

From Consent to Crop Tops

Helping our kids become astute critics of our gendered culture is crucial, but we're missing a huge piece if we're not also teaching about boundaries and consent. As parents at ground zero, we're in the privileged position of being able to challenge a culture that normalizes sexual harassment and assault. While that may sound like a daunting responsibility, you're probably already teaching your kids the fundamentals of boundaries and consent in ways you don't even realize. When we teach children to ask before touching something, that hands are not for hitting, or that begging is not becoming, we're teaching them about boundaries. When we teach them empathy, we're teaching them to understand their own and others' feelings by cultivating emotional intelligence, a useful tool for setting boundaries and understanding consent. When we teach them to treat those of all genders with dignity and respect, we're strengthening their ability to develop caring, responsible relationships. Those who learn empathy and egalitarianism are less likely to violate the boundaries of others.

Still, our children require more specific skills to ensure they'll recognize when someone is pushing their boundaries or when they aren't getting full, unadulterated consent. They need to hear from us that their body is theirs alone and no one else is entitled to it. They need the vocabulary to describe uncomfortable experiences and practice setting boundaries. They need to know how to use their voices to defend themselves and where to go and whom to call to make themselves safe when they're out in the world. A generation that grows up learning and practicing these things will stop accepting and perpetrating mistreatment and regrettable sexual encounters considered ordinary behavior today.

We often use the word "consent" in a sexual context, but in its simplest form it refers to permission to give or take something. Building safe sexual relationships begins long before kids even know about sex. Proactive parenting is a concept that includes introducing strategies to your children that reflect your family's values. We can teach kids they have a choice about their bodies from the day they're born by modeling informed consent. Before they even have language, we can let them know we're going to pick them up, put them in a nice warm bath, and so on. As they get older, we can ask (for example, "Are you ready for me to wipe your bottom now?"). All kids need to know they have a right to what happens to their bodies. If they don't feel like hugging Grandpa, ask if they'd be more comfortable giving a high five or a fist bump or not being touched at all. This can seem odd or insulting, especially to older generations who might view affection as a sign of deference. Sometimes it's hardest to accept when it's *our* love or nuzzle they're rejecting, but if we tolerate it gracefully, we're letting them know they own their bodies, and we're also modeling how to abide someone else's request for space. (How do you do that when your teen bristles when you merely pat her back? Asking for a friend.)

With young kids, the word "consent" can be replaced with "space," "touch," or "body," as in "This is my body, and I don't want to be touched right now." Other age-appropriate ways to grant bodily autonomy to tots are allowing them to decide what they wear, how they want their hair cut, and what snack they want to eat. Of course, there are times we have to veto kids' choices for hygiene and safety reasons. But we can still acknowledge we understand they're not giving consent. We can say,

"You're the boss of your body, and most times you get to decide what to do with it. But you're still learning how to take care of it, and it's my job to teach you so you can stay safe and healthy. We can't leave the bathroom until you wash your hands."

I often think of a beautiful example of gaining toddler consent modeled to me by an X-ray technician. When Jonah was two, he developed a fever of 105.6 degrees. He needed a chest X-ray stat, but the machine terrified him. We explained how an X-ray works and assured him it wouldn't hurt at all, but my strong-willed kid wasn't having it. I was already pondering the ethics (and picturing the nightmare) of having to hold him down when the tech, eyeing the ratty little lamb Jonah clutched in his hand, suggested they X-ray his lovey first. Jonah calmed down, thought for a moment, kissed Lambie, and handed him over. "Whoa!" Jonah said, admiring Lambie's X-ray, then quickly agreed to his own. "All" it takes is time, patience, and some creative ingenuity—those things most parents are running low on in the toddler years.

As kids get older, we can introduce them to the importance of tone of voice and body language. We can role-play what it means when someone says yes only because they're too uncomfortable to say no, or because they're not sure what they want. You might get them to ask you if they can hold your hand. Once they ask, you can say without certainty, "Um, I guess so?" and pull your hand behind your back or into a fist. This is the beginning of teaching them to attend to body language and learn that consent must be enthusiastic. They should learn to live by the rule "Don't guess. Ask!" if they're uncertain. Questions like "Are you sure?" and "Would you rather just talk without holding hands?" build mutuality. Remind them it has to be not only enthusiastic but ongoing and specific (with my kids, I use the acronym EOS for easy recall), meaning consent can be withdrawn at any time and consent to hold hands isn't consent to hug or touch somewhere else. For teenagers, that means a yes at the beginning of the night isn't a yes at the end of the night, and a yes to making out isn't a yes to oral sex. They need to hear they're allowed to change their minds at any point and to check in with their partner periodically to make sure they're still consenting. They can ask questions such as "Is this okay?" "Are you having fun?" or "Do you want to keep going?" And they should understand consent can be given freely only if there's a sufficient balance of power in the relationship, meaning there are no significant age, developmental, or status differences. Make sure you're teaching boys and girls in the same way. Boys are allowed to say no, too, and we want to avoid painting one gender as passive and the other as having agency.

There are only so many times, though, we can have planned conversations or role-plays before kids will tune us out. Thankfully, kids (and adults) provide plenty of spontaneous teachable moments. When Jonah was four, I found him sticking close to me at a BBQ we attended with other families we regularly hung out with. This was unusual for him, a social kid who loved to run around with his friends, legs and arms flying joyfully in ten different directions. I probed a little and found out he was afraid of being tickled by the teddy-bear-of-a-dad who routinely had all the kids shrieking with laughter and asking for more. "I thought you loved being tickled by him," I said. His lip quivered and he shook his head no. "Did you change your mind? You're allowed to change your mind," I reminded him. "Can you tell him you don't want to be tickled?" Jonah shook his head no again. "Would you like me to tell him?" I asked. "Yes, please!" he said, running off to join his friends. Not two minutes later I saw the dad scoop him up and Jonah start kicking and screaming no. "What's wrong, you can't take it?" the dad said playfully, tickling him. My mind flashed to Mickey Mouse spanking me on my fifth birthday during a trip to Disney World. Someone must have told Mickey it was my special day, because all I remember is the joy I felt at coming face-to-face with him turning to horror when I found myself draped over his knee. My family and a small crowd of people looked on, laughing at what felt like my humiliation. I don't know if I cried or played it off, but I know Mickey left a bad taste in my mouth unhappily ever after.

I didn't want my son to feel as unprotected as I had. I jogged over to them and told this dad, my friend, that Jonah was serious. I explained that he might change his mind one day, but until that day he doesn't want to be tickled again. The dad put Jonah down but didn't let it go. I think he knew he'd missed the mark—or maybe he felt shamed by me (though I tried hard to be nonchalant about it)—and wanted to explain himself. "What's up, Jonah? You love being tickled. Don't you like me anymore? You know it's just a game, right?" I winked at my friend to put him at ease and said, "And sometimes games stop being fun for some-one." He got it and apologized to Jonah but then added, "But I'm sad you don't want to play with me anymore."

It was an awkward situation. I wanted that dad to see he was making it about himself when it was really about Jonah's wishes and learning to prioritize his bodily autonomy. But Jonah was backing away, making it clear he was uncomfortable, and I knew this man meant well. I reasoned with myself that I was there not to teach a grown man about consent but to teach it to Jonah, so I left it at that—for the moment.

The next day, I told Jonah I was happy he'd told me what he needed and reminded him he always has the right to say no, even if it hurts some-one's feelings. That caught his attention; in a small voice, he said, "But I don't like hurting someone's feelings." I asked if he felt sad about what our friend had said. He did. Then I asked if he would've felt sad if he'd just let the man continue the tickling. "Yes! And mad. I don't like tickling any-more!" "So don't you think your feelings count as much as anyone else's? It's wonderful to be sensitive to other people, but it's not your job to make them happy. Your body boundaries come first." He nodded his head sol-emnly. We practiced variations of what he could say in similar situations: "I still like you. I just don't like being tickled," or "We could play a differ-ent game, but this one doesn't feel good anymore."

It takes practice to clearly say no without being hurtful, but we don't want our kids diluting their no in an attempt to be polite. To adult women in my practice who agree to things just to avoid conflict, I say something like "We face disappointment daily—like when a lunch buddy opts for someone else or a colleague gets the assignment. But we manage our feelings and don't expect others to always cater to our desires just to fix our disappointment. It's worth wondering how it became your responsibility to manage everyone else's feelings."

After the tickle incident, I started noticing how much pressure is exerted in everyday interactions, especially when it comes to men interacting with girls. *C'mon just one smile. Sure, I'll help you, but I need a hug first. I'm not letting go until I get a kiss. Oh, you're breaking my heart!* This needling sends the message of quid pro quo—a favor for your affection—or tells girls that withholding affection is mean. Girls learn the nice thing to do is to override their own instincts and give people what they want. In other words, boundaries are unkind. Is it any wonder why so many girls are sending nude photos against their better judgment? *If you liked me, you'd send one.*

Sometimes even parents are the unintended culprits of boundary crossing. We often think the rules don't apply to us, the people who wiped their butts and let them drape their bodies all over us any time of the day or night for years. Once, as my then fourteen-year-old daughter slung her purse over her shoulder and stepped out of the house to go meet up with friends, I reached over and tugged the bottom of one side of her shorts, which was riding up and exposing her butt cheek. She whipped around and angrily demanded to know what I was doing. I apologized and told her I knew she wouldn't want to walk out like that. "So tell me, don't touch me!" she snapped. And she was right. If it were a friend, I'd have used my voice, not taken the liberty of adjusting her shorts.

Sibling interactions are a hotbed of mini coercions, providing parents many opportunities for lessons in consent. There was the time little Jonah goaded his younger sister into wrestling with him, despite the many ways she tried to say she wasn't in the mood and that her knee was hurting from falling on the ice. In front of Gabi, I told Jonah it was okay to ask once if she was sure, but it was never okay to press or to try to humiliate her or anyone into getting what he wanted. Then I said to Gabi, "I know how hard it is when someone doesn't listen to your 'no,' but you have every right not to participate no matter how hard someone pushes." I praised her for voicing her refusal.

There was also that time I overheard her relentlessly complaining and asking Jonah to change the Wii game to one she preferred. At dinner, I told her I'd heard her badgering her brother and asked Jonah how it felt. "Miserable," he said, "that's why I changed to *Just Dance* to shut her up." *Just Dance* is a game they both enjoyed but not one he was in the mood for that day. I turned to Gabi. "It's not fair to make him or anyone so miserable they feel like they have no choice but to give in." Then I offered an alternative: "Maybe next time you can ask when he'll be ready to change games and then come back later." "See, Gabi!" he said, happy for once it wasn't him being scolded. It's not that either of these examples is so egregious—and I don't advocate jumping in every time there's a negotiation going on because kids can figure out a lot on their own—but there are times it goes too far, and parents can seize the moment to help kids understand that.

➲ *Fostering a Sexual Morality*

Around fourth or fifth grade, kids generally have a good grasp of physical boundaries, but with emerging puberty and swelling crushes, plus the continuation of "battle of the sexes," it can be harder than ever to quell impulses and adhere to appropriate boundaries. This is the age to begin linking consent to discussions about romantic relationships and misogyny, because it's also the age when there's a startling increase in sexual harassment and assault. The message is still the same—"You don't get to touch anyone without permission, and they don't get to touch you without permission" (or you can say "without consent" at this age)—but now we can be more specific. We can acknowledge they might feel tempted to comment on or even touch other kids' bodies or to say sexual things because they're experiencing new feelings, learning new information and new words. We want them to know unequivocally, though, that that behavior can be bothersome, distracting, or embarrassing and can have enduring effects. The key is to get this across without shaming them. Remember, they don't yet know the rules explicitly. They're getting unreliable information from their friends, the internet, and probably pornography about relationships and sex. Validate their curiosity; let them know that they can come to you with any and all questions or concerns and that you won't laugh or get mad and will always try to answer earnestly. We don't want to give them a bunch of rules about safe and unsafe touch and not keeping secrets that adults ask them to keep, without making clear that if anything like that does happen, it's not their fault, they're not in any trouble, and they should come and tell us. Otherwise, they may feel they're complicit in breaking a rule and be too scared or ashamed to come to us.

"Slut, whore, slut, whore" was the breathy chant my friend's fifth grader, Avery, heard as a male classmate passed her in the hall at school. Avery froze. Why had he chosen her? What had he heard? A false rumor? Her mind began spinning and her breath quickened. She withdrew into herself, unable to tell a teacher what had happened or concentrate for the rest of the day. Thankfully, she later told her mom, who took her seriously. Especially at this stage of development, kids need to hear gender-based insults are not okay; using someone's sexuality against them not only is hurtful but can be damaging. Avery, like nearly one-third of students who experience harassment, began not wanting to go to school. I'm willing to bet the kid who slung gender slurs wasn't a wildly misogynistic boy, but he was definitely testing those limits. It's incumbent upon adults to go beyond simple platitudes about being respectful and help kids understand the long-term pain discrimination causes. Helping fifth and sixth graders develop a sexual morality—an understanding of care and ethics in relationships—can nip poor behavior in the bud before they get older and harassment becomes more serious.

Mutuality and consent in relationships aren't the stuff of rom-coms in which no obstacle is too big to overcome, stalking has a happy ending, and female passivity is sexy. We're driving home the idea of boundaries and consent to our daughters not to scare them but—and this is crucial—to give them a sense of true body sovereignty that will one day allow for a sexuality free from shame and relationships full of pleasure, love, and intimacy. But remember, if we teach only consent, and forget to mention the joy and pleasure of sex, we're teaching our kids to have low expectations. We might consent to a root canal, but that doesn't mean we're going to like it. As you'll see in the next chapter about body literacy and healthy sexuality, we can learn a lot from the Dutch, who teach their children to expect not just consent but also pleasure and reciprocation. The slow building of our daughters' sexism detectors doesn't rob them of their innocence, but instead buttresses their sense of themselves as fully entitled to safety, respect, autonomy, and pleasure.

The Sexy Dress Battle

As I settled into a booth with a bunch of moms I'd invited to my favorite brunch spot to discuss their feelings about their daughters' ways of presenting themselves to the world, a woman named Wendy jumped in with a dilemma she was facing with her seventh grader. She'd used her allowance to buy a top that revealed her belly and cleavage. "She's busty, and I don't think she's prepared to handle the attention it might attract. But I don't want to shame her just for being a girl wearing the latest fashions. And if there's nothing to be ashamed of, why should she hide her body?"

Another woman jumped in: "It's a matter of safety. My kid's only ten, but I've already decided no makeup and crop tops until she's sixteen."

"Ha!" said another woman. "Good luck. I tried banning crop tops and was accused of slut shaming my daughter. What we see as objectifying and sexualized, they find empowering."

A mother with a twelve-year-old said, "So far, Janie's not interested in revealing clothing, but I let her dress how she wants. I don't want to send the message that a certain type of person gets harassed or assaulted. The creepiest creeps of my teenage years harassed me while I was wearing running clothes or school clothes."

Someone else chimed in then: "My creep was a riding instructor. I was wearing long pants and coats. He was arrested eventually, years later."

A woman with sixteen-year-old twin girls said, "I just wish empowered didn't mean sexy. The old marm in me would like them to be able to find self-worth in their brains and their character as well as with their boobs."

Wendy jumped in again, "That's exactly it. I hit puberty early just like my girl. I was dating in sixth grade and had sex in seventh. All that sexualizing both by me and other people was terrible for me. It felt like I was popular because of my body, and it took years of therapy to know there was more to me."

The day will come for most parents of girls when they'll have to reckon with exposed bellies, butt cheeks, and cleavage. That day came for my friend Julie when her fifteen-year-old daughter, Annie, was dressing in a way the school deemed inappropriate (and Julie admitted she found trashy). Annie was proud of how her body had developed and received lots of attention from boys. She was ordered to report to the school office each morning for two weeks to have her outfit approved. Annie would get approval, then head to the girls' bathroom to change into the more revealing clothes she preferred. Julie didn't want people to think poorly of Annie, and wished people would judge her mind and character first. But she didn't want to forbid certain clothing, because she wanted to support Annie finding herself. She encapsulated the double bind perfectly: "I was stuck between 'You go, girl!'" (happy her daughter was able to hold on to her own desires) "and 'Don't you realize people will see you and treat you as a sex object?'" (sad her daughter had internalized the male gaze).

We want our kids to embrace their budding sexuality, or at least be unashamed of it, but seeing themselves through a system that values young women packaged for the marketplace of male desire leaves little room for pimples or tummy rolls. We want them to be relaxed about their appearance but understand they might suffer socially if they don't fit conventions of attractiveness. When we express concern about a sexualized presentation, we risk aligning with the dominant culture and slut shaming them. But saying nothing might risk their safety and self-esteem.

Here's what I hear from girls, at least until the older teen years: They're not doing it to attract attention from boys. They're interested in being fashionable, not sexy, and skimpy is what teen brands are selling. When we call attention to their clothing choices, they feel sexualized by us and become self-conscious and defensive. The popularity of revealing clothing has stripped it of its sexual power in the eyes of girls who may not understand sexual signaling, mostly because they don't yet have a sense of their erotic power. Their mothers sure do, though, and their concerns spring from personal experiences of unsolicited comments on their outfits, being catcalled, followed, or assaulted. They know looking older and sexier attracts grown men. They know that sexy girls aren't seen as smart or respectable and that being sexualized can inhibit academic achievement. They grew up when women's outfits were used as proof they were "asking for it" if they were assaulted and in the wake of second-wave feminism, which wanted women to know their bodies were about more than sex, beauty, and others' pleasure. They know the costs of feeling as if you were constantly on display. Their daughters, however, are growing up in a wave of feminism that values individualism, embraces sex positivity, and vehemently opposes body shaming, a feminism that refuses to be mistaken for hairy, man-hating women.

So, what's a parent to do when dressing like the latest TikTok star might get your daughter social points and a confidence boost, but you worry it might also get her unwanted attention and have a negative effect in the long run? How do you teach her there's nothing wrong with her developing body, nothing she can wear or do that would warrant being hurt, but tell her she still needs to hide it sometimes to be safe?

⮕ Help Her Think Critically About Her Choices, Don't Control Them

Keeping our kids safe and guiding them to a healthy sense of themselves—without disrupting the process of self-discovery—aren't always straightforward. As the mother of teens and a therapist to many adolescents over the years, I've found the only "answer" is ongoing conversation and encouragement to think critically about cultural messages. Hand-wringing and moral panic just make us seem old-fashioned and do nothing to earn our kids' respect, which is what we need if they're going to listen to us. Sure, we can forbid them to wear the clothes they like and that help them fit in, but that does little for our relationships with them. Rather than make it us against the culture, it makes it us against them. The fight over autonomy in general, and clothing in particular, harms too many parent-child relationships.

My daughter, like me, is deeply attached to the mantra "my body, my choice," which, to her, means free rein to bare her midriff when she so pleases. It's true; female bodies have been subject to evaluation and blame for far too long. It's also true, as I once said to Gabi, sometimes a cigar is just a cigar but a crop top, dieting, or a Brazilian wax is never as simple as free choice. I tell her fashion is ephemeral; it takes courage to be an original. I've brought her up to understand her body is hers and hers alone, but when she asked if she could start shaving like the rest of her friends, I didn't just say, "Your choice." I asked her to do some research on the pros and cons of hair removal and to read what I'd written about it for this book. It's not that I cared if she shaved; I just didn't want it to be a mindless, conditioned response to the culture. I wanted to help slow down her decisions without shaming her. The truth is, her leg hair was barely visible; shaving was more a rite of passage to feeling grown up in our culture. My goal has always been to help her think critically about her choices, not to control them. I try to let her make her own decisions but also help her think honestly about how those choices are made within a system that believes girls' value lies mainly in their sex appeal.

I find it helps to discuss the idea of faux empowerment—the idea that *feeling* empowered isn't the same thing as *actual* power. Celebrities like Kim Kardashian present self-objectification as a source of power. Succeeding at sexiness, especially one that adheres to the straight male fantasy, may feel good, but as the feminist critic Jill Filipovic writes in *Cosmopolitan,* it's a cultural "head-pat to keep us satisfied with subservience." Real power is about the fair distribution of resources, political influence, and personal agency. We can express to our daughters, "I want you to feel great in your body and in the clothes you wear, but it's also important to remember you deserve real power, which doesn't come from being hot for the gratification of others." When girls understand that, they'll understand why they can feel simultaneously powerful and disempowered by something as seemingly innocuous as a selfie.

> *Feeling* empowered isn't the same thing as *actual* power. . . . When girls understand that, they'll understand why they can feel simultaneously powerful and disempowered by something as seemingly innocuous as a selfie.

When you're female, liking how you look is a revolutionary act, but it's nearly impossible to tell the difference between what we're doing for ourselves because we want to and what we're doing because we feel as if we have to in order to appear acceptable to others. This is particularly true for teenagers in the throes of figuring out their identities and trying to express them through personal style. If we're heavy-handed in bringing up cultural influences, it can come across as critical of their process. Rather than debating the dangers of their sexuality or assuming you know why they're choosing to dress a certain way, remain curious. Be gentle and inquisitive and have meaningful conversations about the various influences that affect these choices. Once they've got your number, they'll get annoyed, so keep in mind your relationship is more important than capitalizing on every teachable moment. It helps, too, to keep the focus off them. A mom might comment on something uncomfortable she's wearing herself and say, "It's weird how we're trained to ignore irritation and pain in the name of beauty." We can ask them what they make of thong underwear for eight-year-olds and women-sized underwear imprinted with princesses and Hello Kitty in order to highlight the "adultification" of girls and the "youthification" of women.

➲ *Have Her Reflect on What Story She Wants Her Clothes to Tell*

When it comes to being judged poorly by others, we can tell them we're conflicted. "I want you to be able to wear what you want. You're not responsible for other people's reactions, and yet some people will judge, so it's important to reflect on what story you want your clothes to tell about you." If her clothing choices are bringing her attention she doesn't like or making her feel unsafe, she should listen to those cues. Ultimately (we're playing the long game here), we want them to make choices based on both physical and emotional comfort.

So much of the conversation about girls' clothing choice is about what it "does" to boys. The Bible instructs women to dress modestly. Spiritual leaders and school administrators tell girls if they dress in a sexual way, they tempt boys to sin, placing the responsibility for male virtue on girls' shoulders. Imagine my surprise, then, when my friend Cheryl Lynn, a pastor, referenced scripture where Jesus says, "If your eye causes you to stumble, pluck it out. It is better for you to enter the kingdom of heaven with one eye than to have both eyes and be thrown in hell." Translation: lust is your responsibility, not the responsibility of what you consider temptation. Then she told me about meeting with the director of her daughter's church youth group to ask if there was a box for boys' eyeballs after learning about the box of baggy clothes girls could choose from if they didn't meet dress code guidelines. The baggy clothes disappeared. We'll have more credibility if we shift the conversation away from how our daughters' outfits affect boys, and instead encourage them to notice whether their clothes reflect who they are (not who the culture says they should be) and how they affect their ability to think, learn, and move easily.

➔ *Pay Attention to the Messages You're Sending Her*

Consider the mixed messages you give as you're deciding how you want to manage clothing issues that come up with your daughter. If you frequently admire her appearance, why wouldn't she want to emphasize it? If she emphasizes it, remember that even girls in sweatpants or winter coats aren't safeguarded from being catcalled and followed, or, for that matter, interrupted and assumed to be unintelligent. It's fun to feel attractive and wanted, so it's okay to acknowledge her sexual energy. Moms, just as your daughter is starting to seem like a teen sex kitten, you may be facing middle-age changes in your own sexuality and appearance, so take care that your responses to her aren't driven by envy. Dads, you may be tempted to pull away as your daughter's body matures, but keep showing appropriate physical affection. Girls feel the loss of closeness and can take it as a rejection of their developing body.

ULTIMATELY, WE'RE ON the same team as our daughters, infuriated that their wish for independence is obstructed by their lack of emotional and physical safety. Girls are a pawn in this unwinnable game; we need to focus on changing systems, not what girls wear. We can join forces with our daughters and "girlcott" padded bikinis for six-year-olds and teach all children that girls deserve dignity and respect, no matter what they wear.

CHAPTER 11

Sex and Pizza

The Power of Comprehensive Sex Education

When the students at my kids' school reached fifth grade, parents were invited to an evening informally dubbed "Sex and Pizza." Together, everyone ate pizza and watched an animated film about puberty and sex, with a catchy song about body changes that had the kids loudly chiming in to defend against the awkwardness.

It might have been awkward, but the excitement the students felt about finally reaching this rite of passage seemed to overshadow it. They'd already watched the film in class and had written anonymous questions that a nurse answered with the parents present. This allowed parents to hear what kids were curious about ("What's a blow job?" "Do guys always have to make the first move?" "Does your period come out the same hole as your pee?") and made sex a less forbidden topic.

After the film, everyone completed a questionnaire about their values regarding dating and sex and what they thought their child/parent would answer (for example, the age it's okay to start dating). Then each family huddled and compared answers. In sixth grade, there was an added component where parents wrote anonymous letters with embarrassing, funny, and meaningful stories about navigating their own lives at that age that were then read aloud. "Sex and Pizza" helped facilitate conversations about an often rocky part of life and encouraged parents and kids to continue discussing it at home. It was fabulous. Unfortunately, because of an army of social norms, religious restrictions, and moral taboos around sex in the United States, sex education is often considered a corrupting influence on children, and many schools may teach it inaccurately or not at all. Because helping our daughters thrive emotionally is as much about changing the behavior of boys and men as it is about helping girls decode bad behavior, this chapter is for all parents, regardless of their child's gender.

How the Dutch Do It

Before Bonnie J. Rough wrote *Beyond Birds and Bees,* she temporarily relocated to the Netherlands from the United States with her husband and toddler, and was struck by a dramatic difference in parenting norms between the two countries. The Dutch, she observed, normalize bodies and human sexuality from birth, whereas in the United States these topics are loaded with shame and stereotypes. Dutch parents have conversations with their children about gender, sex, power, autonomy, diversity, and consent. Rough draws a clear line from the Dutch parents' and educators' easygoing, egalitarian attitudes about bodies and sex to better outcomes for teens in the Netherlands compared with those in the United States. Indeed, the Dutch have fewer teenage pregnancies, abortions, and STIs than almost any other country. Meanwhile, the United States boasts the highest rates of teen pregnancy, births, and abortions of any industrialized nation. In fact, American girls aged fifteen to nineteen give birth at four times the rate of their Dutch peers and have twice the rate of abortions. Fewer abortions occur in the Netherlands because there are fewer unwanted pregnancies, even though (shocking to us "not under my roof!" Americans) Dutch parents tend to allow their teens to have sleepovers with their partners.

One study of college women set out to understand how two similarly industrialized nations could have such disparate outcomes. They asked the women, just emerging from adolescence, to reflect on their earliest sexual behavior and what influenced it. The American women reported becoming sexually active at a younger age and with more partners and were less likely to use contraception than the Dutch teens. The Americans' responses also reflected a high level of discomfort with their bodies and sex, whereas the Dutch women seemed to positively relate to their bodies and sexuality, as well as their pleasure. Just as I hear from my patients, the U.S. girls were significantly more likely to say the reason for first intercourse was that opportunity presented itself or pressure from partners and friends. They painted a picture of feeling unprepared for their sex lives, which they described as driven by hormones or boyfriends who were in charge and whom they aimed to please.

The Dutch women, on the other hand, pointed to love and commitment as the most important reason for first intercourse. They described taking their time to explore their sexuality and their own desires, planning ahead, and having open communication with their partners. Planning ahead, the Americans said, meant a girl was a slut.

The Dutch's secret sauce seems to contain two important ingredients: attitudes and sex education. Of course, the availability of free birth control and health services doesn't hurt, but the studies and stories tell us Dutch children are surrounded by adults—doctors, teachers, and parents—who make it a point to be body and sex positive. They seem to understand teenage sexuality is normal and they couldn't control it even if they wanted to, so instead they impart knowledge and instill responsibility about bodies and sex in their children. Mandatory sex ed in schools begins at age four, focusing on hygiene, anatomy, and respect for one's own and others' boundaries. Over the years, it progresses to discussions about puberty, masturbation, sexual orientation, consent, oral sex, intercourse, and orgasm. And these things are addressed in the context of a loving relationship, where responsibility, equality, and pleasure are central components.

By contrast, there's no federal mandate for sex ed in the United States, and as of 2023 only twenty-five states and D.C. mandate both sex and HIV education. In states where sex ed is required, programs typically stress abstinence and focus on the perils of sex. Largely absent is meaningful discussion of relationships, including consent and the complex emotions that often accompany sex and desire. Seventeen of those twenty-five don't require sex education to be medically accurate. That's right, your children might be deliberately fed misinformation about, say, the effectiveness of condoms and other contraception to skew their behavior in favor of the morality standards of the adults who run the state. Inconceivably, many states that don't teach kids about sex and pregnancy also restrict or ban abortion. One Harvard report about abstinence-only programs was titled *Sex, Lies, and Stereotypes.* Not only are these programs unethical for keeping young people in the dark about critical, potentially lifesaving information, but research conclusively shows they're ineffective. Teenagers who've received abstinence-only information still have sex before marriage, but they're less likely to use contraception or to be tested for STIs. Our refusal to talk about sex and sexuality is a public health emergency.

The most noteworthy cross-cultural difference, for our purposes anyway, is the openness between Dutch teens and their parents, compared with the typical sneaking around American teenagers do. Kids take their cues from us, so when they sense we're willing to discuss any topic that arises, they feel freer to ask questions and talk about their bodily changes and sexual concerns.

The American college women told researchers they got the message from their parents that sex was bad or dirty and not something "decent" girls did, so they kept their sexuality to themselves. If their parents did mention it, it was usually in the form of a warning about pregnancy and STIs (mothers) or jokes (fathers).

So, while parents of preschoolers in the United States rush to put an end to any games of Doctor or I'll Show You Mine, If You Show Me Yours, Rough tells us Dutch parents are setting clear rules for *Doktertje Spelen,* the Dutch name for Doctor: "Don't play unless you want to, don't do anything against another person's will, don't stick anything in body openings (mouth, ear, nose, vagina, anus), and do no pain." Those are actual rules spelled out in a pamphlet for parents in the widely used sex ed curriculum developed by the International Center of Expertise on Sexual and Reproductive Health and Rights in the Netherlands. The pamphlet also assures parents, "Playing doctor can do no harm; it's totally normal for children to do so. Teach your child some rules." The rules of *Doktertje Spelen* clearly set the stage for future relationships: consent, equality, safety.

Similarly, while parents in the United States are studiously avoiding the topic of masturbation, Dutch parents are explaining it's a great way for girls to develop an empowered sexuality because it allows them to know their own bodies and what brings them sexual pleasure. By the time children in the Netherlands reach adolescence, it's not embarrassing, or at least not unbearably so, to talk to their parents about when and how they want sex to happen and how best to protect themselves. Some Dutch women in the college study reported they'd even talked to their parents about how the experience was afterward. This brings us back to the sleepovers (I know you've been waiting).

"I stepped on a used condom in Brady's room this morning," Miranda confesses to Carrie and Charlotte over brunch in the premiere of the *Sex and the City* reboot. Brady is Miranda's seventeen-year-old son, who's having sex (loudly) in his childhood bedroom with the permission of his parents. Fans were hotly divided on whether this was a big "hell no" because it lacked boundaries or a good idea because teenagers will find a way to have sex anyway, and possibly in dangerous or illegal places. Amy Schalet, author of the book *Not Under My Roof,* which traces the cultural differences in attitudes toward teenage sex between Dutch and American parents, says sex is a source of conflict in American homes whereas Dutch parents prioritize family cohesiveness. She found two-thirds of Dutch teens aged fifteen to seventeen said their significant other was allowed to spend the night at their home. Individualistically minded Americans see sex as something that's okay after their child has separated from the family or is married, whereas in the Netherlands children become independent adults within the context of their relationships with their parents and don't need to leave to establish themselves as independent.

When we pretend teen sexuality doesn't exist, we're asking them to split off an important aspect of themselves. Over and over again, I hear from girls in my practice that they hide their romantic lives from their parents because "it's embarrassing." The girls tell me their parents would be mortified if they knew they were doing sexual things because it would shatter their image of them as their "little princess" or "Daddy's little girl." Dutch teens, Schalet writes, are allowed to "integrate different parts of themselves into their family life." This isn't to suggest anyone would find it acceptable for their children to have loud, wall-banging sex or leave used condoms strewn about. And that doesn't seem to be what it's like for the Dutch. Instead, they see sleepovers as an opportunity to exert their parental influence by discussing respect and boundaries, making sure their kids are having sex in a warm and safe environment with someone they're in a steady relationship with and where contraception is only one drawer away. It also serves as an opportunity to show they trust their children to make responsible romantic decisions. In the United States, we tend to view teenagers like cats in heat, unable to be smart under the influence of lust.

> When we pretend teen sexuality doesn't exist, we're asking them to split off an important aspect of themselves.

Of course, it's overly simplistic to see these differences as purely a function of puritanical Americans versus permissive Europeans. Even liberal parents in the United States jump to eliminate games of Doctor, not because they think there's anything to be ashamed of but because they're trying to teach their kids clear boundaries and protect them from abuse.

Harriet, a mother of four, was emphatic that it's dangerous to normalize this so-called game because it can be used as an excuse to cover up abuse or lead to confusion. She found this out firsthand when her youngest daughter was in kindergarten. When she noticed scratch marks on her daughter's bottom, her daughter explained a classmate was touching her vagina and bottom even though she didn't want him to. She hadn't told anyone, because two other girls also being touched had gone to the teacher but nothing happened to stop it. She thought she had to put up with it. When Harriet met with the teacher and school principal—both women—they chalked it up to "normal exploration" and "playing Doctor." Harriet pulled her daughter out of school until a safety plan was put in place, which happened only weeks later after the situation escalated to threats. The school principal had threatened to call child protective services on Harriet for her daughter's absences, and Harriet accepted the challenge, saying she thought it was a good idea for the agency to assess whether it believed this school was a safe environment for her daughter. Her daughter's therapist and pediatrician didn't think it was. With that, the school agreed it would never put the two in class together, and her daughter would be supervised whenever there was a chance the two could interact (recess, field trips, even passing each other in the hall).

Harriet doesn't think the boy ever got the help he needed. He was held back one year, but his behavior progressed to threatening to kill members of other girls' families if they told on him, blocking them in the school bathroom, and so on. Eventually, he was transferred to another school. "Obviously, what my daughter went through was *not* playing Doctor, but I'm really concerned that when we normalize Doctor games, it grooms girls to tolerate abuse and it's used to cover it up," Harriet told me. "By age five, my daughter got the message she had no agency over her body, and being abused was perceived as a game by the adults at her school who were supposed to protect her."

Along with issues of abuse, others wonder if we allow kids to play out their curiosity in these games with their friends, how will they know it's wrong with an adult? How will they know when it's no longer age appropriate? How will they ever learn good boundaries? These are all the reasons I quietly redirected my own toddlers when show-me games arose, but it turns out there's no evidence these games condition kids to become perpetrators or victims, and all the literature I could find says it's a common and innocent rite of passage. While it's possible for children to be abused by other children, as in Harriet's story, it's rare. More typically, children are extending their natural physicality and curiosity to their own and others' bodies. That's not to say parents should just ignore their kids' exploratory games, but we should try not to project our adult perceptions of arousal and intercourse onto it.

Given the statistics on teenage pregnancy, STI rates, the diminishing ability to obtain an abortion, tainted reputations, and the lack of social support for single mothers, it's understandable for us to warn our daughters about the risks and dangers of partnered sex and withhold information about pleasure. Sex could literally ruin their lives. But as the research has shown over and over again, teaching abstinence backfires. Comprehensive sexuality education—positive and medically accurate—is repeatedly proven to reduce teens' sexual activity, increase their use of contraception and disease protection, and improve their ability to navigate relationships.

Sex-Positive Parenting

Normalizing bodies and sex early and often is an enormous part of building your child's sexism detector. Why? Because children who are secure in their knowledge of their bodies will be better able to identify when something or someone is amiss, and because teenagers who understand their bodies and feel unashamed of their sexuality make better choices, have more equal romantic relationships, and seem to maintain closer family bonds. Being body and sex positive simply means being open and honest about bodies and sex, and replaces shame with facts, wonder, and pleasure.

But how exactly do we put this into practice?

We start by creating an open channel of judgment-free communication so they'll take their questions and concerns to us first, whether they're asking about where babies come from when they're six or about STIs when they're sixteen. Or, in the case of a woman named Angie, BDSM (bondage, discipline, dominance, and submission) when her daughter was fifteen. It might feel like jumping the gun to discuss BDSM before we even get to how to talk about bodies, sex, masturbation, and pleasure, but there's a lot to learn from Angie about open communication.

A mother of two, Angie told me she'd always been open with her kids about bodies, gender, sexuality, and sex. "At first, I felt really awkward because I was raised in a conservative, evangelical household with no talk of sex at all. But it's gotten easier with time. My kids have grown up with it and seem to feel pretty comfortable asking questions or having conversations. I try, when having these conversations, to approach them from a neutral position, just presenting the facts."

When I asked if she'd chosen to parent differently because not discussing it had been damaging or shame inducing to her growing up, she responded, "Absolutely. I had so much shame around sex and sexuality for years, and I also was subjected to a lot of sexual abuse that I didn't know how to say no to or escape from because of my upbringing. I wanted my kids to feel empowered by their own bodies and choices around their bodies."

Angie is queer, and her younger child came out as nonbinary when they were seven, so both kids have been exposed to a variety of gender and sexual orientations. When, at age eleven, her child grabbed a free condom from a booth at their local gay pride parade, she explained matter-of-factly what condoms are used for, "including," she told me, "more than just penis-in-vagina sex, but also for use on sex toys and such."

Now that her kids are teenagers, their questions and conversations go further. The BDSM discussion came up at dinner one evening because her younger child's girlfriend had texted a picture of some handcuffs. Her child was in their first romantic relationship and learning how to navigate the sexual aspects. They wanted to know why their girlfriend had sent that. "It made me a bit uncomfortable, as I'm sure it would most parents. But it provided a good opportunity to talk about consent, which we've been talking about since they were very young, and what it means both in terms of a 'traditional' relationship, as well as one that involves kink or power dynamics. We talked about how BDSM, as it's portrayed in media and in porn, isn't an accurate or often healthy portrayal, and how in any relationship (be it romantic, sexual, kinky, platonic, whatever), communication is a necessary thing, even if it's uncomfortable."

Let's talk a little bit about best practices for creating the sort of relaxed communication Angie has managed with her kids. Children tend to absorb and respond better to information when it comes up organically. TV, movies, and music provide endless fodder for questions and discussion. Certainly, there will be times you need to bring up a topic, so consider doing it on a walk, in the car, or while playing a game because less eye contact can often mean more communication. Remember, your kid is reading your body language; if you're uncomfortable or embarrassed, they will be too. But don't let your (or their) discomfort shut you down.

Feel free to name the awkwardness by saying something like "I'm uncomfortable too, but that's okay because it's important for you to know this stuff." The deeper and more actively we can listen to our kids without reacting, the more we create space for open communication. The poker face is especially useful once they become teens. If we can listen and reflect back what we're hearing when they come to us with their thoughts and confusion, they'll be more likely to come to us when they have questions or concerns about birth control, STIs, or their sexuality. You want them coming to you first, or they'll rely on inaccurate information from friends and porn. That's not to say you have to have all the answers. Telling them you need to learn more about it is perfectly acceptable! Then you can check out (with them or alone) the resource section of SexPositiveFamilies.com.

Body Talk

Body literacy is an essential tool in healthy sexual development and for keeping kids safe. Using anatomically correct terms for genitalia shows a child there's nothing embarrassing about their or anyone else's body. Terms like "penis" and "vulva" are simply descriptive, same as "neck" and "knee." When they know their own bodies, they can also more accurately tell you when and where something hurts.

Notice I said vulva, not vagina? The vulva is the visible part of the genitals—the urethra, clitoris, labia, and vaginal opening. You can't see the actual vagina, which is the scientific name for the canal linking the uterus to the outside of the body. Why vagina became the name we use instead of the more accurate term is anyone's guess, but I'm going with the ignorance and sexism that's surrounded female anatomy for most of history (it took until 1994 for the National Institutes of Health to mandate that clinical trials include women!). Before the mysterious female canal finally got a name in the seventeenth century, "vagina" meant a scabbard or sheath for a sword. Perhaps the doctors (who were mostly men) were thinking with their "swords" when they decided to use "vagina" instead of "vulva."

As a means to both correct history and assist in health-care and abuse communication, let's be sure our daughters know each and every one of their body parts. This is easily accomplished by showing girls a diagram and suggesting they look at their vulva in the mirror. And yes, once genital names are well understood and there's no shame associated with them, feel free to mix it up a little with "vajajay" or whatever your "down there" was called as a child.

Real talk doesn't end there. Just as we use correct terms for genitalia to reduce shame or discomfort about bodies, we need to talk about body changes and body differences casually and factually when our kids are young. Puberty is a huge transformation, both physically and emotionally, and if kids aren't prepared for the changes, it can feel more awkward and disruptive to the whole family. Normalizing changes also provides a good foundation for more difficult conversations later and helps reduce the embarrassment that can occur as kids get older. By talking with both sons and daughters about the relationship between the ovaries and the testicles, the clitoris and the penis, we reduce the mystery of the other sex.

Periods

Menstruating, for example, needn't be gross or mysterious. The shame and misinformation associated with periods leads to teasing, regularly missed school days, and "othering" half the planet. Normalizing periods doesn't mean pretending they're like nosebleeds. It means talking openly about them, answering factually about that string your preschooler sees when he barges into your bathroom, and embracing the wonder of the female body. Boys learn their reproductive abilities—their erections and semen—are a source of virility and pride, while girls speak in hushed, embarrassed voices about theirs. Disney's film *Turning Red* about periods and the sexual awakening of young girls demonstrated how an attempt to familiarize the public with female development led to outrage and scorn. At this writing, Florida is trying to pass a bill prohibiting young girls from discussing their period in school (what could go wrong?). Why is menstrual blood taboo when it's fundamental to the continuation of the human race?

One way to help reduce the shame and instead honor womanhood is to mark or celebrate a girl's first period. Some people have parties, go out for a special family dinner, or create a rite-of-passage "First Moon" Ceremony. In the Navajo tradition, a girl's first period is celebrated in a four-day ceremony called a Kinaaldá. For my daughter, I decided not to mark the occasion with the cultural Jewish custom (*not* in accordance with Jewish law) of a slap in the face. Instead, I decided to put together a period kit that included pads and tampons in different sizes, a menstrual cup, period underwear, a strawberry-printed period wallet that holds pads, a tiny pillbox with kitten decor, a microwavable heating pad in the form of a stuffed sloth (perfect for laying across her belly), a tips-and-tricks sheet with important period information, and of course chocolate. I waited and waited, sizing up in the underwear as time passed, and of course her period finally came while she was at overnight camp. Her basket of goodies tied with helium balloons was waiting for her when she returned. At fifteen, she seems to have no shame or even self-consciousness around her period and can talk casually about it even in front of her father and brother. In contrast, I swore my mother to secrecy with regard to my dad and brothers.

Nudity

While I might've found periods and other puberty markers humiliating, I seemed to have no body shame early on about nudity. As tots, my little brother and I ran around the house naked after our bath chanting with full-throated joy, "The nudies, the nudies, we are the nudies." My parents weren't nudists (other than at that nude beach we happened upon when I was six and didn't want to be considered voyeurs), but they also weren't uptight about nudity. Maintaining neutrality or even a sense of humor is another way to normalize bodies and ensure they're seen first as bodies and not sexual objects. Without the weight of sexuality and close-up shots of breasts and bottoms, there's no fuel for the male gaze. My husband and I took baths with our kids until either the bath could no longer accommodate two people or the kids wanted privacy. Even now, I'm comfortable changing my clothes in front of my kids if it so happens. Bodies aren't inherently sexual or erotic; it's the adults who sexualize nudity, not the children.

When Rough lived in Amsterdam, she found nudity was no big deal, though she notes now body shame seems to be seeping into Dutch culture. It was common to see little kids playing naked in the public wading pool and neighbors changing their clothing. Covering your windows at home signaled you had something to hide, so Rough and her husband learned to keep their shades open. "We never totally got used to being so visibly bare," she writes, "but over time I know we both had proud moments when we thought task first, clothing whenever." After reading her book, I stopped worrying if my shades were up when I went from the shower to my closet. And I've tried to stop reminding Gabi to close her shade when she changes. I want to disrupt a lifetime of social norms to cover up because I want her to know the freedom Dutch children experience. But it's difficult to shake the cultural dictate about a woman's duty to be modest and control men's arousal. I can't shut off that part of my mind that says, "Why invite trouble?" "What if some creep is getting off on looking at a child's body?" "What if he starts to follow her?" And then I nonchalantly shut her blinds myself. The chance is so minuscule (voyeurism has gone digital, so I probably should worry more about her computer's webcam than her window), and yet, given the statistics of violence against women, it's hard to just relax and believe our daughters are safe.

We're sexualizing nudity when our prepubescent sons but not our daughters can whip off their shirts on a sticky summer day or jump in a lake in their shorts and nothing else if they've forgotten their suits. As Rough puts it, "The everyday assumption that nudity represents eroticism is a profound entanglement sitting deep in the modern American psyche. It's why women don't go topless on our beaches (we're not there to have sex). It's why our wading pools require 'appropriate swimming attire' for every age (we can't have tots attracting sexual attention)." It's also why some people find public breast-feeding lewd. Or in a reversal of sorts, my husband was admonished by a five-year-old for changing into his swimsuit in a pool locker room. "Next time, please don't let me see your privates," the boy said to his backside, seemingly having learned privates are inherently shameful or icky.

You might be surprised to learn toplessness is technically legal in most states, even for adult women. But topless women have been relegated to sexual environments like live nude shows. So here comes the circular logic: if topless women are seen only in the context of pornography, is it any wonder we objectify breasts and have trouble dealing with them in other contexts? If seeing breasts was made more matter-of-fact, the joy of spontaneously swimming and going braless would be at girls' disposal.

Sex Talk

"But where does the daddy get the seed to fertilize the egg?" my friend's five-year-old son asked for the umpteenth time since she'd rather vaguely answered his question about how babies are made. "Does he go to the planting store to buy it?" She was relieved to have been driving with him in his car seat so she could silently giggle without him seeing. She told him it was a great question, and they'd talk all about this exciting process when the picture book arrived. In truth, she was trying to buy time until school was out for the summer the following week. Knowing her incredibly curious and verbal child loved wielding the power of knowledge, we'd been conspiring about how to delay answering. She didn't want him being that kid—the precocious one who reveals all to his classmates before their parents decide it's time. The day of kindergarten graduation, she took him to their favorite chocolate shop, where she picked out some salted caramel truffles and he some vanilla ice cream. They settled on the wicker love seat with *It's Not the Stork!*, the first in a series of three books that takes a straightforward approach to explaining bodies, boundaries, and how babies are made. They spent over an hour reading and discussing it. He was fascinated by the pictures of babies growing in their mothers' wombs but took little interest in the pages on sex and fertility. So, before they left, she checked in to make sure his questions had been answered, and he was clear about the seed coming through the daddy's penis. "Yup!" he said happily, licking the now-dried ice cream from his fingers. A few weeks later, though, he asked again how babies are made. She reminded him of the basics and where he could find the book but didn't go into more detail. He didn't ask. Kids absorb what they're ready for, and that told her he wasn't quite ready to learn more. It's a good reminder we don't really have to worry about providing too much information.

Once kids have started asking about how babies are made, you'll be surprised how often sex-related topics and questions arise. Parents tell me they're concerned they won't know the answers to their kids' questions or how much to tell them. They also fear talking about sex will give their children permission to do it. In fact, sex education and parent-child communication about sexuality are associated with delayed sexual activity and more consistent contraceptive use. Regular and ongoing two-way discussions support and reinforce bodily concepts so kids will be more likely to recall them when they need them most. Easier said than done, of course.

Messages about sex take root in us when we're young. Most of us lack good examples of how to parent around sexuality. There was "the Talk" (one talk!) that was laden with shame and awkwardness or "the Book" (one book!). And many people—women especially—have experienced some form of sexual trauma, so, sometimes, fear and shame can affect how we parent around sexuality, leading to hypervigilance or denial of a child's sexuality. If you've been assaulted or abused in your lifetime, or even just grew up with negative messages about sex, working through that in therapy can be a helpful bridge to relating to inquisitive, puberty-bound children and sexually interested teens.

My goal has been to give sex enough airtime to make it as mundane a topic as, well, pizza. Treat it as you would their wonder about the stars and galaxies: affirming the curiosity, pride, and pleasure they show in their genitalia and avoiding shaming them for touching themselves. One of my favorite examples of this easygoing approach occurred in a friend's kitchen. While cooking, she offhandedly asked her toddler if he could please put away his penis for now and play with something else.

Ideally, we should start having conversations and reading body books with our kids by age five when they're still open, curious, and unselfconscious. Around age eight, they should understand their body is going to change, so we want to make the topic of puberty ordinary. By age nine, they become more modest, and discussing bodies and sexuality gets a little more touchy. By age twelve, if you haven't yet broached the topic (or maybe even if you have), expect to be critiqued and shut down by your kids. That doesn't mean don't talk about this stuff when they're tweens and teens (definitely do), but if you've been doing it all along in age-appropriate ways, it won't be nearly so awkward. You can always say you realize you haven't been as open as you wish you had about topics like bodies and sex, and consider explaining why. By late middle school, kids should know all about sex—the different kinds, birth control, and STIs—so when sexual experimenting and dating starts, they can make good choices for themselves. Keep in mind, kids develop at different paces, so adjust these loose guidelines as you see fit.

You may decide to have family rules about dating. Maybe your child has to bring home their love interest at least twice before there's a private date. Deciding what age is appropriate to start hanging out or "talking to" someone (kid nomenclature for flirting and exploring possibilities) depends on your kid's level of maturity. Can they speak up for themselves? Can they protect their own bodily autonomy and respect someone else's boundaries? We can help our kids become savvy daters and relaters by giving them scenarios to ponder: How can a girl let a boy know if she wants to date him? What if someone is flirting with a girl but she's not interested? What if a friend (or a boyfriend) is pressuring her to do something/go somewhere she doesn't want to?

It's one thing to talk about sex in the abstract; it's a whole other ball of sweaty mortification to talk directly about our teens' sex lives. But parents have to let their kids know exactly where they stand because, though they grossly underestimate their power, they're the single largest influence on their adolescents' decisions about sex. We can be proactive while also remembering that being a sexually active teen isn't the same as being a sexually promiscuous teen. Let them know what milestones you'd want them to hit. Do you want them to be a certain age? In a loving relationship? Prepared with birth control? We also want them to have a clear sense of their own rules and limits. We can encourage them to consider how many dates or how they want to feel before there's any physical touch, what they're willing to do and not do in a car or public place, how far they're willing to go that night with that particular person. Of course, they're not robots and may not always stick to the plan, but having guidelines in place helps in the heat of the moment. The ultimate goal is for our daughters to tune in to what's right for them. We can communicate our preferences, but pressuring them just adds to the cacophony, making it harder to hear their own voices. We might say, "I think it's best to be in a loving relationship, but if you decide you're ready before you feel in love, just make sure you feel valued."

> We can be proactive while also remembering that being a sexually active teen isn't the same as being a sexually promiscuous teen.

Pleasure Talk

While tweens and teens need to hear about the risks of partnered sex, they also need to hear that most partnered sex isn't about reproduction but about the pursuit of emotional and physical pleasure. Telling kids otherwise is dishonest, and they know it. That's why they keep doing it despite pledges to wait until marriage and warnings it could ruin their life or reputation. Even stressing that sex happens only between two people who love each other can be confusing. I don't want my daughter confusing lust or infatuation with love. I don't want her to think if someone agrees to have sex with her, it's because they love her, or she has to have sex with someone because she loves them.

Many parents focus on their values and on providing factual and mechanical information about sex but leave out the bit about pleasure. They worry that if they admit sex feels good, it'll entice their children to experiment too early. When a friend's ten-year-old daughter asked her mother to explain a condom commercial, she said, "Condoms are pieces of rubber that men put on their penises during sex so that the sperm stays inside. That way, the woman doesn't get pregnant and neither of them can get a disease from each other." Her daughter asked, "Why would they have sex if the woman doesn't want to get pregnant?" Her mom responded, "Because, for grown-ups, sex feels good." Her daughter said, "Oh," and moved on.

Remember, all the research tells us open, honest conversations with kids about sex, which include brief yet repetitive reminders of health and safety, lead to better sexual outcomes for teens, including delayed sex. Your daughter probably already understands the power of sensual pleasure from the lifetime of soothing, cuddling, and caressing you've provided her, examples of loving and attentive touch that are one of life's greatest joys. Doesn't she deserve to know she should expect that in a romantic relationship? We want our teens to be safe, *and* we want them to grow up to be adults with vibrant, intimate, healthy sex lives. By saying sex feels good, we validate our daughters' longings, rather than drive them and that part of her underground, where they risk being kept secret not just from us but from them too.

Your daughter probably already understands the power of sensual pleasure from the lifetime of soothing, cuddling, and caressing you've provided her, examples of loving and attentive touch that are one of life's greatest joys. Doesn't she deserve to know she should expect that in a romantic relationship?

Talking about pleasure in the context of sex may seem radical, but it's all about being sex positive. To be clear, sex positive doesn't mean encouraging your kids to have sex. Saying yes to their sexuality is a yes not to sexual intercourse but to connection with themselves and you. It communicates we don't think sex is bad or they're bad for wanting it. It's less about whether they're going to have sex and more about how to have deeply meaningful, intense relationships that call for respect, consent, communication, and self-expression. With all the facts, they can both enjoy and keep their bodies safe. That's an important message, even if we expect them to wait until a certain age or even until marriage, because we're communicating that sex is an essential ingredient for sustained happiness in long-term relationships for most people.

Sex-positive conversations can still communicate boundaries and values. You might explain the exciting, safe feeling that happens when someone is kissing *them* and not just their lips, when someone is really present, not in a race to get further. Or explain that sex can be transcendent when it's saved for someone they feel connected to in a spiritual way. They should also hear sex is a commitment to deal with any consequences because, even with protection, it can lead to pregnancy and disease. By balancing the hazards and pleasures of sex, we're being real with our kids.

There are many ways to communicate to our kids that being sexual is an essential and amazing part of being human. I used to deliberately play and sing along to songs like Marvin Gaye's "Sexual Healing" and Salt-N-Pepa's "Let's Talk About Sex" just so my kids would know sex wasn't a taboo topic. When we hug, kiss, and hold our significant others in front of our kids, we're modeling positive intimacy. And some people, like my patient Judy, are more explicit.

Judy was in her mid-sixties and came to see me after her husband, Bruce, died suddenly of a heart attack. Her eldest daughter and son-in-law brought her to the first session because she was in a fragile state. All three squeezed onto the small couch, ignoring the armchair next to it. Judy's daughter, Michelle, sat between them and took her mother's hand as her husband took hers. Judy didn't talk much that first session, but her daughter and son-in-law waxed on about the strong physical and emotional connection Judy and Bruce had had. "I credit my happy marriage with watching my parents," Michelle told me, looking radiantly at her husband as he reached over to stroke her hair. "Even when I was little, they were all over each other. I'm not meaning they were inappropriate, but they wouldn't shy away from flirting and kissing in front of us kids. You just knew they really enjoyed each other. Once, in middle school, they were playing footsie under the table like teenagers, and I told them to get a room. Mom looked at me with a twinkle in her eye and said, 'Maybe we will,' which of course I rewarded with a giant 'ew.' Then Mom got serious and said, 'Michelle, what we do when the sign is on the door is part of what makes a marriage great. I hope you'll have the same thing when you get married.' Well, that shut me up, and I've always remembered that."

At that moment Judy spoke up to explain the sign. When she and Bruce wanted to have sex, they hung a "Do not disturb" sign on their door. Michelle jumped in, "They called it 'sacred time,' but eventually we figured out what that meant." Judy smiled and said, "We knew we were lucky to have a good marriage and we wanted them to know it too."

Then Judy's son-in-law spoke up: "I've been with Michelle since we were twenty-four, and a big part of why that was possible was witnessing how Bruce did it. My dad was kinda unplugged, and I wasn't what you'd call the greatest boyfriend before I met Michelle. Somehow, I could tell Michelle wouldn't have given me a second look if I'd acted like a knucklehead with her, so I didn't. I started kind of studying Bruce. He always seemed happy when Judy walked in the room, and he wasn't afraid to let her know it." Judy explained they deliberately shared that affection openly in hopes their three daughters would seek and expect similarly satisfying relationships. From the many stories I heard, all three were in warm, happy relationships. Judy and Bruce made it clear to their children a satisfying sex life within an intimate relationship was important to them even though they never came right out and said it. Not all marriages have to be as "hot" as Judy's to be forthright that parents are having sex. One couple I know in a more typical marriage choose to be even more direct by explaining to their kids they're having grown-up time that probably includes sex and the kids aren't invited.

What I've noticed is when girls aren't put in a position by their parents of having to disavow their sexuality, they tend to remain more open in general than teens who have to pretend nothing has changed. Terrified of their daughters facing a sexual crisis, many parents simply ignore their daughters' budding sexuality, hoping it'll go away, or they give strict warnings about the perils of sex and encourage them to avoid it altogether. This leaves the hyper-sexualized media as our kids' primary source of information. The problem is, we know teens engage in sexual activity anyway because they have sexual urges and a need for intimacy; because it represents growing up and individuating from their parents; because it's part of the bumpy road to finding loving, pleasurable relationships.

Teens are in the tricky position of balancing the developmental need for autonomy with the still deep, if secret, longing for our approval and connection. I can't count the number of times I've reflected back to adolescents the simultaneous wishes to be held and to be set free. Parents are in the tricky position of navigating those mixed messages while both facilitating that autonomy and keeping their kids safe. If we make space for the teenage project of self-discovery and experimentation within a set of clear boundaries and understanding, rather than hamper them with guilt and fear, we give our children a chance to thrive in our presence. This approach fosters open communication and nourishing relationships where they won't feel the need to subjugate their own needs for the sake of maintaining connection.

Masturbation

When Freud first introduced the concept of infantile sexuality, it was considered outrageous. The idea that children could experience pleasure at their mother's breast, for example, apart from the nourishment they were enjoying, was viewed as depriving them of the idealized innocence with which adults viewed them. But in the twenty-first century, the sensual nature of breast-feeding and defecation and the pleasurable, sexual feelings associated with discovery of the body in childhood are generally accepted. During potty training, one friend's son would groan, "I love you, Mama," when he was having a bowel movement. Through their caregivers, children can begin to attain control over their biological needs and make them acceptable. This is all part of their sexual development that contributes significantly to their adult personalities, so how we respond matters a lot.

Most parents observe their kids from a young age exploring their bodies, touching, rubbing, and pulling various body parts, including their genitals. While this is often curiosity-driven, and made even more interesting by the fact that we cover up those parts and call them private, the pleasurable feelings they come to enjoy play a part in the origin and development of sexual feelings. Yet even parents who easily validate their kids' curiosity and pride in their body parts find themselves stumped when it comes to outright masturbation. One mother named Marla told me she found herself flustered when her eight-year-old asked her how to masturbate because he wanted to "do it right." She quickly consulted her Facebook parenting group and was advised to ask first what he thought and why he was asking. Turns out he thought masturbating was when you put lotion on your body after you bathe, as he'd seen Marla do. He'd overheard his teenage brothers joking about lotion and masturbation. Marla clarified, and he of course wanted to know what masturbation really was.

"This time I was prepared—thank you, Facebook. So I told him it's about exploring your body to see what feels good and what doesn't, like when he sometimes puts his hands in his pants because it feels nice; that it's a way to really get to know your own body, which can be useful because one day when he's much older, he might choose to share it with another person." By normalizing self-pleasure and partnered sex, Marla helped her son understand his pleasure was not only nothing to be ashamed of but important for his development.

Children's growing awareness of their genitals' capacity for pleasure isn't adult sexuality; it's a way to self-soothe just like thumb-sucking. Red flags should be raised if children are inserting objects into genital openings, referencing adult sex acts, or, as they get older, are unable to be redirected. But otherwise, there's no reason to interrupt the private, enjoyable moment they're having, especially if they are young children under five, so long as they're in a safe space and not bothering anyone. If they're in public, or when they're older, you can use it as a shame-free teachable moment: "I know it feels good to rub yourself. Adults do that too. It's something to do in private like in your room or in the bath." Kids are always calibrating their comfort against ours, so when we manage our reactions appropriately, we send the message that there's nothing unnatural about them and their bodily pleasure.

Pam, a relatable, funny mother of two girls, didn't wait until she found her kids rocking back and forth on an inanimate object to explain masturbation. "I talked about it with my girls (six and eight) in the context of talking about vulvas, vaginas, and all the parts that are hard to see but important to know about," she wrote in an email to me. "When I got to the clitoris, I was like 'This is a really cool body part because the WHOLE POINT OF IT is to make you feel good!' I told them if they ever wanted to rub it or do whatever feels good, to go ahead, but it's a thing you do in private. And I told them they could borrow my hand mirror any time they wanted to get a good look at what's happening between their legs."

When I asked whether sex or masturbation had come up again with her girls, Pam said no but then added, "Well, except when my younger child who's now eight found one of my vibrators and asked what it was.

At first, I was like 'nothing.' My fear was she'd tell my in-laws and they'd be mortified. My husband says they never once talked about sex with him. But then I thought, what the hell. If I say it's nothing, she's smart enough to know it's obviously something, and when she figures it out, I don't want her to think it's anything to be ashamed of. So I just told her: 'look, it's basically a massager for your vulva and clitoris and you use it to make yourself feel good when you're in private.' I was so tempted to say 'DO NOT mention this to Grandma and Grandpa' but then I decided that would basically be giving her instructions to tell them, so I said nothing." Pam felt good about coming clean for at least a full second until she flashed to "kids at school going home and being like 'Guess what Mia's mom has!?' and parents being alarmed." So she added, "There's nothing wrong with having a vibrator, but it's probably better if you don't tell your friends about this conversation until you're a little older." I could practically hear Pam groan through the screen when she wrote, "I really hope that didn't make the whole thing seem shameful." Pam wants her kids to be proud of who they are and to erase the shame girls all over the world grow up with, but that means forcing herself to face head-on her own internalized shame that many of us also share around sex.

Parenting is not for the faint of heart.

Conclusion

Girls Together: Joining Forces, Redirecting Anger

The fight between my sixteen-year-old patient Priya and her friend Eve began when Eve sided with their male friends who were tired of Priya's "feminist bullshit." *Roe v. Wade* had just been overturned, and Priya was trying to grasp how girls in Florida seeking judicial bypasses could be told by judges they weren't mature enough to end their pregnancies but were presumably mature enough to parent. Priya stomped into my office declaring, "Eve just doesn't care about women's rights. How am I supposed to relate to her!"

When you wake up to sexism, you find out quickly that what you hope to eradicate and the harm you experience because of it seem nonexistent to others. That's exactly what Priya, who'd begun doing antiracist gender justice work for a local organization, was discovering. So accustomed to my own compartmentalizing, I found it painful to watch Priya experience the sting of each new instance of unfair treatment and its denial.

What might have been a fruitful discussion between Priya and Eve about sexism and what it means to be female devolved instead into a hotbed of envy and competition between them—the kind of fighting that's culturally sanctioned and expected among girls. You'd think something as pervasive as sexism would draw girls and women together, but by its very nature it often does the opposite. A patriarchal society does its most effective work when it turns women against each other, making them afraid to be feminists and encouraging competition and distrust between them. Girls learn early to compete both for male attention (which allows boys to do little to earn admiration) and for a limited number of token spots at the top.

Nobody wants to be *that* kind of girl—the aggressive one, the needy one, the uptight one, the slutty one, the prudish one. In a culture that sees human attributes as divisible into "masculine" and "feminine" and assigns those it doesn't value to the latter pile, any kind of girl may be viewed as "less than," prompting girls to declare themselves different from the other girls.

There are three related reasons girls sometimes deny the existence of sexism:

1) Sexism is normalized, so speaking out seems whiny and abrasive. Rather than lose social capital or risk safety, girls learn to accept being dismissed, belittled, and harassed as normal and maybe funny.

2) Not only are they taught by society to self-blame, but psychologically it may also feel safer to blame themselves for being annoying, demanding, slutty, and so on, rather than see that the world they live in dislikes women. If they feel bad or defeated by how they're treated, it must mean something's wrong with them.

3) Being the girl who adapts most readily to sexist structures comes with rewards. Individual girls are made to feel stronger than other girls or like "one of the boys." By defensively overidentifying with men, as Eve was doing, they get to feel as if they figured out something others struggle with; they're chill. In short, by agreeing with the dominant assessment of girls and women, they avoid considerable stress. But they end up participating in their own oppression and then project that blame onto other girls who protest, deeming them difficult or weak.

I watched in nearly real time as Priya and Eve drew directly from the patriarchal script and attacked each other with stereotypes. Priya decided

Eve was "a bimbo who drank the sexist Kool-Aid," while Eve viewed Priya as "one of those girls who moans about everything" and repeatedly demanded she lighten up. Before Priya found her megaphone, she, a girl with Indian roots and brown skin, had felt "wrong." Eve's accusations both enraged her and stirred up latent insecurities. She said of Eve, "It must be nice to be rich and white so you don't have to worry about anything."

When Priya complained that Eve had called her "a fucking whore," I said, "I can imagine, but can you say what bothers you about that?" Priya answered, "It's just not okay for one girl to call another girl a whore, or even a bitch."

"What about a bimbo?" I countered.

"Oh, bro," she said, recognizing her role in the drama. "I guess I have some things to figure out."

Their fight might have been made more dramatic by the poisonous fumes of patriarchy, but we tend to dismiss girls' attention to intricate relationship dynamics as "girl drama"—ironic given that we socialize them to invest more in relationships. We live in a system that reflexively considers girls' and women's concerns less important than those of boys and men. While this relational work can be exhausting and painful, it's also fundamental to human connection. Girls form deep bonds and expect more, which they get, for better and worse. By femininizing emotional labor, we give boys and men license to opt out, generating loneliness and placing an unfair burden on girls and women to shoulder the social and emotional load of life.

When our daughters share conflicts they're having with a friend, we should neither dismiss them nor join them. Instead, we can empathize without taking sides and, if they're open to it, help them problem solve. While it was satisfying for Priya to call out chauvinism for what it was, it didn't get her any closer to being understood. When she went after Eve's character, calling her a sexist bimbo, Eve felt cornered and, not surprisingly, doubled down rather than apologizing or becoming introspective. Instead of focusing on the hurtful attitudes and behaviors, the argument was derailed and became a debate about who's a good or bad person. Priya and I discussed the idea of "calling in" rather than calling someone out. That would involve describing to Eve how sexism harms people and communities and how Eve's behavior affected Priya, without using language that would make her feel judged.

Priya nervously approached Eve and said she realized she was doing to her exactly what she was accusing Eve of, and wondered if she could tell her about her justice work. Eve coldly agreed but after four hours of deep discussion, of which I got the play-by-play, she warmed up considerably. Priya told Eve about atrocities that we think of as bygone in the United States like child marriage and clitoridectomies but that are still happening. They discussed legislation related to women's bodies, and burdens that tend to fall specifically on girls and women in relationships, in part because of the lingering myth that women belong in the home—which, Priya explained, allows the government to be stingy when it comes to parental leave and childcare. She was naming the political issues that deeply and directly affect women's lives but, despite women being half the population, are considered "specialty issues."

Priya told Eve about less appalling but still inexcusable sexism like the "pink tax," where almost all products and services marketed for women are given a higher price tag. Walk into any dry cleaner and you're likely to find men's (usually larger) shirts cost less than women's to clean. Walk into any pharmacy and you're likely to find two razors side by side made by the same company, but the one packaged for women costs more. A woman living in the United States will pay a whopping $300,000 more than a man over the course of her lifetime simply by virtue of being a woman.

Period poverty was the issue that really got Eve's attention. She was "beyond pissed" to learn the United States places a "luxury tax" on period products. In 2021, two-thirds of low-income menstruating people in this country couldn't afford period essentials, with half choosing between those and food. Improvising with rags and newspapers leads to leakage; teasing and cultural shame of menstruation in general lead to missed school and work days.

By the end of their talk, both girls were angry. But they found a productive outlet for their anger rather than each other, deciding to team up for their service learning requirement, choosing to educate about period poverty and raise money for menstrual products. The power of female friendship is transformative.

GIRLS OFTEN FEEL angry, enraged even, when they realize they've been betrayed by the laws and institutions they assumed were there to protect them. When that betrayal is brushed off, it's compounded by "the injustice of having one's social experience denied and hidden from communal understanding," as Soraya Chemaly writes in her book about women's anger. This is both the blessing and the curse of having an intact, functional sexism detector: anger at injustice remains sharp, clear, and focused, rather than diffused and turned in all directions. In a culture that pathologizes female anger, we can help our daughters use this anger constructively. Unlike guilt or shame, anger is rousing, galvanizing; it can clarify who you are and what you care about and help you find others who share those frustrations. With the right guidance, anger can spark activism and organizing, and in the process—as it did with Priya and Eve—generate confidence and leadership skills, rather than spur conformity or depression. With the right guidance, girls can use their anger to demand equality, which, at its heart, is an assertion of self-worth.

For girls and women, the best revenge against a culture that demeans them is to stick together. Being with girlfriends (or anyone who's faced gender discrimination) is a balm against the limitations of constantly feeling Other. It's freedom from having to adjust your behavior and conversation due to the fear that a man may perceive it as tedious or unrelatable.

Mothers are in a particularly powerful position to model solidarity and to dismantle the competition among girls roused by cultural deprivation. By reserving judgment—or better yet embracing, admiring, and showing we can learn from other women—we can interrupt the destructive cycle that interferes with girls and women joining forces to oppose sexism and demand better. When we distance ourselves from other women, elevating our choices and ideas over theirs, we teach our girls that their best allies are their adversaries. Individual successes won't lead to liberation on a larger scale. We must underscore for girls the power of collective action and standing together, which begins with standing with our daughters.

. . .

AS OUR DAUGHTERS neared adolescence and the requests for crop tops and bikinis rolled in—a mixture of patriarchy taking hold and a celebration of their new bodies—my friends and I wondered how to encourage their autonomy and enjoyment of their bodies while still keeping them safe physically and whole emotionally. How could we teach them they have a right to reject a boy's advances, knowing it might risk their well-being? How could we request they walk to the store alone, knowing there are men who might comment in explicit detail about their bodies or do something worse? How could we inspire healthy sexuality in them, knowing they could be forced to have babies if they got pregnant? How could we ask them to take on a world that would one day dismiss their intellect, deny them promotions, pay them less, use their appearances against them, and blame them for their own assaults?

Short of locking our daughters in their rooms until they're thirty, as more than one friend has ruefully joked, there's no way to shield them completely from misogyny. There are no hard-and-fast rules that will ensure they hold on to the cake-baking, Quidditch-playing, openhearted people they were before puberty and the slow degrading process of objectification. We can't protect our daughters from the things they'll see and hear, but we can equip them with the power to swiftly decode it.

My hope is that this book has helpfully outlined a two-pronged approach to a girl's psychological and physical well-being: (1) instilling an understanding of boundaries and consent so that the likelihood of something undesirable happening decreases; (2) cultivating the critical thinking skills needed to detect gender bias and sexism so that what she chooses—everything from pastimes to clothing to whom she trusts—rests on a profound understanding of her culture. The cornerstone of this approach is pleasure. If girls feel good in and about their bodies and believe their own pleasure is important, they'll be able to identify when something feels bad, wrong, or inappropriate, and trust their concerns are worthwhile. Just like the nascent wishes I had as a girl reading my mother's envelope, I want for our girls to see themselves addressed as whole people, filled with potential—to freely feel joy and pleasure and friendship and intimacy and courage and determination.

We can't protect our daughters from the things they'll see and hear, but we can equip them with the power to swiftly decode it.

At various points while I was writing this book, the stories and statistics illustrating the sheer breadth of sexism were disheartening to say the least. But then I'd remember that where there's growth, there's always backlash. As a society we're growing every single day. I think of my mother and how much pleasure I felt baking with her in our kitchen—if only we could redo that conversation about her name on the envelope. But now my concerns are her concerns too, and I delight in the open-minded conversations we have, or I overhear her having with my daughter.

As we're fine-tuning our daughters' sexism detectors, we can pull back the lens to show them the arc of progress—the hope and inspiration needed to believe in themselves, stand up for what they know is right, and divest from the structures that benefit from their self-loathing so they can live a life unashamedly in their own skin, focusing less on fixing themselves and more on fixing a broken world. Like girls today, equality is primed to be a powerful force that brings economic and social benefits to everyone, not just girls and women.

ACKNOWLEDGMENTS

Making a book is a massive team effort. There is no other way. I am so lucky that my debut book was shepherded into this world by a literary dynamic duo: my agent, Gail Ross, and my editor, Marnie Cochran. Special thanks to Dara Kaye, the proposal whisperer, and to the amazing team at Penguin Random House. In addition to their wise and generous guidance, this manuscript benefited immensely from conversations with and early reads by friends, colleagues, and acquaintances.

Thanks go to Debi Lewis, who championed this book from the beginning and provided generous editorial feedback; Jennifer Wells for her exquisite eleventh-hour edits; Leslie Danzig for the countless walks and talks and thoughtful input; Ruth Whippman for camaraderie, commiseration, and consultation; Devorah Heitner for patiently deciphering the publishing business for me; and Deborah Siegel, Kimberly Kol, Sarah Liebov, Monica Bisgaard, Liz Jackson, Jane Isay, Bonnie Alexander, Suzanne Bost, Carrie Goldman, Esther Warkov, Emily Rothman, Lisa Selin Davis, and Jenn Wilson for helping me believe I was on the right path or nudging me in that direction.

I was fortunate to find John Lyons, intern extraordinaire, who took on simple and complicated responsibilities with equal passion, as well as the Podstars—you know who you are—who took (most of) the *ew* out of platform building. Much gratitude and love to my parents and brothers for cheering me on with this book and in this life, and to David Goldberg for his grace (and fantastic cooking) during this writing process, which kept me consumed and distracted. And to my kids, who were given veto power over the stories about them and still (mostly) let me go forth, I love you boundlessly.

Finally, there would be no book without my therapist, Nancy Burke, who steadily, often wordlessly, communicated that I was somebody, not some *body*. And most important, the girls and women who were brave enough to share their stories with me.

Introduction

xii   **Even the youngest children:** Ziv, T., & Sommerville, J. (2016). Developmental differences in infants' fairness expectations from 6 to 15 months of age. *Child Development, 88.* 10.1111/cdev.12674.

xiii   **In fact, a recent:** England, P., Levine, A., & Mishel, E. (2020). Progress toward gender equality in the United States has slowed or stalled. *Proceedings of the National Academy of Sciences of the United States of America, 117*(13), 6990–97. doi.org/10.1073/pnas.1918891117.

xiv   **One in six women:** National Institute of Justice and Centers for Disease Control and Prevention. (1998). *Prevalence, incidence, and consequences of violence against women survey.* U.S. Department of Justice. Retrieved from rainn.org/statistics/victims-sexual-violence.

xiv   **Equal pay has been:** Payscale. (2023). *Gender pay gap report.* www.payscale.com/research-and-insights/gender-pay-gap/.

xiv   **Women work long hours:** Chavda, J. (2023, April 14). *Husbands and wives earn similar wages in a growing share of marriages.* Pew Research Center's Social and Demographic Trends Project. www.pewresearch.org/social-trends/2023/04/13/in-a-growing-share-of-u-s-marriages-husbands-and-wives-earn-about-the-same/.

xiv **Women make up just:** Hinchliffe, E. (2023). Women CEOs run 10.4% of Fortune 500 companies. A quarter of the 52 leaders became CEO in the last year. *Fortune.* fortune.com/2023/06/05/fortune-500-companies-2023-women-10-percent/.

xiv **Only 13 percent of directors:** Women and Hollywood. (2021). *2021 statistics.* womenandhollywood.com/resources/statistics/2021-statistics/; Lauzen, M. (2023). It's a man's (celluloid) world: Portrayals of female characters in the top grossing U.S. films of 2022. Center for the Study of Women in Television and Film. San Diego State University. womenintvfilm.sdsu.edu/wp-content/uploads/2023/03/2022-its-a-mans-celluloid-world-report-rev.pdf.

xiv **In a large-scale survey:** *Weissbourd, R. (2017). The talk: How adults can promote young people's healthy relationships and prevent misogyny and sexual harassment. Making Caring Common Project. Harvard Graduate School of Education.*

Chapter 1: Egalitarian Relationships, Equal Parenting

3 **Many fathers are in:** Pipher, M. (1994). *Reviving Ophelia: Saving the selves of adolescent girls.* Putnam.

4 **One gender expert calls:** Ward, J. (2020). *The tragedy of heterosexuality.* New York University Press.

4 **In their 2018 book:** Gilligan, C., & Snider, N. (2018). *Why does patriarchy persist?* Polity Press.

7 **Girls between the ages:** Livingston, G. (2019, Feb. 20). The way U.S. teens spend their time is changing, but differences between boys and girls persist. Pew Research Center. www.pewresearch.org/short-reads/2019/02/20/the-way-u-s-teens-spend-their-time-is-changing-but-differences-between-boys-and-girls-persist/.

7 **This is no small thing:** Goldin, C., Pekkala Kerr, S., Olivetti, C., & Barth, E. (2017). The expanding gender earnings gap: Evidence from the LEHD-2000 census." *American Economic Review, 107*(5), 110–14.

8 **Even if they work:** Chavda. *Husbands and wives earn similar wages in a growing share of marriages.*

8 **No wonder couples who:** Gager, C. T., & Yabiku, S. T. (2010). Who has the time? The relationship between household labor time and sexual frequency. *Journal of Family Issues, 31*(2), 135–63. doi.org/10.1177 /0192513X09348753; Carlson, D., Miller, A., Sassler, S., & Hanson, S. (2016). The gendered division of housework and couples' sexual relationships: A reexamination. *Journal of Marriage and Family Therapy, 78*(4), 975–95.

13 **Research shows when kids:** Dinella, L., Claps, J., & Lewandowski, G., Jr. (2017). Princesses, princes, and superheroes: Children's gender cognitions and fictional characters. *Journal of Genetic Psychology, 178*(5), 262–80. doi:10.1080/00221325.2017.1351417.

16 **When fathers share housework:** Croft, A., Schmader, T., Block, K., & Baron, A. S. (2014). The second shift reflected in the second generation: Do parents' gender roles at home predict children's aspirations? *Psychological Science, 25*(7), 1418–28. doi:10.1177/0956797614533968.

17 **Our kids absorb:** Knudson-Martin, C., & Rankin Mahoney, A. (2009). *Couples, gender, and power: Creating change in intimate relationships.* Springer.

19 **A global study:** Blum, R. W., Mmari, K., & Moreau, C. (2017). It begins at 10: How gender expectations shape early adolescence around the world. *Journal of Adolescent Health, 61*(4 Suppl.), S3–S4. doi:10.1016/j .jadohealth.2017.07.009.

19 **Researchers discovered that the constraints:** Lennox, R. (2021). "There's girls who can fight, and there's girls who are innocent": Gendered safekeeping as virtue maintenance work. *Violence Against Women, 28*(2), 641–63. doi.org/10.1177/1077801221998786.

22 **In 2018, the American:** American Psychological Association, Boys and Men Guidelines Group. (2018). *APA guidelines for psychological practice with boys and men.* www.apa.org/about/policy/psychological-practice -boys-men-guidelines.pdf.

23   **A study out of Duke:** Stanaland, A., & Gaither, S. (2021). "Be a man":
The role of social pressure in eliciting men's aggressive cognition.
Personality and Social Psychology Bulletin, 47(11), 1596–611.
doi:10.1177/0146167220984298.

24   **By almost every measure:** Schore, A. N. (2017). All our sons: The
developmental neurobiology and neuroendocrinology of boys at risk.
Infant Mental Health Journal, 38(1), 15–52. doi:10.1002/imhj.21616;
Chaplin, T. M., Cole, P. M., & Zahn-Waxler, C. (2005). Parental
socialization of emotion expression: Gender differences and relations
to child adjustment. *Emotion, 5*(1), 80–88. doi.org/10.1037/1528
-3542.5.1.80.

24   **And one study observing:** Ross, H. E., Tesla, C., Kenyon, B., & Lollis, S.
(1990). Maternal intervention in toddler peer conflict: The socialization
of principles of justice. *Developmental Psychology, 26*(6), 994–1003. doi
.org/10.1037/0012-1649.26.6.994.

24   **The male characters in movies:** Heldman, C., Narayanan, S.,
Cooper, R., Conroy, M., Cooper-Jones, N., Burrows, E., Campos, P.,
Christensen, S., Fava-Pastilha, M., Juliano, L., Lorísdóttir, M.,
McTaggart, N., Perez, R., Phillips, H., Virgo, J., Yoder, J., Baruah, S.,
Bose, D., . . . Young, A. (2020). *See Jane 2020 TV report.* Geena Davis
Institute for Gender in Media. seejane.org/wp-content/uploads
/2020-tv-historic-screen-time-speaking-time-for-female-characters
-report.pdf.

25   **Male privilege is usually:** Oster, M. (2017). Preventing sexual violence
starts with what we teach our boys. *Child Trends.* www.childtrends.org/
blog/preventing-sexual-violence-starts-teach-boys.

26   **One group of boys:** Milkovits, A. (2022, Sept. 9). The middle school
boys thought their teacher was a "creep." So they tracked how he treated
the girls. *Boston Globe.* www.bostonglobe.com/2022/09/09/metro
/middle-school-boys-thought-their-teacher-was-creep-so-they-tracked
-how-he-treated-girls/.

Chapter 2: Reconsidering Her Life Script

28   **Dating rituals, marriage proposals:** Wanic, R., & Kulik, J. (2011). Toward an understanding of gender differences in the impact of marital conflict on health. *Sex Roles, 65,* 297–312. doi.org/10.1007/s11199-011 -9968-6.

30   **Our daughters should hear:** Munsey, C. (2010). Does marriage make us happy? *Monitor on Psychology, 41*(9). www.apa.org/monitor/2010/10 /marriage.

31   **In a phenomenon researchers:** Rudman, L. A., & Heppen, J. B. (2003). Implicit romantic fantasies and women's interest in personal power: A glass slipper effect? *Personality and Social Psychology Bulletin, 29*(11), 1357–70. doi:10.1177/0146167203256906.

32   **I've certainly noticed:** Twenge, J. M., & Park, H. (2019). The decline in adult activities among U.S. adolescents, 1976–2016. *Child Development, 90*(2), 638–54. doi:10.1111/cdev.12930; Noenickx, C. (2022, Dec. 13). "Situationships": Why Gen Z are embracing the grey area. *BBC Worklife.* www.bbc.com/worklife/article/20220831-situationships-why-gen-z-are -embracing-the-grey-area.

37   **Not surprisingly, studies show:** Rosenfeld, M. (2017). Who wants the breakup? Gender and breakup in heterosexual couples. In D. F. Alwin, D. Felmlee, & D. Kreager (Eds.), *Social networks and the life course: Integrating the development of human lives and social relational networks* (pp. 221–43). Springer.

38   **They're also happier:** Kingston University London. (2013, July 8). *Research shows divorce spells big boost to women's happiness.* www. kingston.ac.uk/news/article/1055/08-jul-2013-research-shows-divorce -spells-big-boost-to-womens-happiness/.

38   **Just as research shows:** Halim, M. L., & Martin, C. L. (2022, March 16). *Friendships with different genders reduce sexism.* Society for Personality and Social Psychology. spsp.org/news-center/character-context-blog /friendships-different-genders-reduce-sexism.

38   **In a study of nine:** Gansen, H. M. (2017). Reproducing (and disrupting) heteronormativity: Gendered sexual socialization in preschool classrooms. *Sociology of Education, 90*(3), 255–72. doi:10.1177/0038040717720981.

39   **In her book *Beyond*:** Rough, B. J. (2018). *Beyond birds and bees: Bringing home a new message to our kids about sex, love, and equality.* Seal Press.

40   **I chose to tell:** Serbin, L. A., Tonick, I. J., & Sternglanz, S. H. (1977). Shaping cooperative cross-sex play. *Child Development, 48*(3), 924–29. doi.org/10.2307/1128342.

41   **A project out of Harvard:** Weissbourd. *Talk.*

43   **Perhaps the best way:** hooks, b. (1999). *All about love: New visions.* William Morrow.

43   **When we help them:** Thomae, J. (2023). Love is a verb. *Mind Body Align.* mindbodyalign.com/love-is-a-verb/.

45   **As the novelist-philosopher:** de Botton, A. (1993). *On love.* Atlantic Monthly Press.

45   **There's plenty of research:** *Early family experience affects later romantic relationships.* (2018, Aug. 14). National Institutes of Health. www.nih .gov/news-events/nih-research-matters/early-family-experience-affects -later-romantic-relationships.

Chapter 3: Stereotypes and the Gender Binary

48   **Indeed, a majority of:** Twenge, J. (2023, May 1). How Gen Z changed its views on gender. *Time.* time.com/6275663/generation-z-gender -identity/.

50   **As the neuroscientist Lise Eliot:** Eliot, L. (2009). *Pink brain, blue brain: How small differences grow into troublesome gaps—and what we can do about it.* Houghton Mifflin Harcourt.

50   **So why, then, if science:** Hyde, J. S. (2005). The gender similarities hypothesis. *American Psychologist, 60*(6), 581–92. doi:10.1037/0003 -066X.60.6.581.

50   **Mothers who know they're:** Katz Rothman, B. (1988). *Tentative pregnancy: Prenatal diagnosis and the future of motherhood.* Pandora.

50   **Once born, infant daughters:** Rubin, J. Z., Provenzano, F. J., & Luria, Z. (1974). The eye of the beholder: Parents' views on sex of newborns. *American Journal of Orthopsychiatry, 44*(4), 512–19. doi.org/10.1111 /j.1939-0025.1974.tb00905.x; Karraker, K. H., Vogel, D. A., & Lake, M. (1995). Parents' gender-stereotyped perceptions of newborns: The eye of the beholder revisited. *Sex Roles, 33,* 687–701. doi.org/10.1007 /bf01547725.

51   **Those labeled boys:** Burnham, D. K., & Harris, M. B. (1992). Effects of real gender and labeled gender on adults' perceptions of infants. *Journal of Genetic Psychology, 153*(2), 165–83. doi:10.1080/00221325 .1992.10753711; BBC Stories. (2017, Aug. 16). *Girl toys vs boy toys: The experiment—BBC stories* [Video]. YouTube. www.youtube.com /watch?v=nWu44AqF0iI.

51   **Judith Butler's theory of gender:** Butler, J. (2006). *Gender trouble: Feminism and the subversion of identity.* Routledge.

53   **One-quarter of Gen Z kids:** Kenney, L. (2020, April 8). Companies can't ignore shifting gender norms. *Harvard Business Review.* hbr .org/2020/04/companies-cant-ignore-shifting-gender-norms.

54   **The lucrative rise:** Ruble, D. N., Lurye, L. E., & Zosuls, K. M. (2011). Pink frilly dresses (PFD) and early gender identity. *Princeton Report on Knowledge, 5.*

56   **There's research showing that kids:** Pauletti, R. E., Menon, M., Cooper, P. J., Aults, C. D., & Perry, D. G. (2016). Psychological androgyny and children's mental health: A new look with new measures. *Sex Roles, 76,* 705–18. doi.org/10.1007/s11199-016-0627-9; Korlat, S., Holzer, J., Schultes, M., Buerger, S., Schober, B., Spiel, C., & Kollmayer, M. (2022). Benefits of psychological androgyny in adolescence: The role of gender

role self-concept in school-related well-being. *Frontiers in Psychology, 13.* doi.org/10.3389/fpsyg.2022.856758.

58   **As for gender reveal:** Langmuir, M. (2020, June 29). I started the "gender reveal party" trend. And I regret it. *Guardian.* www.theguardian .com/lifeandstyle/2020/jun/29/jenna-karvunidis-i-started-gender-reveal -party-trend-regret.

59   **When girls are given:** Tzuriel, D., & Egozi, G. (2010). Gender differ- ences in spatial ability of young children: The effects of training and processing strategies. *Child Development, 81*(5), 1417–30. doi:10.1111 /j.1467-8624.2010.01482.x.

59   **And children who play:** Peterson, E. G., Weinberger, A. B., Uttal, D. H., Kolvoord, B., & Green, A. E. (2020). Spatial activity participation in childhood and adolescence: Consistency and relations to spatial thinking in adolescence. *Cognitive Research: Principles and Implications, 5,* 43. doi:10.1186/s41235-020-00239-0.

59   **For starters, try not:** Think again: Men and women share cognitive skills. (2014, Aug. 1). American Psychological Association. www.apa .org/topics/neuropsychology/men-women-cognitive-skills.

Chapter 4: Beauty Is the Beast

68   **To wit, teen girls:** Dahl, M. (2014, Feb. 24). Stop obsessing: Women spend 2 weeks a year on their appearance, TODAY survey shows. *Today.* www.today.com/health/stop-obsessing-women-spend-2-weeks-year -their-appearance-today-2D12104866.

68   **As Renee Engeln writes:** Engeln, R. (2017). *Beauty sick: How the cultural obsession with appearance hurts girls and women.* Harper.

69   **Worth $579 billion globally:** Statista. (2023). Beauty & personal care—worldwide. Statista Market Forecast. www.statista.com/outlook /cmo/beauty-personal-care/worldwide.

69   **Total revenue from surgical:** Michas, F. (2022, Aug. 31). Revenue from surgical and nonsurgical cosmetic procedures in the U.S. 2021. Statista. www.statista.com/statistics/281357/total-us-expenditure-on-surgical -and-nonsurgical-cosmetic-procedures/.

69   **On skin care alone:** Skinstore. (2021). *The skincare report—an analysis of beauty in the US.* www.skinstore.com/blog/skincare/the-skin-report/; Skinstore. (2017). *How much is your face worth? Our survey results revealed!* www.skinstore.com/blog/skincare/womens-face-worth -survey-2017/.

69   **Women who say they:** Looking good isn't cheap: Groupon finds people will spend almost a quarter of a million on their appearance over their lifetime. (2017, June 21). Business Wire. www.businesswire.com/news /home/20170621006357/en/.

70   **The UK professors Rosalind Gill:** Gill, R., & Elias, A. S. (2014). "Awaken your incredible": Love your body discourses and postfeminist contradictions. *International Journal of Media and Cultural Politics, 10*(2), 179–88. doi:10.1386/macp.10.2.179_1.

71   **Promisingly, younger consumers:** Beauty is child's play: 80% of US tweens use beauty and personal care products. (2016, July 28). Mintel. www.mintel.com/press-centre/beauty-is-childs-play-80-of-us-tweens -use-beauty-and-personal-care-products/.

72   **Girls as young as three:** Di Pasquale, R., & Celsi, L. (2017). Stigmatization of overweight and obese peers among children. *Frontiers in Psychology, 8*, 524. doi:10.3389/fpsyg.2017.00524.

72   **The World Health Organization:** Inchley, J., et al. (Eds.). (2016). *Growing up unequal: Gender and socioeconomic differences in young people's health and well-being.* World Health Organization, Regional Office for Europe. apps.who.int/iris/handle/10665/326320.

73   **Decades of research show:** Santos, R. (2022, Nov. 15). A psychologist explains why life is easier for attractive people. Vice.com. www.vice .com/en/article/epz8pk/psychology-pretty-privilege-attractive-people.

73   **In court, attractive people:** Gunnell, J. J., & Ceci, S. J. (2010). When emotionality trumps reason: A study of individual processing style and juror bias. *Behavioral Sciences and the Law, 28*(6), 850–77. doi.org/10 .1002/bsl.939.

74   **Gender policing has reverberating:** Hart, D. (2021, June 4). Girls want to lead but fear harassment and discrimination. Plan International. www.plan.org.au/media-centre/girls-want-to-lead-but-fear-harassment -and-discrimination/.

74   **Research supports this:** Ramati-Ziber, L., Shnabel, N., & Glick, P. (2020). The beauty myth: Prescriptive beauty norms for women reflect hierarchy-enhancing motivations leading to discriminatory employ-ment practices. *Journal of Personality and Social Psychology, 119*(2), 317–43. doi.org/10.1037/pspi0000209.

74   **The author Peggy Orenstein:** Orenstein, P. (2016). *Girls and sex: Navigating the complicated new landscape.* Harper.

76   **This Eurocentric ideal:** Gay, R. (2018, Jan.). Fifty years ago, protesters took on the Miss America pageant and electrified the feminist move-ment. *Smithsonian Magazine.* www.smithsonianmag.com/history /fifty-years-ago-protestors-took-on-miss-america-pageant-electrified -feminist-movement-180967504/.

76   **"are determined by our proximity":** Ijeoma, O. (2018). *So you want to talk about race.* Seal Press.

76   **"For young people of color":** Kendall, M. (2020). *Hood feminism: Notes from the women that a movement forgot.* Viking.

78   **It wasn't until the late:** Wolchover, N. (2012, Jan. 26). The real skinny: Expert traces America's thin obsession. LiveScience.com. www .livescience.com/18131-women-thin-dieting-history.html.

79   **An eight-year longitudinal study:** Stice, E., Marti, C. N., Shaw, H., & Jaconis, M. (2009). An 8-year longitudinal study of the natural history of threshold, subthreshold, and partial eating disorders from a commu-nity sample of adolescents. *Journal of Abnormal Psychology, 118*(3), 587–97. doi.org/10.1037/a0016481.

79   **Eating disorders are among:** Arcelus, J., Mitchell, A. J., Wales, J., & Nielsen, S. R. (2011). Mortality rates in patients with anorexia nervosa and other eating disorders. *Archives of General Psychiatry, 68*(7), 724–31. doi.org/10.1001/archgenpsychiatry.2011.74.

79   **The trend toward thinness:** Nelson, L. D., & Morrison, E. L. (2005). The symptoms of resource scarcity. *Psychological Science, 16*(2), 167–73. doi .org/10.1111/j.0956-7976.2005.00798.x.

79   **Even the size of Playboy:** Pettijohn, T. F., & Jungeberg, B. J. (2004). Playboy Playmate curves: Changes in facial and body feature prefer- ences across social and economic conditions. *Personality and Social Psychology Bulletin, 30*(9), 1186–97. doi.org/10.1177 /0146167204264078.

80   **As Gabi and I researched:** Depilatory advert.jpeg. Wikimedia Com- mons. (n.d.). commons.wikimedia.org/wiki/File:Depilatory_advert.jpeg.

80   **As hemlines got shorter:** Tschachler, H., Devine, M., & Draxlbauer, M. (Eds.). (2003). *The embodyment of American culture.* LIT.

81   **Sixty-two percent of all women:** Rowen, T. S., Gaither, T. W., Awad, M. A., Osterberg, E. C., Shindel, A., & Breyer, B. N. (2016). Pubic hair grooming prevalence and motivation among women in the United States. *JAMA Dermatology, 152*(10), 1106. doi.org/10.1001 /jamadermatol.2016.2154.

81   **Some researchers believe:** Desruelles, F., Cunningham, S. A., & Dubois, D. (2013). Pubic hair removal: A risk factor for "minor" STI such as molluscum contagiosum? *Sexually Transmitted Infections, 89*(3), 216. doi.org/10.1136/sextrans-2012-050982.

82   **Doctors suggest leaving:** Marturana Winderl, A. (2016, July 22). 6 reasons your gyno wishes you'd leave your pubic hair the f alone. *Self.* www.self.com/story/6-reasons-your-gyno-wishes-youd-leave-your -pubic-hair-the-f-alone.

82   **Cosmetic vaginal surgery increased:** Viscione, C. (2020, Aug. 3). Nips, tucks, and . . . designer vaginas? Hype or help? National Center for Health Research. www.center4research.org/nips-tucks-designer-vaginas/.

82   **A huge spike among teens:** Breast and labial surgery in adolescents. American College of Obstetricians and Gynecologists. www.acog.org/clinical/clinical-guidance/committee-opinion/articles/2017/01/breast-and-labial-surgery-in-adolescents.

86   **Research suggests such "self-objectification":** TEDxYouth. (2013, Jan. 21). *The sexy lie: Caroline Heldman at TEDxYouth@SanDiego* [Video]. YouTube. www.youtube.com/watch?v=kMS4VJKekW8.

86   **Girls who self-objectify:** Tiggemann, M., & Slater, A. (2015). The role of self-objectification in the mental health of early adolescent girls: Predictors and consequences. *Journal of Pediatric Psychology, 40*(7), 704–11. doi.org/10.1093/jpepsy/jsv021; Tiggemann, M. (2011). Mental health risks of self-objectification: A review of the empirical evidence for disordered eating, depressed mood, and sexual dysfunction. In R. M. Calogero, S. Tantleff-Dunn, & J. K. Thompson (Eds.), *Self-objectification in women: Causes, consequences, and counteractions* (pp. 139–159). American Psychological Association.

86   **Before looks and femininity:** Kay, K., & Shipman, C. (2018). *The confidence code for girls.* HarperCollins.

87   **Research shows self-objectification:** Szymanski, D. M., Moffitt, L. B., & Carr, E. (2010). Sexual objectification of women: Advances to theory and research. *Counseling Psychologist, 39*(1), 6–38. doi.org/10.1177/0011000010378402; Kahalon, R., Shnabel, N., & Becker, J. C. (2018). "Don't bother your pretty little head": Appearance compliments lead to improved mood but impaired cognitive performance. *Psychology of Women Quarterly, 42*(2), 136–50. doi.org/10.1177/0361684318758596.

88   **That was the finding:** Fredrickson, B. L., Roberts, T., Noll, S. M., Quinn, D. M., & Twenge, J. M. (1998). That swimsuit becomes you: Sex differences in self-objectification, restrained eating, and math performance. *Journal of Personality and Social Psychology, 75*(1), 269–84. doi.org/10.1037/0022-3514.75.1.269.

88   **Men's cognitive abilities:** Parisi, C., & Wogan, P. (2006). Compliment topics and gender. *Women and Language, 29*(2), 21. Parisi-Wogan/172cea9aa9ec49405860df6601d2ea7b77a78760.

88   **Every man interviewed:** Halliwell, E., & Dittmar, H. (2003). A qualitative investigation of women's and men's body image concerns and their attitudes toward aging. *Sex Roles, 49,* 675–84.

88   **And in a maddening:** Calogero, R. M. (2013). Objects don't object. *Psychological Science, 24*(3), 312–18. doi.org/10.1177/0956797612452574.

90   **I'm heartened by a recent study:** Karazsia, B. T., Murnen, S. K., & Tylka, T. L. (2017). Is body dissatisfaction changing across time? A cross-temporal meta-analysis. *Psychological Bulletin, 143*(3), 293–320. doi.org/10.1037/bul0000081.

92   **Negative body image:** Salk, R. H., & Engeln-Maddox, R. (2012). Fat talk among college women is both contagious and harmful. *Sex Roles, 66,* 636–45. doi.org/10.1007/s11199-011-0050-1; Stice, E., Maxfield, J., & Wells, T. T. (2003). Adverse effects of social pressure to be thin on young women: An experimental investigation of the effects of "fat talk." *International Journal of Eating Disorders, 34*(1), 108–17. doi.org/10.1002/eat.10171.

92   **It's also true that:** Hahn-Smith, A. M., & Smith, J. E. (2001). The positive influence of maternal identification on body image, eating attitudes, and self-esteem of Hispanic and Anglo girls. *International Journal of Eating Disorders, 29*(4), 429–40. doi.org/10.1002/eat.1039.

92   **Active engagement around the topic:** Arroyo, A., Southard, B.A.S., & Martz, D. M. (2022). Feminist embodiment, body talk, and body image among mothers and daughters. *Body Image, 41,* 354–66. doi.org/10.1016/j.bodyim.2022.04.005.

92   **The best-known environmental:** Culbert, K. M., Racine, S. E., & Klump, K. L. (2015). Research review: What we have learned about the causes of eating disorders—a synthesis of sociocultural, psychological, and biological research. *Journal of Child Psychology and Psychiatry, 56*(11), 1141–64. doi.org/10.1111/jcpp.12441.

93   **Weight is the most common:** Puhl, R. M., Latner, J. D., O'Brien, K., Luedicke, J., Forhan, M., & Daníelsdóttir, S. (2015). Cross-national perspectives about weight-based bullying in youth: Nature, extent, and remedies. *Pediatric Obesity, 11*(4), 241–50. doi.org/10.1111/ijpo.12051.

94   **A large-scale study:** Hunger, J. M., & Tomiyama, A. J. (2018). Weight labeling and disordered eating among adolescent girls: Longitudinal evidence from the National Heart, Lung, and Blood Institute Growth and Health Study. *Journal of Adolescent Health, 63*(3), 360–62. doi.org/10.1016/j.jadohealth.2017.12.016.

94   **Indeed, research shows it:** Augustus-Horvath, C. L., & Tylka, T. L. (2011). The acceptance model of intuitive eating: A comparison of women in emerging adulthood, early adulthood, and middle adulthood. *Journal of Counseling Psychology, 58*(1), 110–25. doi.org/10.1037/a0022129.

94   **Researchers have identified:** Belluz, J. (2022, Nov. 22). Opinion | Scientists don't agree on what causes obesity, but they know what doesn't. *New York Times.* www.nytimes.com/2022/11/21/opinion/obesity-cause.html.

95   **We've all heard that fat:** Tomiyama, A. J., Carr, D., Granberg, E. M., Major, B., Robinson, E., Sutin, A. R., & Brewis, A. (2018). How and why weight stigma drives the obesity "epidemic" and harms health. *BMC Medicine, 16*(1). doi.org/10.1186/s12916-018-1116-5.

95   **Similarly, research repeatedly tells us:** Pietiläinen, K. H., Saarni, S., Kaprio, J., & Rissanen, A. (2011). Does dieting make you fat? A twin study. *International Journal of Obesity, 36*(3), 456–64. doi.org/10.1038/ijo.2011.160; Lissner, L., Odell, P. M., D'Agostino, R. B., Stokes, J., Kreger, B. E., Belanger, A. J., & Brownell, K. D. (1991). Variability of body weight and health outcomes in the Framingham population. *New England Journal of Medicine, 324*(26), 1839–44. doi.org/10.1056/nejm199106273242602; Neumark-Sztainer, D., Wall, M. M., Guo, J., Story, M., Haines, J., & Eisenberg, M. E. (2006). Obesity, disordered eating, and eating disorders in a longitudinal study of adolescents: How do dieters fare 5 years later? *Journal of the American Dietetic Association, 106*(4), 559–68. doi.org/10.1016/j.jada.2006.01.003.

95   **A recent review of hundreds:** Gaesser, G. A., & Angadi, S. S. (2021). Obesity treatment: Weight loss versus increasing fitness and physical activity for reducing health risks. *iScience, 24*(10), 102995. doi.org/10.1016/j.isci.2021.102995.

95   **It's not inherently unhealthy:** Tylka, T. L., Annunziato, R. A., Burgard, D., Daníelsdóttir, S., Shuman, E., Davis, C., & Calogero, R. M. (2014). The weight-inclusive versus weight-normative approach to health: Evaluating the evidence for prioritizing well-being over weight loss. *Journal of Obesity,* 1–18. doi.org/10.1155/2014/983495.

95   **If we're going to help:** Ulian, M. D., Aburad, L., Oliveira, M. S., Poppe, A., Sabatini, F., Perez, I., Gualano, B., Benatti, F. B., Pinto, A. J., Roble, O. J., Vessoni, A., De Morais Sato, P., Unsain, R. F., & Scagliusi, F. B. (2018). Effects of health at every size® interventions on health-related outcomes of people with overweight and obesity: A systematic review. *Obesity Reviews, 19*(12), 1659–66. doi.org/10.1111/obr.12749.

96   **Some core elements:** Tribole, E., & Resch, E. (2019, Dec. 19). *10 principles of intuitive eating.* IntuitiveEating.org. www.intuitiveeating.org/10-principles-of-intuitive-eating/.

97   **The body politics literature:** Craig, M. L. (2006). Race, beauty, and the tangled knot of a guilty pleasure. *Feminist Theory, 7*(2), 159–77. doi.org/10.1177/1464700106064414.

97   **While this has largely:** Cheng, Z. H., Perko, V. L., Fuller-Marashi, L., Gau, J. M., & Stice, E. (2019). Ethnic differences in eating disorder prevalence, risk factors, and predictive effects of risk factors among young women. *Eating Behaviors, 32,* 23–30. doi.org/10.1016/j.eatbeh.2018.11.004.

97   **Furthermore, when thickness is idealized:** Hughes, E. (2020). "I'm supposed to be thick": Managing body image anxieties among Black American women. *Journal of Black Studies, 52*(3), 310–30. doi.org/10.1177/0021934720972440.

Chapter 5: Plugged In

100   **As it happens, I had:** Framke, C. (2015, Feb. 4). On *MasterChef Junior,* innate biases are hard to beat. *Atlantic.* www.theatlantic.com/entertainment/archive/2015/02/masterchef-junior/385079/.

101   **There's little doubt that TV:** Martins, N., & Harrison, K. (2011). Racial and gender differences in the relationship between children's television use and self-esteem. *Communication Research, 39*(3), 338–57. doi.org /10.1177/0093650211401376.

102   **A Common Sense Media:** Ward, L. M., & Aubrey, J. S. (2017). *Watching gender: How stereotypes in movies and on TV impact kids' development.* Common Sense.

102   **Another study showed:** Halim, M. L., Ruble, D. N., & Tamis-LeMonda, C. S. (2012). Four-year-olds' beliefs about how others regard males and females. *British Journal of Developmental Psychology, 31*(1), 128–35. doi .org/10.1111/j.2044-835x.2012.02084.x.

102   **Fortunately, research finds that co-viewing:** American Psychological Association, Task Force on the Sexualization of Girls. (2007). *Report of the APA Task Force on the Sexualization of Girls.* www.apa.org/pi/women /programs/girls/report-full.pdf.

102   **But before we get:** Wood, J. T. (1994). *Gendered lives: Communication, gender, and culture.* Wadsworth.

102   **With recent progress:** Lemish, D., & Johnson, C. R. (2019). *The landscape of children's television in the US and Canada.* Center for Scholars & Storytellers.

102   **And as Geena Davis:** Ward & Aubrey. *Watching gender.*

102   **One twenty-year-long study:** *Visualizing the data: Women's representation in society.* (2020, Feb. 20). UN Women. www.unwomen.org/en /digital-library/multimedia/2020/2/infographic-visualizing-the-data -womens-representation.

102   **The popular hashtag:** Morgenroth, T., Ryan, M. K., & Peters, K. (2015). The motivational theory of role modeling: How role models influence role aspirants' goals. *Review of General Psychology, 19*(4), 465–83. doi .org/10.1037/gpr0000059.

103   **In 2022, the videos:** Varner, A. (2022, Sept. 12). *Representation matters, beautiful Black girls reaction to the Little Mermaid trailer* [Video]. YouTube. www.youtube.com/watch?v=Qp4yfmOOv6Q.

103 **Only 2 percent of characters:** Heldman et al. *See Jane 2020 TV report;* U.S. Census Bureau. (2022, Dec. 20). National Poverty in America Awareness Month: January 2023. Census.gov. www.census.gov/newsroom /stories/poverty-awareness-month.html; *Disability impacts all of us.* (2023, May 15). Centers for Disease Control and Prevention. www.cdc .gov/ncbddd/disabilityandhealth/infographic-disability-impacts-all.html.

103 **And there's reason to believe:** Bond, B. J. (2016). Fairy godmothers > robots: The influence of televised gender stereotypes and counter-stereotypes on girls' perceptions of STEM. *Bulletin of Science, Technology, and Society, 36*(2), 91–97. doi.org/10.1177/0270467616655951.

104 **Girls in children's television:** Lemish & Johnson. *Landscape of children's television in the US and Canada;* Heldman et al. *See Jane 2020 TV report.*

104 **In a damning report:** American Psychological Association, Task Force on the Sexualization of Girls. *Report of the APA Task Force on the Sexualization of Girls.*

104 **This is important because:** Ward, L. M., & Grower, P. (2020). Media and the development of gender role stereotypes. *Annual Review of Developmental Psychology, 2*(1), 177–99. doi.org/10.1146/annurev -devpsych-051120-010630.

104 **Teens who think reality TV:** Behm-Morawitz, E., Lewallen, J., & Miller, B. (2016). Real mean girls? Reality television viewing, social aggression, and gender-related beliefs among female emerging adults. *Psychology of Popular Media Culture, 5*(4), 340–55.

104 **Worse, screen use predicts:** Galdi, S., & Guizzo, F. (2020). Media-induced sexual harassment: The routes from sexually objectifying media to sexual harassment. *Sex Roles, 84,* 645–69. doi.org/10.1007/s11199 -020-01196-0; Manganello, J. A. (2008). Teens, dating violence, and media use. *Trauma, Violence, and Abuse, 9*(1), 3–18. doi.org/10.1177 /1524838007309804.

104 **Girls who internalize these sexist messages:** Impett, E. A., Schooler, D., & Tolman, D. L. (2006). To be seen and not heard: Feminist ideology and adolescent girls' sexual health. *Archives of Sexual Behavior, 35*(2), 131–44. doi:10.1007/s10508-005-9016-0.

105 **unfortunate depictions of girls:** Ward, L. M. (2004). Wading through the stereotypes: Positive and negative associations between media use and Black adolescents' conceptions of self. *Developmental Psychology, 40*(2), 284–94. doi.org/10.1037/0012-1649.40.2.284.

105 **Research shows that when adults:** Nathanson, A. I., Wilson, B. J., McGee, J. S., & Sebastian, M. (2002). Counteracting the effects of female stereotypes on television via active mediation. *Journal of Communication, 52*(4), 922–37. doi.org/10.1111/j.1460-2466.2002.tb02581.x.

106 **After an episode of the sitcom:** Collins, R. L., Elliott, M. N., Berry, S. H., Kanouse, D. E., & Hunter, S. B. (2003). Entertainment television as a healthy sex educator: The impact of condom-efficacy information in an episode of *Friends. Pediatrics, 112*(5), 1115–21. doi.org/10.1542/peds.112.5.1115.

106 **Our kids see anywhere:** How many ads do we see a day? 17 insightful stats from 2023. (2023, March 6). WebTribunal. webtribunal.net/blog/how-many-ads-do-we-see-a-day.

107 **Knowing heterosexual male desire:** Tzoutzou, M., Bathrellou, E., & Matalas, A. (2021). Cartoon characters in children's series: Gender disparities in body weight and food consumption. *Sexes, 2*(1), 79–87. doi.org/10.3390/sexes2010007; Kim, S. (2016, Jan. 10). The subtle sexism in movie ratings. *ATTN.* archive.attn.com/stories/4978/sexist-movie-ratings.

108 **By the time the CDC report:** Centers for Disease Control and Prevention. (2023). *The youth risk behavior survey data summary and trends report: 2011–2021.* www.cdc.gov/healthyyouth/data/yrbs/pdf/YRBS_Data-Summary-Trends_Report2023_508.pdf.

108 **As the NYU professor:** Haidt, J. (2023, Feb. 22). Social media is a major cause of the mental illness epidemic in teen girls. Here's the evidence. *After Babel.* jonathanhaidt.substack.com/p/social-media-mental-illness-epidemic.

108 **Boys can have a hard time:** Centers for Disease Control and Prevention. *Youth risk behavior survey data summary and trends report: 2011–2021.*

109   Research shows it's much harder: Papageorgiou, A., Fisher, C., & Cross, D. (2022). "Why don't I look like her?": How adolescent girls view social media and its connection to body image. *BMC Women's Health, 22*(1). doi.org/10.1186/s12905-022-01845-4.

109   Seeing social media posts: Jiang, S., & Ngien, A. (2020). The effects of Instagram use, social comparison, and self-esteem on social anxiety: A survey study in Singapore. *Social Media and Society, 6*(2). doi.org/10 .1177/2056305120912488.

109   Not surprisingly, girls: Kelly, Y., Zilanawala, A., Booker, C. L., & Sacker, A. (2018). Social media use and adolescent mental health: Findings from the UK Millennium Cohort Study. *EClinicalMedicine, 6*, 59–68. doi.org/10.1016/j.eclinm.2018.12.005.

109   Even beyond the greater: Nesi, J., & Prinstein, M. J. (2015). Using social media for social comparison and feedback-seeking: Gender and popularity moderate associations with depressive symptoms. *Journal of Abnormal Child Psychology, 43*(8), 1427–38. doi:10.1007/s10802-015-0020-0.

110   As the psychologist Jean Twenge: Twenge, J. M. (2023, June 8). Yes, we do know social media isn't safe for kids. *Generation Tech.* jeanmtwenge. substack.com/p/yes-we-do-know-social-media-isnt; Riehm, K. E., Feder, K. A., Tormohlen, K. N., Crum, R. M., Young, A., Green, K. M., Pacek, L. R., La Flair, L. N., & Mojtabai, R. (2019). Associations between time spent using social media and internalizing and externalizing problems among US youth. *JAMA Psychiatry, 76*(12), 1266. doi.org/10 .1001/jamapsychiatry.2019.2325.

110   But rather than hyper-monitoring: Heitner, D. (2023). *Growing up in public: Coming of age in a digital world.* TarcherPerigee.

112   @Sophthickfitnesss, whose profile reads: Sophie. [@Sophthickfitnesss] (n.d.). Instagram. Retrieved Aug. 8, 2023, from www.instagram.com /sophthickfitnesss/.

113   Nearly half of U.S. teens: Vogels, E. A. (2022, Dec. 15). Teens and cyberbullying. Pew Research Center: Internet, Science & Tech. www .pewresearch.org/internet/2022/12/15/teens-and-cyberbullying-2022/.

113   **Boys who are harassed:** Hill, G., & Kearl, H. (2011). Crossing the line: Sexual harassment at school. American Association of University Women. www.aauw.org/research/crossing-the-line/.

115   **A 2020 survey asked:** Thorn. (2021). Self-generated child sexual abuse material: Youth attitudes and experiences in 2020. info.thorn.org /hubfs/Research/SGCSAM_Attitudes&Experiences_YouthMonitoring _FullReport_2021.pdf.

117   **A study called "Damned":** Lippman, J. R., & Campbell, S. W. (2014). Damned if you do, damned if you don't . . . if you're a girl: Relational and normative contexts of adolescent sexting in the United States. *Journal of Children and Media, 8*(4), 371–86. doi.org/10.1080/17482798 .2014.923009.

119   **And kids who aren't coerced:** Temple, J. R., Strasburger, V. C., Zimmerman, H., & Madigan, S. (2019). Sexting in youth: Cause for concern? *Lancet Child & Adolescent Health, 3*(8), 520–21. doi.org/10.1016 /s2352-4642(19)30199-3.

119   **There is such a thing:** *Weinstein, E., & James, C. (2022). Behind their screens: What teens are facing (and adults are missing). MIT Press.*

Chapter 6: From Unentitled to Healthy Entitlement

124   **Adolescence is, as the Bill:** Bill & Melinda Gates Foundation. (2019). *The goalkeepers report 2019. Examining inequality: How geography and gender stack the deck for (or against) you.* www.gatesfoundation.org /goalkeepers/report/2019-report//#ExaminingInequality.

124   **In a study of four:** Arnold, S. H., & McAuliffe, K. (2021). Children show a gender gap in negotiation. *Psychological Science, 32*(2), 153–58. doi.org/10.1177/0956797620965544.

124   **It's a fact:** *"Do you speak American?" What speech do we like best?* PBS. (n.d.). www.pbs.org/speak/speech/prejudice/women/.

124   **A study at George Washington:** Hancock, A. B., & Rubin, B. A. (2014). Influence of communication partner's gender on language. *Journal of*

Language and Social Psychology, 34(1), 46–64. doi.org/10.1177 /0261927x14533197.

125   **Decades of research find:** How often are women interrupted by men? Here's what the research says. (2017, July 7). Advisory Board. www .advisory.com/daily-briefing/2017/07/07/men-interrupting-women; Snyder, K. (2014, July 23). How to get ahead as a woman in tech: Interrupt men. *Slate.* slate.com/human-interest/2014/07/study-men -interrupt-women-more-in-tech-workplaces-but-high-ranking-women -learn-to-interrupt.html.

125   **Men are actually the more talkative:** Cutler, A., & Scott, D. (1990). Speaker sex and perceived apportionment of talk. *Applied Psycholinguistics, 11*(3), 253–72. doi.org/10.1017/s0142716400008882.

125   **Even female Supreme Court:** Jacobi, T., & Schweers, D. (2021). How men continue to interrupt even the most powerful women. *Aeon.* aeon .co/ideas/how-men-continue-to-interrupt-even-the-most-powerful -women.

125   **In schools, boys are:** Sadker, M., & Sadker, D. (1994). *Failing at fairness: How America's schools cheat girls.* Scribner.

125   **Nearly 50 percent of girls:** Hull, S. (2020). *Stronger, smarter, bolder: Girls take the lead.* Girls Inc.

125   **When you add race and class:** Fine, M., & Weiss, L. *Silenced voices and extraordinary conversations: Re-imagining schools.* (2003). Teachers College Press.

125   **The term for that:** Editors of Merriam-Webster. (2022). Mansplaining. In *Merriam-Webster.* www.merriam-webster.com/wordplay/ mansplaining-definition-history.

126   **First, decades of research:** Bales, R. F., Strodtbeck, F. L., Mills, T. M., & Roseborough, M. E. (1951). Channels of communication in small groups. *American Sociological Review, 16*(4), 461. doi.org/10.2307 /2088276.

126 **Second, experiencing sexual harassment:** McLaughlin, H., Uggen, C., & Blackstone, A. (2017). The economic and career effects of sexual harassment on working women. *Gender and Society, 31*(3), 333–58. doi .org/10.1177/0891243217704631.

127 **Instead, it fits with research:** *Women face backlash for speaking up at work.* (2015, Jan. 20). Association for Psychological Science. www .psychologicalscience.org/news/minds-business/women-face-backlash -for-speaking-up-at-work.html.

129 **Equivocating—considered more feminine:** Grant, A. (2023, Aug. 5). Opinion | How women's "weak language" is a source of strength. *New York Times.* www.nytimes.com/2023/07/31/opinion/women-language -work.html.

129 **And in the end:** Cameron, D. (2015, July 27). An open letter to Naomi Wolf: Let women speak how they please. *In These Times.* inthesetimes .com/article/naomi-wolf-speech-uptalk-vocal-fry.

129 **It's unclear, though, whether:** Tannen, D. (2019, Oct. 15). The power of talk: Who gets heard and why. *Harvard Business Review.* hbr.org/1995 /09/the-power-of-talk-who-gets-heard-and-why.

130 **Soraya Chemaly, an author:** Chemaly, S. (2014, Aug. 30). 10 words every girl should learn. *HuffPost.* www.huffpost.com/entry/10-words -every-girl-should-learn_b_5544203.

132 **Instead, our brains and hormones:** Gordon, I., Zagoory-Sharon, O., Leckman, J. F., & Feldman, R. (2010). Oxytocin and the development of parenting in humans. *Biological Psychiatry, 68*(4), 377–82. doi.org /10.1016/j.biopsych.2010.02.005.

137 **As Brené Brown writes:** Brown, B. (2015). *Daring greatly: How the courage to be vulnerable transforms the way we live, love, parent, and lead.* Avery.

139 **Mounting scientific evidence:** Harvard Health. (2017, Oct. 9). *Women and pain: Disparities in experience and treatment.* www.health.harvard .edu/blog/women-and-pain-disparities-in-experience-and-treatment -2017100912562.

139 **Their pain often has:** Adachi, T., Yamada, K., Fujino, H., Enomoto, K., & Shibata, M. (2021). Associations between anger and chronic primary pain: A systematic review and meta-analysis. *Scandinavian Journal of Pain, 22*(1), 1–13. doi.org/10.1515/sjpain-2021-0154.

139 **The girl guru Rachel Simmons:** Simmons, R. (2010). *The curse of the good girl: Raising authentic girls with courage and confidence.* Penguin Books.

140 **Lisa Damour calls it:** Damour, L. (2023). *The emotional lives of teenagers: Raising connected, capable, and compassionate adolescents.* Ballantine.

140 **One study found more than half:** Ackard, D. M., Neumark-Sztainer, D., Story, M., & Perry, C. L. (2006). Parent-child connectedness and behavioral and emotional health among adolescents. *American Journal of Preventive Medicine, 30*(1), 59–66. doi.org/10.1016/j.amepre.2005.09.013.

142 **When women don't negotiate:** Leech, M. (2022, July 28). The million-dollar mistake: Women fall short when negotiating salaries. *Business Journals.* www.bizjournals.com/bizwomen/news/profiles-strategies/2022/07/the-million-dollar-mistake-women-fall-short-on.html.

143 **When incoming college students:** Heatherington, L., Daubman, K. A., Bates, C. H., Ahn, A., Brown, H., & Preston, C. (1993). Two investigations of "female modesty" in achievement situations. *Sex Roles, 29,* 739–54. doi.org/10.1007/bf00289215.

143 **The tendency for men:** Furnham, A., Hosoe, T., & Tang, T. L. (2001). Male hubris and female humility? A crosscultural study of ratings of self, parental, and sibling multiple intelligence in America, Britain, and Japan. *Intelligence, 30*(1), 101–15. doi.org/10.1016/s0160-2896(01)00080-0.

143 **It's hard to imagine a man:** Epstein, J. (2020, Dec. 11). Is there a doctor in the White House? Not if you need an M.D. *Wall Street Journal.* www.wsj.com/articles/is-there-a-doctor-in-the-white-house-not-if-you-need-an-m-d-11607727380.

144 **The annual T. Rowe Price:** T. Rowe Price Insights. (2014, Aug. 18). *Boys and girls not equally prepared for financial future.* Sixth Annual Parents,

Kids & Money Survey. www.troweprice.com/corporate/us/en/press
/t--rowe-price--boys-and-girls-not-equally-prepared-for-financial.html.

144   **They also pay boys:** Aleksandra. (2018, June 29). Gender pay gap starts
with kids in America. BusyKid. busykid.com/blog/gender-pay-gap
-starts-with-kids-in-america/.

144   **The World Economic Forum:** *Global gender gap report 2020.* (2021,
April 23). World Economic Forum. www.weforum.org/reports/gender
-gap-2020-report-100-years-pay-equality/.

144   **Being more cautious financially:** Osborne, H. (2019, April 8). Why
women need to stop saving their cash—and start investing. *Guardian.*
www.theguardian.com/lifeandstyle/2019/apr/08/why-women-need-to
-stop-saving-their-cash-and-start-investing.

144   **Even so, a 2021:** Fidelity Investments. (2021). *Fidelity's 2021 women and
investing study.* www.fidelity.com/bin-public/060_www_fidelity_com
/documents/about-fidelity/FidelityInvestmentsWomen&Investing
Study2021.pdf.

145   **Pro tip: investing in:** Fatemi, F. (2019, March 29). The value of
investing in female founders. *Forbes.* www.forbes.com/sites/falonfatemi
/2019/03/29/the-value-of-investing-in-female-founders/?sh
=57d7ce055ee4.

145   **For a more typical learning:** *Free finance programs for high school girls.*
(n.d.). Invest in Girls. www.investingirls.org/for-students/.

145   **A large and growing body:** Cingano, F. (2014). Trends in income
inequality and its impact on economic growth. *OECD Social, Employ-
ment, and Migration Working Papers,* No. 163. OECD Publishing, Paris.
doi.org/10.1787/5jxrjncwxv6j-en.

Chapter 7: Discovering All Geniuses Born Girls

146   **By the age of fourteen:** Do you know the factors influencing girls'
participation in sports? (2019, Oct. 11). Women's Sports Foundation.

www.womenssportsfoundation.org/do-you-know-the-factors-influencing
-girls-participation-in-sports/.

147   **The answer to why:** The Style O.G. (2021, Feb. 4). *8 reasons women want men with money and why they should* [Video]. YouTube. www .youtube.com/watch?v=rVRakUX9Sq0.

148   **Parents are two and a half times:** Stephens-Davidowitz, S. (2014, Jan. 19). Opinion | Google, tell me. Is my son a genius? *New York Times.* www.nytimes.com/2014/01/19/opinion/sunday/google-tell-me-is-my -son-a-genius.html.

148   **Still, across the globe:** Furnham, A., & Gasson, L. (1998). Sex differences in parental estimates of their children's intelligence. *Sex Roles, 38,* 151–62. doi.org/10.1023/a:1018772830511.

148   **One in three girls:** Hinkelman, L. (2017). *The Girls' Index: New insights into the complex world of today's girls.* Ruling Our eXperiences Inc. bit .ly/TheGirlsIndexReport.

148   **This has long-term implications:** Jacobs, J. E., Chhin, C. S., & Bleeker, M. (2006). Enduring links: Parents' expectations and their young adult children's gender-typed occupational choices. *Educational Research and Evaluation, 12*(4), 395–407. doi.org/10.1080/13803610600765851.

148   **That changes by age six:** Bian, L., Leslie, S., & Cimpian, A. (2017). Gender stereotypes about intellectual ability emerge early and influence children's interests. *Science, 355*(6323), 389–91. doi.org/10.1126/science.aah6524.

148   **As kids grow up:** Meyer, M., Cimpian, A., & Leslie, S. (2015). Women are underrepresented in fields where success is believed to require brilliance. *Frontiers in Psychology, 6.* doi.org/10.3389/fpsyg.2015.00235.

149   **A Google search for:** TheTopTens. (n.d.). *Top 10 smartest TV characters.* www.thetoptens.com/television/smartest-tv-characters/.

149   **The same is true:** TheTopTens. (n.d.). *Top 10 greatest geniuses of all time.* www.thetoptens.com/people/geniuses/.

149   **Other women's legacies have:** Shetterly, M. L. (2016). *Hidden figures: The American dream and the untold story of the Black women mathematicians who helped win the space race.* William Morrow.

149   **In one experiment, she divided:** Bigler, R. S. (1995). The role of classification skill in moderating environmental influences on children's gender stereotyping: A study of the functional use of gender in the classroom. *Child Development, 66*(4), 1072. doi.org/10.2307/1131799.

150   **Math achievement for boys:** U.S. Department of Education. Institute of Education Sciences, National Center for Education Statistics, National Assessment of Educational Progress. (2017). NAEP Mathematics & Reading Assessments. www.nationsreportcard.gov/reading_math_2017 _highlights/; 2018 NAEP Technology and Engineering Literacy (TEL) Assessment at Grade 8. nces.ed.gov/pubsearch/pubsinfo.asp?pubid =2019068.

151   **One study, for example:** Lavy, V., & Sand, E. (2015). On the origins of gender human capital gaps: Short and long term consequences of teachers' stereotypical biases. Working paper 20909. National Bureau of Economic Research. doi.org/10.3386/w20909.

151   **Another similar study found:** Copur-Gencturk, Y., Cimpian, J. R., Lubienski, S. T., & Thacker, I. (2019). Teachers' bias against the mathematical ability of female, Black, and Hispanic students. *Educational Researcher, 49*(1), 30–43. doi.org/10.3102/0013189x19890577.

151   **Parents too hold biased views:** Parsons, J. E., Adler, T. F., & Kaczala, C. M. (1982). Socialization of achievement attitudes and beliefs: Parental influences. *Child Development, 53*(2), 310. doi.org/10.2307 /1128973.

151   **Girls themselves express less:** Zander, L., Höhne, E., Harms, S., Pfost, M., & Hornsey, M. J. (2020). When grades are high but self-efficacy is low: Unpacking the confidence gap between girls and boys in mathematics. *Frontiers in Psychology, 11.* doi.org/10.3389/fpsyg.2020.552355.

151   **While this is technically:** Barrett, K. (2018, July 24). When school dress codes discriminate. *NEA Today.* www.nea.org/nea-today/all-news -articles/when-school-dress-codes-discriminate.

152   **Twelve-year-old Ari:** Bruk, D. (2022, Aug. 6). OMG yet another teen was told to "cover up" for wearing an "inappropriate" formal dress!

Seventeen. www.seventeen.com/fashion/a28757/teen-told-to-cover-her
-bare-arms-during-formal-dance/.

152 **Their learning process is:** Krischer, H. (2021, Sept. 4). Is your body
appropriate to wear to school? *New York Times.* www.nytimes.com
/2018/04/17/style/student-bra-nipples-school.html; Winslow, H. (2014,
Sept. 4). Student assigned to wear bright clothes as school's punishment.
WJXT. www.news4jax.com/news/2014/09/04/student-assigned-to-wear
-bright-clothes-as-schools-punishment/.

152 **By the end of:** Leaper, C., & Brown, C. S. (2008). Perceived experiences
with sexism among adolescent girls. *Child Development, 79*(3), 685–704.
doi.org/10.1111/j.1467-8624.2008.01151.x.

152 **Trevor Wilkinson, a gay boy:** Riley, J. (2020). Texas male high school
student gets in-school suspension for wearing nail polish. *Metro Weekly.*
www.metroweekly.com/2020/12/texas-male-high-school-student-gets
-in-school-suspension-for-wearing-nail-polish/.

153 **This is particularly true:** Barrett. When school dress codes discriminate.

153 **Black girls in particular:** National Women's Law Center. (2018). *Dress
coded: Black girls, bodies, and bias in D.C. schools.* Washington, D.C.
nwlc.org/wp-content/uploads/2018/04/5.1web_Final_nwlc_DressCode
Report.pdf.

153 **It becomes a self-fulfilling prophecy:** Reilly, D. (2022, March 15). Men
think they're brighter than they are and women underestimate their IQ.
Why? phys.org. phys.org/news/2022-03-men-theyre-brighter-women
-underestimate.html.

153 **To wit, a nationwide survey:** T. Rowe Price Insights. (2017, Sept. 18).
*Parents of only boys place greater priority on college than parents of only
girls.* Ninth Annual Parents, Kids & Money Survey. www.troweprice
.com/corporate/us/en/press/t--rowe-price--parents-of-only-boys
-place-greater-priority-on-co.html.

154 **It's concerning, then, that:** Carter, A. J., Croft, A., Lukas, D., & Sand-
strom, G. M. (2018). Women's visibility in academic seminars: Women
ask fewer questions than men. *PLOS ONE, 13*(9), e0202743. doi.org
/10.1371/journal.pone.0202743.

155   **Carol Dweck, who coined:** Dweck, C. S. (2006). *Mindset: The new psychology of success.* Random House.

155   **It turns out how we praise:** Gunderson, E. A., Gripshover, S., Romero, C., Dweck, C. S., Goldin-Meadow, S., & Levine, S. C. (2013). Parent praise to 1- to 3-year-olds predicts children's motivational frameworks 5 years later. *Child Development, 84*(5), 1526–41. doi.org/10.1111/cdev .12064.

155   **And here's the important part:** Gunderson, E. A., Sorhagen, N., Gripshover, S., Dweck, C. S., Goldin-Meadow, S., & Levine, S. C. (2018). Parent praise to toddlers predicts fourth grade academic achievement via children's incremental mindsets. *Developmental Psychology, 54*(3), 397–409. doi.org/10.1037/dev0000444.

156   **I wonder what my friend's son:** Zimmerman, J. (2017, Aug. 11). Who's benefiting from affirmative action? White men. *Washington Post.* www .washingtonpost.com/opinions/who-benefits-from-affirmative-action -white-men/2017/08/11/4b56907e-7eab-11e7-a669-b400c5c7e1cc_story .html.

157   **In one famous experiment:** Mondschein, E. R., Adolph, K. E., & Tamis-LeMonda, C. S. (2000). Gender bias in mothers' expectations about infant crawling. *Journal of Experimental Child Psychology, 77*(4), 304–16. doi.org/10.1006/jecp.2000.2597.

159   **The American Psychological Association:** American Psychological Association, Task Force on the Sexualization of Girls. *Report of the APA Task Force on the Sexualization of Girls.*

159   **To boot, gender differences:** Notarnicola, A., Maccagnano, G., Pesce, V., Tafuri, S., Novielli, G., & Moretti, B. (2014). Visual-spatial capacity: Gender and sport differences in young volleyball and tennis athletes and non-athletes. *BMC Research Notes, 7*(1). doi.org/10.1186/1756-0500-7-57.

159   **There are numerous other:** Benefits—why sports participation for girls and women. (2016, Aug. 30). Women's Sports Foundation. www .womenssportsfoundation.org/advocacy/benefits-sports-participation -girls-women/.

159   **They also have significant:** Do you know the factors influencing girls' participation in sports? Women's Sports Foundation.

159   **Indeed, girls are considered:** Norman, L. (2016). Is there a need for coaches to be more gender responsive? A review of the evidence. *International Sport Coaching Journal, 3*(2), 192–96. doi.org/10.1123 /iscj.2016-0032.

159   **They list teasing and taunting:** Slater, A., & Tiggemann, M. (2010). "Uncool to do sport": A focus group study of adolescent girls' reasons for withdrawing from physical activity. *Psychology of Sport and Exercise, 11*(6), 619–26. doi.org/10.1016/j.psychsport.2010.07.006.

159   **Three-fourths of adolescent girls:** Brown, C.S. & Stone, E.A. Gender Stereotypes and Discrimination: How Sexism Impacts Development. In S.S. Horn, M.D. Ruck and L.S. Liben, (Eds) Advances in Child Development and Behavior, Vol. 50, Academic Press, 2016, (pp. 105-133). doi .org/10.1016/bs.acdb.2015.11.001.

159   **A third of parents:** Zarrett, N., Veliz, P. T., & Sabo, D. (2020). Keeping girls in the game: Factors that influence sport participation. Women's Sports Foundation. www.womenssportsfoundation.org/wp-content /uploads/2020/02/Keeping-Girls-in-the-Game-Executive-Summary -FINAL-web.pdf.

160   **Specific sports are coded:** Brown & Stone. Gender stereotypes and discrimination.

160   **While girls notice these:** Few parents and students know about Title IX and the protections it offers. (2022, April 19). Ipsos. www.ipsos.com /en-us/news-polls/few-parents-and-students-know-about-title-ix-and -protections-it-offers.

160   **Interviewed on the *PBS*:** After Title IX, girls still face discrimination in sports. (2022, April 11). [Video]. *PBS NewsHour.* www.pbs.org/newshour /show/decades-after-title-ix-girls-face-tough-battles-on-and-off-the -sports-field.

161   **In her best-selling book:** Wiseman, R. (2016). *Queen bees and wan-nabes: Helping your daughter survive cliques, gossip, boys, and the new realities of girl world.* Harmony.

164   **Fathers spend about three:** Mascaro, J. S., Rentscher, K. E., Hackett, P. D., Mehl, M. R., & Rilling, J. K. (2017). Child gender influences paternal behavior, language, and brain function. *Behavioral Neuroscience, 131*(3), 262–73. doi.org/10.1037/bne0000199.

165   **It turns out not only:** Bettes, K. (2018, Jan. 9). Study finds link between dads who treat daughters like "princesses" and anxiety. *Sydney Morning Herald.* www.smh.com.au/lifestyle/life-and-relationships/study-finds -link-between-dads-who-treat-daughters-like-princesses-and-anxiety -20180109-h0feqb.html; Majdandžić, M., Lazarus, R. S., Oort, F. J., Van Der Sluis, C., Dodd, H. F., Morris, T., De Vente, W., Byrow, Y., Hudson, J. L., & Bögels, S. M. (2017). The structure of challenging parenting behavior and associations with anxiety in Dutch and Australian children. *Journal of Clinical Child and Adolescent Psychology, 47*(2), 282– 95. doi.org/10.1080/15374416.2017.1381915.

165   **When the Women's Sports Foundation:** Zarrett, Veliz, & Sabo. Keeping girls in the game.

166   **While it might be tempting:** Chen, S., Li, X., Jin, Y., & Ren, Z. (2021). To be a sportsman? Sport participation is associated with optimal academic achievement in a nationally representative sample of high school students. *Frontiers in Public Health, 9.* doi.org/10.3389/fpubh .2021.730497.

166   **Research finds there's no:** McKay, M. J., Baldwin, J., Ferreira, P. H., Simic, M., Vanicek, N., & Burns, J. (2016). Normative reference values for strength and flexibility of 1,000 children and adults. *Neurology, 88*(1), 36–43. doi.org/10.1212/wnl.0000000000003466.

167   **After the champion golfer:** Lev, J., & Ronald, I. (2023, Feb. 19). Tiger Woods apologizes after handing Justin Thomas a tampon at the Genesis Invitational. CNN. www.cnn.com/2023/02/17/golf/tiger-woods-justin -thomas-tampon-spt-intl/index.html.

167 **Thanks to Title IX:** *50 years of Title IX. (2022). Women's Sports Foundation.* www.womenssportsfoundation.org/wp-content/uploads/2022/04/FINAL6_WSF-Title-IX-Infographic-2022.pdf.

Chapter 8: The Slippery Slope from Gender Bias and Sexism to Sexual Harassment and Assault

169 **But becoming the target:** McDowell, R., Dunklin R., Schmall, E., & Pritchard, J. (2017, May 1). Hidden horror of school sex assaults revealed by AP. Associated Press. apnews.com/article/sports-only-on-ap-sexual-misconduct-sexual-harassment-1b74feef88df4475b377dcdd6406ebb7.

169 **The stats are grim:** Finkelhor, D., Shattuck, M. A., Turner, H. A., & Hamby, S. L. (2014). The lifetime prevalence of child sexual abuse and sexual assault assessed in late adolescence. *Journal of Child and Adolescent Health, 55,* 329–33; Teen dating violence statistics. (n.d.). Domestic Violence Services Inc. www.dvs-or.org/teen-dating-violence-statistics/; Centers for Disease Control and Prevention. *Youth risk behavior survey data summary and trends report: 2011–2021.*

170 **Unfortunately, in a large:** Undem, T., and Wang, A. (2018). *The state of gender equality for U.S. adolescents.* Plan International USA. planusa-org-staging.s3.amazonaws.com/public/uploads/2021/04/state-of-gender-equality-summary-2018.pdf.

170 **The emotional toll it takes:** Hill & Kearl. Crossing the line.

170 **Longitudinal studies show:** Goldstein, S. E., Malanchuk, O., Davis-Kean, P. E., & Eccles, J. S. (2007). Risk factors of sexual harassment by peers: A longitudinal investigation of African American and European American adolescents. *Journal of Research on Adolescence, 17*(2), 285–300. doi.org/10.1111/j.1532-7795.2007.00523.x; Chiodo, D., Wolfe, D. A., Crooks, C. V., Hughes, R., & Jaffe, P. G. (2009). Impact of sexual harassment victimization by peers on subsequent adolescent victimization and adjustment: A longitudinal study. *Journal of Adolescent Health, 45*(3), 246–52. doi.org/10.1016/j.jadohealth.2009.01.006.

171   **We can view this:** Hammack, S. E., Cooper, M. A., & Lezak, K. R. (2012). Overlapping neurobiology of learned helplessness and conditioned defeat: Implications for PTSD and mood disorders. *Neuropharmacology, 62*(2), 565–75. doi.org/10.1016/j.neuropharm.2011.02.024.

174   **In the United States, a sexual assault:** National Crime Victimization Survey 2019. (2020). Bureau of Justice Statistics. Department of Justice. Retrieved from www.rainn.org/statistics/scope-problem.

174   **Every nine minutes, that victim:** *Child maltreatment 2016.* (2018). U.S. Department of Health and Human Services, Administration for Children and Families. Children's Bureau. Retrieved from www.rainn .org/statistics/children-and-teens.

174   **One in seven girls:** Townsend, C., & Rheingold, A. A. (2013). *Estimating a child sexual abuse prevalence rate for practitioners: A review of child sexual abuse prevalence studies.* Darkness to Light. www.d2l.org/wp -content/uploads/2017/02/PREVALENCE-RATE-WHITE-PAPER-D2L .pdf; James, S. E., Herman, J. L., Rankin, S., Keisling, M., Mottet, L., & Anafi, M. (2016). *The report of the 2015 U.S. Transgender Survey.* National Center for Transgender Equality. www.transequality.org/sites /default/files/docs/USTS-Full-Report-FINAL.PDF.

174   **Survivors of sexual assault:** Dworkin, E. R., Jaffe, A. E., Bedard-Gilligan, M., & Fitzpatrick, S. (2021). PTSD in the year following sexual assault: A meta-analysis of prospective studies. *Trauma, Violence, and Abuse, 24*(2), 497–514. doi.org/10.1177/15248380211032213; National Center for PTSD. (n.d.). *PTSD.* U.S. Department of Veterans Affairs. www.ptsd.va.gov/understand/common/common_veterans.asp.

174   **Only 2 to 10 percent:** Lisak, D., Gardinier, L., Nicksa, S. C., & Cote, A. M. (2010). False allegations of sexual assault: An analysis of ten years of reported cases. *Violence Against Women, 16*(12), 1318–34. doi .org/10.1177/1077801210387747; NPR. (2018, Oct. 31). Poll reveals divided understanding of #MeToo. www.npr.org/about-npr/662519588 /poll-reveals-divided-understanding-of-metoo.

174   **As Rebecca Solnit describes:** Solnit, R. (2020). *Recollections of my nonexistence.* Viking.

178   **The comedian and writer Kate Willett:** Altman, D. (2017). Comedian's viral post breaks down the difference between harassment and flirting. WorldWideInterweb. worldwideinterweb.com/comedian-kate-willett -difference-flirting-sexual-harassment/.

185   **A large-scale Harvard study:** Weissbourd. *Talk.*

187   **Here's a parenting tip:** Doepner, A. [@AnneDoepner]. (2019, Sept. 27). Twitter. twitter.com/AnneDoepner/status/1177616690068090880.

Chapter 9: Deconstructing the World of Girls' Sexuality

197   **Maybe they did what:** Hirsch, J. S., Khan, S., Wamboldt, A., & Mellins, C. A. (2019). Social dimensions of sexual consent among cisgender heterosexual college students: Insights from ethnographic research. *Journal of Adolescent Health, 64*(1), 26–35. doi.org/10.1016/j.jadohealth .2018.06.011.

198   **The data tell us:** Thompson, A. E., & O'Sullivan, L. F. (2012). Gender differences in associations of sexual and romantic stimuli: Do young men really prefer sex over romance? *Archives of Sexual Behavior, 41,* 949–57. doi.org/10.1007/s10508-011-9794-5.

199   **Often, girls end up:** Halpern-Felsher, B. L. (2007). Adolescents' reported consequences of having oral sex versus vaginal sex. *Pediatrics, 119*(2), 229–36.

200   **Sex toys, often designed:** 7 actual love laws in the US that are so unbelievable yet real. (2021, July 14). Halt.org. www.halt.org/love-laws -in-the-us-that-are-so-unbelievable-yet-real/.

200   **Women might be less:** Conley, T. D., & Klein, V. (2022). Women get worse sex: A confound in the explanation of gender differences in sexuality. *Perspectives on Psychological Science, 17*(4), 960–78. doi.org /10.1177/17456916211041598.

201 **Consider that, at every age:** Laumann, E., Michael, R. T., & Kolata, G. (1995). *Sex in America.* Grand Central.

201 **The truth is:** McClelland, S. I. (2010). Intimate justice: A critical analysis of sexual satisfaction. *Social and Personality Psychology Compass, 4*(9), 663–80. doi.org/10.1111/j.1751-9004.2010.00293.x.

201 **I was introduced to:** Orenstein. *Girls and sex.*

201 **If "good sex" means:** Kaestle, C. E. (2009). Sexual insistence and disliked sexual activities in young adulthood: Differences by gender and relationship characteristics. *Perspectives on Sexual and Reproductive Health, 41*(1), 33–39. doi.org/10.1363/4103309.

202 **Still, "virgin" is a slur:** Centers for Disease Control and Prevention. (2020). *National survey of family growth, 2015–2019.* www.cdc.gov/nchs/nsfg/key_statistics/s.htm#sexualactivity.

202 **In a piece for *The Cut*:** Traister, R. (2015, Oct. 20). Why sex that's consensual can still be bad. And why we're not talking about it. *Cut.* www.thecut.com/2015/10/why-consensual-sex-can-still-be-bad.html.

202 **A study by Common Sense Media:** Robb, M. B., & Mann, S. (2023). *Teens and pornography.* Common Sense. www.commonsensemedia.org/sites/default/files/research/report/2022-teens-and-pornography-final-web.pdf.

203 **Indeed, studies show teens:** Häggström-Nordin, E., Hanson, U., & Tydén, T. (2005). Associations between pornography consumption and sexual practices among adolescents in Sweden. *International Journal of STD and AIDS, 16*(2), 102–7. doi.org/10.1258/0956462053057512.

203 **The more porn boys:** Herbenick, D., Fu, T., Wright, P. J., Paul, B., Gradus, R., Bauer, J., & Jones, R. (2020). Diverse sexual behaviors and pornography use: Findings from a nationally representative probability survey of Americans aged 18 to 60 years. *Journal of Sexual Medicine, 17*(4), 623–33. doi.org/10.1016/j.jsxm.2020.01.013; Ybarra, M. L., Mitchell, K. J., Hamburger, M. E., Diener-West, M., & Leaf, P. J. (2010). X-rated material and perpetration of sexually aggressive behavior among children and adolescents: Is there a link? *Aggressive Behavior, 37*(1), 1–18. doi.org/10.1002/ab.20367.

203   **And erotic asphyxiation:** Herbenick, D., Guerra-Reyes, L., Patterson, C., Gonzalez, Y. R. R., Wagner, C. S., & Zounlome, N. O. O. (2021). "It was scary, but then it was kind of exciting": Young women's experiences with choking during sex. *Archives of Sexual Behavior, 51*(2), 1103–23. doi.org/10.1007/s10508-021-02049-x.

203   **Research that followed adolescents:** Brown, J. D., & L'Engle, K. L. (2009). X-rated: Sexual attitudes and behaviors associated with U.S. early adolescents' exposure to sexually explicit media. *Communication Research, 36*(1), 129–51. doi.org/10.1177/0093650208326465.

203   **Subsequent studies confirm pornography:** Hald, G. M., Malamuth, N. N., & Lange, T. (2013). Pornography and sexist attitudes among heterosexuals. *Journal of Communication, 63*(4), 638–60. doi.org/10.1111/jcom.12037; Seabrook, R. C., Ward, L. M., & Giaccardi, S. (2019). Less than human? Media use, objectification of women, and men's acceptance of sexual aggression. *Psychology of Violence, 9*(5), 536–45. doi.org/10.1037/vio0000198.

204   **But seeing the odd *Playboy*:** Kohut, T., & Štulhofer, A. (2018). Is pornography use a risk for adolescent well-being? An examination of temporal relationships in two independent panel samples. *PLOS ONE, 13*(8) doi.org/10.1371/journal.pone.0202048; Pizzol, D., Bertoldo, A., & Foresta, C. (2015). Adolescents and web porn: A new era of sexuality. *International Journal of Adolescent Medicine and Health, 28*(2), 169–73. doi.org/10.1515/ijamh-2015-0003.

206   **Such curricula can teach:** Vandenbosch, L., & Van Oosten, J. M. F. (2017). The relationship between online pornography and the sexual objectification of women: The attenuating role of porn literacy education. *Journal of Communication, 67*(6), 1015–36. doi.org/10.1111/jcom.12341.

209   **I suspect this is one reason:** Lehman, C. F. (2020, Sept. 1). Fewer American high schoolers having sex than ever before. Institute for Family Studies. ifstudies.org/blog/fewer-american-high-schoolers-having-sex-than-ever-before.

209   **As Hayley Phelan aptly:** Phelan, H. (2018, March 12). How does submissive sex work in the age of #MeToo? *New York Times.* www.nytimes.com/2018/03/12/style/submissive-sex-me-too.html.

Chapter 10: Giving the Gift of Bodily Autonomy

219   **They know that sexy girls:** Graff, K., Murnen, S. K., & Smolak, L. (2012). Too sexualized to be taken seriously? Perceptions of a girl in childlike vs. sexualizing clothing. *Sex Roles, 66,* 764–75. doi.org/10 .1007/s11199-012-0145-3; Choate, L., & Curry, J. R. (2009). Addressing the sexualization of girls through comprehensive programs, advocacy, and systemic change: Implications for professional school counselors. *Professional School Counseling, 12*(3), 213–22. www.jstor.org/stable /42732779.

221   **Succeeding at sexiness:** Filipovic, J. (2021, Nov. 2). How Kim Kardashian killed the term "empowerment." *Cosmopolitan.* www .cosmopolitan.com/entertainment/a55017/kim-kardashian-naked -selfie-empowerment/.

222   **Imagine my surprise:** Mark 9:47. www.thenivbible.com.

Chapter 11: Sex and Pizza

225   **Before Bonnie J. Rough:** Rough, *Beyond birds and bees.*

225   **In fact, American girls:** Sedgh, G., Finer, L. B., Bankole, A., Eilers, M. A., & Singh, S. (2015). Adolescent pregnancy, birth, and abortion rates across countries: Levels and recent trends. *Journal of Adolescent Health, 56*(2), 223–30. doi.org/10.1016/j.jadohealth.2014.09.007; *Abortion Rates by Country 2023.* (2023). World Population Review. worldpopulation review.com/country-rankings/abortion-rates-by-country.

225   **One study of college women:** Brugman, M., Caron, S. L., & Rademakers, J. (2010). Emerging adolescent sexuality: A comparison of American and Dutch college women's experiences. *International Journal of Sexual Health, 22*(1), 32–46. doi:10.1080/19317610903403974.

226   **By contrast, there's no:** Sex and HIV education. (2023, Aug. 8). Guttmacher Institute. www.guttmacher.org/state-policy/explore/sex -and-hiv-education.

227   **One Harvard report about:** Kay, J. F. (2008). *Sex, lies, and stereotypes: How abstinence-only programs harm women and girls.* Legal Momentum.

227   **Not only are these programs:** Guttmacher Institute. (2022, Aug. 24). Abstinence-only-until-marriage programs are ineffective and harmful to young people, expert review confirms. Press release. www.guttmacher .org/news-release/2017/abstinence-only-until-marriage-programs-are -ineffective-and-harmful-young-people.

228   **Amy Schalet, author of the book:** Schalet, A. (2011). *Not under my roof: Parents, teens, and the culture of sex.* University of Chicago Press.

231   **But as the research has shown:** Guttmacher Institute. Abstinence-only -until-marriage programs are ineffective and harmful to young people, expert review confirms.

231   **Because children who are secure:** Elliott, M., Browne, K. D., & Kilcoyne, J. (1995). Child sexual abuse prevention: What offenders tell us. *Child Abuse and Neglect, 19*(5), 579–94. doi.org/10.1016/0145-2134(95)00017-3; Kågesten, A., & Van Reeuwijk, M. (2021). Healthy sexuality development in adolescence: Proposing a competency-based framework to inform programmes and research. *Sexual and Reproductive Health Matters, 29*(1), 104–20. doi.org/10.1080/26410397.2021.1996116.

234   **Disney's film *Turning Red*:** Romano, A. (2022, March 17). Pixar's Turning Red is an unlikely culture war battleground. *Vox.* www.vox .com/culture/22981394/turning-red-reviews-controversy-reactions -parents.

234   **At this writing, Florida:** Bella, T. (2023, March 20). Florida bill would ban young girls from discussing periods in school. *Washington Post.* www.washingtonpost.com/politics/2023/03/17/florida-bill-girls-periods -school-gop/.

237   **They settled on the wicker:** Harris, R. H. (2008). *It's not the stork! A book about girls, boys, babies, bodies, families, and friends.* Candlewick.

239   **But parents have to:** Ashcraft, A. M., & Murray, P. J. (2017). Talking to parents about adolescent sexuality. *Pediatric Clinics of North America, 64*(2), 305–20. doi.org/10.1016/j.pcl.2016.11.002.

244   **The idea that children:** *Fonagy, P., & Target, M. (2003). Psychoanalytic theories: Perspectives from developmental psychopathology. Whurr.*

Conclusion: Girls Together

250   **Priya told Eve about atrocities:** Norris, A. (2023, March 13). It's time to end child marriage in the United States. Council on Foreign Relations. www.cfr.org/blog/its-time-end-child-marriage-united-states; Equality Now. (2023, Sept. 5). Female genital mutilation in the United States. www.equalitynow.org/fgm_in_the_us_learn_more/.

250   **A woman living in the United States:** Henderson, A. (2022). Why it costs $300K+ more to be a woman than it does to be a man. *HerMoney.* hermoney.com/invest/why-it-costs-300k-more-to-be-a-woman-than-it -does-to-be-a-man/.

250   **In 2021, two-thirds:** Michel, J., Mettler, A., Schönenberger, S., & Gunz, D. (2022). Period poverty: Why it should be everybody's business. *Journal of Global Health Reports, 6.* doi:10.29392/001c.32436.

251   **When that betrayal is brushed off:** Chemaly, S. (2018). *Rage becomes her: The power of women's anger.* Atria.

masculinity
  aggression/violence and, 23
  boys' sexuality as celebration of,
    199–200
  patriarchal traits/behaviors of, 9–10
  as performance, 23
  sexual intercourse and, 198, 199
  "toxic," 22–23
masturbation
  parents talking about, 228
  in sex education in school, 226
  tools, 245–46
  touching as exploration and, 244–45
  using pornography for, 206
McClelland, Sara, 201
media
  age of first exposure of children to
    sexually explicit, 203, 204
  application of Bechdel-Wallace test
    to, 106
  average number of ads seen by
    children daily, 106
  desensitization of boys to violence
    and promoting aggression, 24
  examples of sexism in, 100, 103–4
  focus on appearance in, 68
  intelligent women on, 149
  normalization of traditional gender
    roles and violence against women,
    104
  objectification of women, 84
  patriarchy and "male gaze" of, 107
  as primary source of children's
    information, 243
  promotion of idea being male is
    more valuable than being female,
    101–2
  resources for combating sexism in,
    105–7
  systematic sexualization and
    commodification of girls in, 104,
    106–7
  underrepresentation of Black-or
    brown-skinned persons in,
    102–3
  underrepresentation of girls and
    women in, 102, 103
#MeToo movement, xiv, 177
menstruation, 234–35, 250

mental health and social media, 110
"mental load," women as carriers of, 8,
  131, 214, 249
"misogyny paradox," 4
Miss America pageant, 76
mothers of daughters
  ability to tolerate conflict, 140
  focus on child's appearance, 67
  as modeling feminine
    self-silencing, 18
  modeling self-respect by, 18–19
  modeling solidarity against sexism by,
    251
  self-objectification of, 91–92
  underestimation of girls' physical
    abilities, 157–58
  untangling own experiences from
    current situations by, xi–xii

Netherlands, 225–29, 235–36
New York Times, 148, 209
Not Under My Roof (Schalet), 228
nudity, 235–37

objectification
  generational views of, 218, 219
  of girls who have sexual intercourse,
    196
  pattern of, 126–27
  rape and, 176
  school dress codes and, 151–53
  self-, 86–88, 91–92, 115, 221
  of women by media, 84
  of women's breasts, 236–37
"Objects Don't Object," 88
Oluo, Ijeoma, 76
On Love (Botton), 45
"On *MasterChef Junior,* Innate Biases
  Are Hard to Beat" (Framke), 100
"Operation Love Your Curls," 88–89
oral sex, 194
Orenstein, Peggy, 74, 193, 201

pain and anger, 139
Paltrow, Gwyneth, 177
pansexuality, 58

ABOUT THE AUTHOR

Jo-Ann Finkelstein, PhD, earned a master's in human development and psychology from the Harvard Graduate School of Education, and a doctorate in clinical psychology from the Northwestern University Feinberg School of Medicine. She completed her fellowship in women's health at Northwestern Memorial Hospital and was a program evaluation consultant for health and sexuality education curricula for the Cambridge and Chicago public schools. Dr. Finkelstein has taught at the Illinois School of Professional Psychology, Northwestern University, and Loyola University Chicago. Her work has been highlighted in *The New York Times, Harvard Business Review, Oprah Daily, Parents,* and *Women's Health,* and on *HuffPost* and CNN. She is the author of numerous academic papers related to parenting and child development, and her writing has appeared in *Psychology Today, Ms.* magazine, *Your Teen Magazine,* and on *Medium,* among other publications. Dr. Finkelstein maintains a psychotherapy practice in Chicago, where she lives with her family.

Joannfinkelstein.com
drjowrites.substack.com
Instagram: @TheFeministParent

ABOUT THE TYPE

This book was set in Minion, a 1990 Adobe Originals typeface by Robert Slimbach. Minion is inspired by classical, old-style typefaces of the late Renaissance, a period of elegant and beautiful type designs. Created primarily for text setting, Minion combines the aesthetic and functional qualities that make text type highly readable with the versatility of digital technology.